# On Creaturely Life

D1153587

# On Creaturely Life

## Life RILKE | BENJAMIN | SEBALD

Eric L. Santner

THE UNIVERSITY OF CHICAGO PRESS

CHICAGO AND LONDON

ERIC L. SANTNER is the Philip and Ida Romberg Professor in Modern Germanic Studies and chair of the Department of Germanic Studies at the University of Chicago. He is a coauthor of *The Neighbor: Three Inquiries in Political Theology* (2005).

The University of Chicago Press, Chicago 60637
The University of Chicago Press, Ltd., London
© 2006 by The University of Chicago
All rights reserved. Published 2006
Printed in the United States of America

15 14 13 12 11 10 09 08 07 06     1 2 3 4 5

ISBN: 0-226-73502-8 (cloth)
ISBN: 0-226-73503-6 (paper)

Library of Congress Cataloging-in-Publication Data

Santner, Eric L., 1955–
    On creaturely life : Rilke, Benjamin, Sebald / Eric L. Santner.
        p.   cm.
    Includes bibliographical references and index.
    ISBN 0-226-73502-8 (cloth : alk. paper) —
    ISBN 0-226-73503-6 (pbk. : alk. paper)
    1. Sebald, Winfried Georg, 1944– —Criticism and interpretation.
2. Psychoanalysis and literature.   3. Rilke, Rainer Maria, 1875–1926—
Influence.   4. Melancholy in literature.   5. Benjamin, Walter, 1892–
1940—Influence.   I. Title.
PT2681.E18Z84 2006
833'.914—dc22
                                                            2005027453

♾ The paper used in this publication meets the minimum requirements of the American National Standard for Information Sciences—Permanence of Paper for Printed Library Materials, ANSI Z39.48-1992.

FOR Slavoj AND Analia

# Contents

# Editions of Sebald's Works

In the text I provide page references to both German and English editions of Sebald's major works (German page numbers follow the slash). I used the following editions:

*Nach der Natur: Ein Elementargedicht*. Frankfurt a.M.: Fischer, 1995.
*After Nature*. Trans. Michael Hamburger. New York: Modern Library, 2003.
*Schwindel. Gefühle*. Frankfurt a.M.: Fischer, 1996.
*Vertigo*. Trans. Michael Hulse. New York: New Directions, 1999.
*Die Ausgewanderten: Vier lange Erzählungen*. Frankfurt a.M.: Fischer, 1996.
*The Emigrants*. Trans. Michael Hulse. New York: New Directions, 1996.
*Die Ringe des Saturn*. Frankfurt a.M.: Fischer, 1998.
*The Rings of Saturn*. Trans. Michael Hulse. New York: New Directions, 1999.
*Austerlitz*. Munich: Hanser, 2001.
*Austerlitz*. Trans. Anthea Bell. New York: Modern Library, 2001.

# Preface

## I

In this book I attempt to develop further certain lines of thought introduced in previous work, above all in my *On the Psychotheology of Everyday Life,* a study of Franz Rosenzweig's thought in light of psychoanalytic theory. More important, what served as an epilogue for that work—a series of short reflections on the implications of "psychotheological" thought for the understanding of literature—moves to the center of this book. I hope that this approach will open up new ways of thinking about literature (and not just the work of my primary point of reference, W. G. Sebald); and I also hope that, by engaging with literary texts, the conceptual relations that make up the field of what I call "psychotheology" will become more tangible.

The basic intuition at the heart of *Psychotheology* was that one could shed new light on the messianic dimension of modern German-Jewish thought by bringing it into contact with the Freudian revolution in psychology. The primary "laboratory" for this thought experiment was Franz Rosenzweig's monumental work *The Star of Redemption,* which offers what is arguably the most extensive and systematic presentation of this "modernist messianism."[1] For Rosenzweig, the messianic dimension of thought and action turns on our understanding of the concept of the *neighbor,* of what it means to engage in acts of neighbor love, and ultimately what it means (and doesn't mean) to work to make room in the world for such love.

A good part of the first volume of the *Star* develops what in many ways looks like a psychoanalytic view of the self, a drive theory of human mindedness—Rosenzweig even speaks of *Eros* and *Thanatos*—without which, he suggests, we could never fully grasp what is at stake when we speak of our "neighbor." As I understand it, Rosenzweig's work suggests that the only way to truly understand the concept of love of neighbor is to grasp what it means that he or she has an unconscious (in Rosenzweig's terms, that he or she is caught up in what he calls a "protocosmic" dimension of being and thought). The being whose proximity we are enjoined to inhabit and open to according to the imperative of neighbor love is always a subject at odds with itself, split by thoughts, desires, fantasies, and pleasures it can never fully claim as its own and that in some sense both do and do not belong to it. To put it in a more Lacanian idiom, the "otherness" of the neighbor, the dimension at issue in our ethical responsiveness to him or her, is at least in part a function of his or her bearing the burden—or perhaps one should say burdensome excitement—of unconscious *jouissance.* This seems to be what Freud intuited when he noted a strange expression on the face of the patient who would become famous as the "Rat Man." As Freud put it in his case study of that analysand, the Rat Man's face manifested a *horror at an enjoyment of which he was unaware.*[2] My argument in *Psychotheology* was that

1. Sigrid Weigel has argued that the trajectory of Walter Benjamin's intellectual career, one that was at least to some extent nourished by Rosenzweig's work, ought to be understood as an ongoing effort to integrate messianism and a psychoanalytically inflected theory of memory. In that sense her project belongs to the "field" I have called "psychotheology." See Weigel, *Entstellte Ähnlichkeit: Walter Benjamins theoretische Schreibweise* (Frankfurt a.M.: Fischer, 1997).
2. See Sigmund Freud, "Notes on a Case of Obsessional Neurosis," in *The Standard Edition of the Complete Psychological Works of Sigmund Freud,* trans. and ed. James E. Strachey (London: Hogarth, 1953–74), 10:166.

Rosenzweig's understanding of neighbor love orbited around the difficult task of turning toward such a face, of becoming responsive, answerable to the new ethical material—he calls it *metaethical*—it manifests. Both Freud and Rosenzweig shared the view that this uncanny—or what I will call *creaturely*—expressivity was an index of a traumatic kernel around which the "ego life" of the other has, at some level, been (dis)organized. The new ethics of neighbor love adumbrated by Rosenzweig locates our responsibility in our capacity to elaborate forms of solidarity with this creaturely expressivity that makes the other strange not only to me but also to him- or herself. What led me in this project to focus so exclusively on the work of W. G. Sebald was my sense that his literary writings were singularly obsessed with developing the means to engage with the "neighbor" in his or her creaturely expressivity, that his entire oeuvre could be seen as the construction of *an archive of creaturely life*.

Winfried Georg Maximillian Sebald, who died in 2001 at the age of fifty-seven in a car accident outside his home in Norwich, England, became something of a literary star in the 1990s after spending some twenty years as a professor of German literature at the University of East Anglia. His meteoric rise to "literary greatness"—a phrase used by Susan Sontag in a review of his work—came through a series of remarkable volumes of semidocumentary prose fiction that he began to write only in midlife. Perhaps because he was himself an emigrant—he moved to England in the late 1960s—his literary reputation was in large part made through his reception—one should perhaps say lionization—in the English-speaking world (though he won a number of major literary prizes in Germany, there his work was met with considerably more skepticism and ambivalence). One might say that he was the first German writer of recent memory whose work was immediately registered as being "canonical"; here was a writer who seemed truly to belong in the company of the very authors to whom he frequently alluded and from whom he freely borrowed in his work: Stendhal, Stifter, Keller, Kafka, Robert Walser, and Thomas Bernhard, among others.

The difficulty of categorizing the sort of literary practice Sebald engaged in is notorious. The genres and hybrid styles his "novels" have been identified with include travel writing, memoir, photo essay, documentary fiction, magical realism, postmodern pastiche, and cultural-historical fantasy, among others. And given that it so often deals, if only indirectly, with the Holocaust and its aftershocks, his work has furthermore been associated with that highly problematic generic and historical constellation, "Holocaust literature." Ultimately, I think James Wood got it right when, in a review of one of Sebald's works, he cited Walter Benjamin's well-known remark apropos of Proust, that all great works found a new genre or dissolve an old one.[3] I will argue that we truly grasp the specificity and stakes of this generic innovation only when we place it in the context of a conception of creaturely life developed, above all, in the writings of a series of twentieth-century German-Jewish writers, most importantly Walter Benjamin. By focusing on Sebald, then, I hope to contribute as well to the elaboration of the legacy of this remarkable cultural formation, which spans from Cohen and Rosenzweig to Kafka, Benjamin, Scholem, Adorno, and Celan, to name just its most prominent representatives.

II

In a review of Sebald's first foray into "creative writing," a book-length prose poem called *After Nature* (*Nach der Natur*), Eva Hoffman adumbrated the notion of "natural history" without ever naming it or the intellectual heritage behind it. The book deals with three figures separated by centuries: the great early modern German painter Matthias Grünewald; the German naturalist Georg Stellar, who turned from theology to become a naturalist and take part in Bering's Arctic expedition; and Sebald himself, who grew up in the aftermath of World War II in a part of southern Germany that was largely spared what Sebald would later call the "natural history of destruction" perpetrated in that war (Sebald was born in 1944). The poem announces all the themes and topics that would preoccupy him in his major work. These include, in Hoffman's words, "the sources of the catastrophic imagination, the continuities between human nature and nature, and the

3. James Wood, "The Right Thread" (review of Sebald, *The Rings of Saturn*), *New Republic*, July 6, 1998, 38.

inexorable interweaving, within both, of desire and destruction, pattern and chaos, proliferation and decay."[4] As Hoffman suggests, Sebald's vision of the mutual exchange of properties between natural and historical worlds leads to a conception of nature that is already "postnatural" and of the human world that is already "post-historical": "not only after nature, but after history."[5] The theme of the ending of time *within time,* a constant of the apocalyptic imagination, clearly haunts Sebald's writing and the figures that populate his work.

But there is a more specific sense of natural history at work in Sebald's vision of the nexus of the natural and the human, one that Walter Benjamin developed over the course of his career. As we shall see, Sebald's writing is deeply indebted to the Benjaminian view that at some level we truly encounter the radical otherness of the "natural" world only where it appears in the guise of historical remnant. The opacity and recalcitrance that we associate with the materiality of nature—the mute "thingness" of nature—is, paradoxically, most palpable where we encounter it as a piece of human history that has become an enigmatic ruin beyond our capacity to endow it with meaning, to integrate it into our symbolic universe. Where a piece of the human world presents itself as a surplus that both demands and resists symbolization, that is both inside and outside the "symbolic order"—for Benjamin, this is the unnerving point of departure of the allegorical imagination—that is where we find ourselves in the midst of "natural history." What I am calling creaturely life is a dimension of human existence called into being at such natural historical fissures or caesuras in the space of meaning. These are sites where the struggle for new meaning—in Nietzsche's terms, the exercise of will to power—is at its most intense. And it is precisely at such fissures—sites that can persist as uncanny loci of alterity within the order of meaning—that we will find W. G. Sebald at work.

At various points in this book I will turn to the work of a poet who has until now not been generally viewed as one of Sebald's key

---

4. Eva Hoffman, "Curiosity and Catastrophe," review of Sebald, *After Nature, New York Times Book Review,* September 22, 2002, 10.
5. Ibid.

precursors: Rainer Maria Rilke. In chapter 1 I develop a notion of creaturely life by way of a reading of Rilke's eighth *Duino Elegy* (along with Martin Heidegger's important critical response to it). In the epilogue I turn to what is perhaps Rilke's most famous poem, "The Archaic Torso of Apollo," to work out the logic of "neighbor love" that I take to be at issue in Sebald's writings. But it is, I think, in Rilke's great novel of urban life, *The Notebooks of Malte Laurids Brigge,* that we find the greatest resources for developing a feel for Sebald's "method," for the "spectral materialism" that informs his project.

In Rilke's novel, the first-person narrator-diarist Malte Laurids Brigge, a young, now impoverished Dane of aristocratic background struggling to become a writer—at least in part as an effort to master the overwhelming impact of life in Paris—repeatedly takes the measure of his own precarious existence by way of the fragile boundary provided by the residues of his upbringing—"a genteel hand, a hand that is washed four or five times a day"—against the multitude of the homeless and impoverished he encounters on the streets.[6] Malte refers to these figures as *Fortgeworfene,* outcasts. What makes them particularly disturbing—even *uncanny*—is that they seem more and more to recognize in Malte one of their own. What is especially important is that Malte's language indicates an awareness that he is confronting not simply an economic class or subculture generated by the contingencies of urban life but a fundamental dimension—what I am calling the "creaturely"—of a new social (or better, *biopolitical*) constellation in which he himself is implicated: "For it is obvious they are outcasts, not just beggars; no, they are really not beggars, there is a difference. They are human trash, husks of men that fate has spewed out. Wet with the spittle of fate, they stick to a wall, a lamp-post, leaving a dark, filthy trail behind them."[7] Malte's great fear is that the

6. Rainer Maria Rilke, *The Notebooks of Malte Laurids Brigge,* trans. Stephen Mitchell (New York: Vintage, 1990), 39.
7. Ibid., 40. Giorgio Agamben has suggested that Malte's intuitions concerning these "husks of men" anticipate Primo Levi's reflections on the "Muselmänner" in the death camps, whom Levi himself characterizes as "husk-men." See Agamben, *Remnants of Auschwitz: The Witness and the Archive,* trans. Daniel Heller-Roazen (Cambridge: MIT Press, 1999), 62. Agamben's work will be a constant point of reference in this volume.

tenuous distinctions he works at sustaining between himself and the outcasts—distinctions sustained only at the cost of a degree of shame he is constantly made aware of—will be shown to be insupportable.

There is even a brief passage in *Malte* where the protagonist, in a sequence taking inventory of a remarkable series of failures and missed opportunities in human history, contemplates the possibility that it might be just such "husks of men" who could provide a radically new perspective—a new and unheard of archive—for the writing of human history: "Is it possible that the whole history of the world has been misunderstood? Is it possible that the past is false, because we have always spoken about its masses, just as if we were telling about a gathering of many people, instead of talking about the one person they were standing around because he was a stranger and was dying?"[8]

Rilke knew, of course, that the record of human history had for the most part been written from the perspective of, and about, its elites—its *masters*. The reference to "masses" here thus cannot be understood as referring to the outcasts Malte encounters in Paris. I take it, rather, to signify those who are in some fashion represented within a given social formation, those who have a more or less defined place within the matrix of relations that constitute it. The "masses" in the cited passage are those who are in one way or another "covered" by, integrated into, the symbolic order. The dying stranger would thus stand in for those who are included but do not count, who are not represented, who "stick out" in some fundamental way (as we will see in chapter 4, such "queerness" does indeed have a sexual dimension). Malte seems to be proposing the possibility of displacing the thinking and writing of history to the sites—we might say to the "neighborhood"—of such "singularities."[9]

---

8. Rilke, *Malte*, 23.

9. A related passage in the same sequence in Rilke's novel reads: "Is it possible that we know nothing about young girls, who are nevertheless living? Is it possible that we say 'women,' 'children,' 'boys,' not suspecting . . . that these words have long since had no plural, but only countless singulars?" (24). It has been suggested that Rilke's language here, as in the earlier passage, is directed against the advent of the sociological gaze embodied above all in the great cultural theorist, Georg Simmel, with whom Rilke briefly studied. See Hans-Jürgen Schings, "Die Fragen des Malte Laurids Brigge und Georg

Malte brings his series of questions to an end on a note of hope, though one not without a certain element of foreboding:

But if all this is possible, if it has even a semblance of possibility, — then surely, for the sake of everything in the world, something must be done. The first comer, the one who has had these alarming thoughts, must begin to do some of the things that have been neglected; even though he is just anyone, certainly not the most suitable person: since there is no one else. This young, insignificant foreigner, Brigge, will have to sit down in his room, five flights up, and keep writing, day and night. Yes, he will have to write; that is how it will end.[10]

As readers of *Malte* know, Rilke's protagonist achieves at best an ambiguous success with this project. I hope to show in the following that W. G. Sebald—this "insignificant foreigner" living and writing in the English provinces from the late 1960s until his death in 2001—might best be understood as Malte's great successor in this endeavor.

III

As I have indicated, in chapter 1 I introduce the central concept of this book, one that will ultimately guide me in my readings of Sebald's fiction: *creaturely life*. My argument will be that this notion, which

---

Simmel," *Deutsche Vierteljahresschrift für Literaturwissenschaft und Geistesgeschichte* 76, no. 2 (2002): 643–72. For Simmel, the birth of sociology is correlated with the emergence of new kinds of collectivities—"*Massen*"—that radically diminish the status and power of individuals and individuality in modern societies (Simmel also noted the double bind that modern society demands of the members of such collectivities that they distinguish themselves from all the others by means of fashion and other mass-produced commodities). I will argue that what Rilke touches on in these passages is a notion of singularity that not only resists absorption into sociological categories (as Malte emphasizes, the outcasts cannot be subsumed by the sociological category of the poor, one of Simmel's objects of study) but is linked in a fundamental way—just how, Sebald will help us see—to the dimension I am calling creaturely life.

10. Ibid., 24–25.

acquired considerable currency in twentieth-century German—and
above all, German-Jewish—thought, opens a new way of understanding how human bodies and psyches register the "states of exception"
that punctuate the "normal" run of social and political life. "Creatureliness" will thus signify less a dimension that traverses the boundaries
of human and nonhuman forms of life than a specifically human way
of finding oneself caught in the midst of antagonisms in and of
the political field. The discussion will lead us from Rilke and Heidegger to Benjamin's numerous reflections on creaturely life and will engage throughout with Giorgio Agamben's important work on these
matters.

In chapter 2 I turn to the "mood" that permeates the universe of
Sebald's fiction, *melancholy*. My discussion of melancholy will focus
largely on the work of Walter Benjamin, who figures, I think, as a kind
of patron saint—not to say "totem"—of Sebald's fictional universe.
The central question of the chapter pertains to the relation between
the knowledge produced by the melancholy gaze on human affairs,
on the one hand, and the realm of action and practice—the ethical and
political intervention in history—on the other. Another way of put-
ting it: What is the relation between melancholy, understood by Benjamin as an immersion into the realm of creaturely life, and redemption? The crux of the problem lies in how we understand the "mythic"
fixations that account for the peculiar passion of melancholy as a subjective stance, that weigh down the objects of the melancholy gaze
and make them *matter* in the specific way they do. Melancholy shows
itself to be both resource and impasse, enabling and disabling, in the
work of historical analysis and action at issue for Benjamin. To get a
better grasp of the nature of such fixations, I will turn to the place in
Freud's writings where the concept of the state of exception and the
work of myth come together, namely in his infamous hypothesis of
the primal father and murder. As we shall see, it is the *manic* side of
melancholy, the peculiar agitation that informs it, that will prove to
be of greatest consequence for our understanding of creaturely life
and the conditions under which it is called into being.

In chapter 3, Sebald's fiction firmly assumes center stage. Sebald
shows himself to be the modern master of a Benjaminian poetics, a

mode of writing in which the materiality of human artifacts and habitations pulsates with the rhythms of natural history. I explore in detail Sebald's privileged substances—dust, ash, bone, silk, and all manner of combustion and entropy—as well as sites that draw his gaze: fortifications, railway stations, the flayed surfaces of urban space. At the center of these explorations will be the various ways Sebald invokes the dimension of *undeadness,* the space between real and symbolic death, which I take to be the ultimate domain of creaturely life. The logic of "petrified unrest" (Benjamin's term) proper to this dimension leads Sebald to key cultural and literary figurations of the undead: the vampire, the Wandering Jew, Kafka's hunter Gracchus, and Balzac's Colonel Chabert. The chapter culminates in a discussion of the question of hope in Sebald's universe, one that brings Sebald into a certain proximity to St. Paul and the latter's understanding of what it might mean to be released from the travails of creatureliness.

I begin chapter 4 by arguing that a series of seemingly heterogeneous features of Sebald's writings ultimately provide further occasions for the exploration of creaturely expressivity in the aftermath of historical violence. Most important in this context is Sebald's signature use of photography in his books. By engaging with Barthes's important reflections on photography as well as with Sebald's own account of the status of photographs in his work, I show that what is at issue in the interplay of image and text in these writings is the task of bearing witness to what exceeds our hermeneutic grasp of historical experience. For Sebald, photography is a "medium" in a double sense, a technological means and substrate for the production and reproduction of images and a locus of commerce with the dead (or undead). Sebald's use of photography constitutes one aspect of his engagement with issues of "postmemory," a term coined by Marianne Hirsch to capture the peculiarities of the memory of events that hover between personal memory and impersonal history, events one has not lived through oneself but that, in large measure through exposure to the stories of those who did experience them, have nonetheless entered into the fabric of the self. In the second half of the chapter

I turn to the status of sexuality in Sebald's texts, an issue that has heretofore been neglected in the literature on this author. The discussion follows the track of Sebald's sexually ambiguous narrators and "informants" into the nexus of homosexual panic and paranoia that Freud analyzed in this famous reading of the Schreber case, one that Sebald clearly knew well. The chapter culminates in an attempt to bring together the notion of creaturely life developed throughout the book with a new understanding of the constellation of issues that Freud grouped under the heading of the "uncanny."

In an epilogue I return to Rilke—and Lacan—as the occasion to open new paths of speculation as to the dimension of hope, the presence of a "weak Messianic power," in the engagement with creaturely life. By bringing together Rilke's "thing poem," "Archaic Torso of Apollo," a poem steeped in the image world of castration, with Lacan's speculations on a jouissance in excess of the phallic register, I try to articulate a new conception of what it means to open to the singularity, the creaturely expressivity, of our neighbor, a figure whose "queerness" exceeds the available categories of sociosexual organization and who provides us with an ethical material we have only begun to explore.

I am grateful to many people for their contributions to my thinking about Sebald and the notion of "creaturely life" elaborated in this book. I first want to thank the students who took part in various seminars in which this work began to take shape, above all the members of the Seminar in Experimental Critical Theory at the Humanities Research Center at the University of California at Irvine (August 2004) and the students in my seminar on Sebald at the University of Chicago (Fall 2004). I also want to single out Catherine Sprecher, who took my seminar on Franz Rosenzweig several years ago and who wrote a fine essay on Sebald in the context of Rosenzweig's thought. I could not have written this book were it not for ongoing conversations with several friends and colleagues: Kenneth Reinhard, Slavoj Žižek, Mladen Dolar, Alenka Zupancic, Joan Copjec, Alan Thomas, Julia Lupton, Amir Eshel, Stanley Corngold,

David Wellbery, and Robert Pippin. Judith Ryan's rigorous and generous evaluation of the manuscript made revising the book a genuine learning experience. My thanks to Alice Bennett for her fine copy-editing. I am, finally, deeply grateful to Janel Mueller and Danielle Allen for everything they have done to make the Division of the Humanities at the University of Chicago such a hospitable environment for teaching, thinking, and writing.

# On Creaturely Life

In his eighth *Duino Elegy,* Rainer Maria Rilke famously sets off human life from the way of being of what he calls, simply, *die Kreatur.* In the elegy, written in 1922, Rilke praises the capacity of plant and animal life to inhabit a seemingly borderless surround that he names, as the environmental correlate or sphere of the creature, *das Offene* — the Open:

With all its eyes the natural world [*die Kreatur*] looks out
into the Open.[1]

Because human life is essentially reflective, mediated through consciousness and self-consciousness, man's relation to things is crossed with borders, articulated within a matrix of representations that

---

1. I refer to the translation in *The Selected Poetry of Rainer Maria Rilke,* trans. Stephen Mitchell (New York: Vintage, 1984).

position him, qua *subject,* over against the world, qua *object* of desire and mastery:

Only *our* eyes are turned
backward, and surround plant, animal, child
like traps, as they emerge into their freedom.

Even the child, Rilke says, is only fleetingly absorbed by the Open:

We know what is really out there only from
the animal's gaze; for we take the very young
child and force it around, so that it sees
objects—not the Open, which is so
deep in animals' faces.[2]

At the end of the first strophe, Rilke suggests that it is ultimately death anxiety that disrupts the free movement in the Open for humankind:

We, only, can see death; the free animal
has its decline in back of it, forever,
and God in front, and when it moves, it moves
already in eternity, like a fountain.

Man is forever caught up in the labor of the negative—the (essentially defensive) mapping and codification of object domains that allow for certain sorts of desire and possession but never what Rilke posits as the unimaginable enjoyment of self-being in otherness manifest by the creature:

Never, not for a single day, do *we* have
before us that pure space into which flowers
endlessly open. Always there is World
and never Nowhere without the No: that pure

---

2. Think of Rilke's earlier poem, "The Grownup" ("Die Erwachsene"): "Till in the midst of play, / transfiguring and preparing for the future, / the first white veil descended, gliding softly // over her opened face, almost opaque there, / never to be lifted off again." Rilke, *Selected Poetry,* 31.

unseparated element which one breathes
without desire and endlessly *knows*.[3]

Man, instead, is condemned to the ceaseless production of mediating representations (in German the word for representation, *Vorstellen,* literally means to place before, in front of, over against the agent of representation):

That is what fate means: to be opposite [*gegenüber sein*],
to be opposite and nothing else, forever.

In the second strophe, Rilke indicates that in certain states or phases of human life one might, as it were, make brief contact with the dimension of the Open. Childhood, as was suggested, provides a brief threshold for such contact:

A child
may wander there for hours, through the timeless
stillness, may get lost in it and be
shaken back.

But so does death:

Or someone dies and *is* it.
For, nearing death, one doesn't see death; but stares
beyond, perhaps with an animal's vast gaze [*mit großem Tierblick*].

Finally, Rilke singles out lovers, who—were it not for the transitiveness of their love, their anxious clinging to the object of their desire—are the ones best positioned to relinquish that fateful, oppositional posture that inhibits access to the Open:

Lovers, if the beloved were not there
blocking the view, are close to it, and marvel . . .
As if by some mistake, it opens for them

3. Rilke's formulation is especially powerful here: "Immer ist es Welt / und niemals Nirgends ohne Nicht."

behind each other . . . But neither can move past
the other, and it changes back to World [*Aber über ihn/kommt keiner fort,
und wieder wird ihm Welt*].

In the third strophe, Rilke seems to introduce a series of distinctions into the world of the creaturely, suggesting that even there one
discovers degrees of purity with respect to the immersion in the
Open, that animal life, too, undergoes forms of breaks and ruptures
in relation to this dimension. The thought here is that only those creatures that never experience a radical break between the sphere of ges-
tation and the sphere of motility, creatures never distracted by memories of the more tender and intimate communion of the womb, as
Rilke puts it, are fully at home in the Open. Thus the otherwise curious celebration of the life of insects:

Oh bliss of the *tiny* creature which remains
forever inside the womb that was its shelter;
joy of the gnat which, still *within,* leaps up
even at its marriage: for everything is womb.[4]

In stark contrast to such apparently seamless emergence into and
absorption by the Open, Rilke's image of the flight of the bat offers a
vision of what one is tempted to call a trauma in the realm of creaturely life:

And how bewildered is any womb-born creature
that has to fly. As if terrified and fleeing
from itself, it zigzags through the air, the way
a crack runs through a teacup. So the bat
quivers across the porcelain of evening.[5]

---

4. In the notes to his translation of the poem, Mitchell cites a notebook entry from
1914 to clarify Rilke's thinking here: "That a multitude of creatures which come from
externally exposed seeds have *that* as their maternal body, that vast sensitive freedom—
how much at home they must feel in it all their lives."
5. The German word for "crack," *Sprung,* opens on to a larger semantic field: it also
means *leap* or *jump* and is connected to the German word for origin, *Ursprung.*

Be that as it may, the crucial distinction for Rilke remains that between man and the "world" of the creature taken as a whole. The word Rilke uses to summarize his claim about man's alienation from the Open, his claustral enclosure within an inner theater of representations and mediations, comes, not surprisingly, from the stage. The poet suggests, that is, that only man lives his separation from the maternal sphere as a kind of permanent homesickness experienced in the modality of a compulsive stance of *spectatorship* over against the world:

And we: spectators, always, everywhere,
turned toward the world of objects, never outward.
It fills us. We arrange it. It breaks down.
We rearrange it, then break down ourselves.

Rilke's understanding of such a posture seems to continue what Robert Pippin has characterized as a romantic tradition of seeing alienation "wherever one can detect the presence of self-consciousness and reflection . . . as if such reflection, a cardinal aspect of modern mindedness, is inherently doubling," that is to say, as if the human mind not only perceived objects but also, by reflection, had a "second-order self-consciousness *of* one's perceptual state as a new, dual object."[6]

II

Martin Heidegger, the twentieth-century philosopher most associated with the analysis and critique of—or perhaps better, diagnosis and therapy for—the spectatorial attitude Rilke identifies with representational thinking, has himself argued that Rilke's elegy is

6. Robert Pippin, "Authenticity in Painting: Remarks on Michael Fried's Art History," *Critical Inquiry* 31 (Spring 2005): 592. The Fourth Elegy includes another statement about the difference between human and creaturely life: "We are not in harmony, our blood does not forewarn us / like migratory birds." Later in the poem, Rilke brings together his conception of angelic being, elaborated throughout the elegies, with Kleist's famous essay on the marionette theater, to project a theater that, as it were, fully overcomes the alienation introduced into Being by our posture of spectatorship: "Angel and puppet: a real play, finally. / Then what we separate by our very presence / can come together."

fundamentally implicated in the stance to the world from which the poem ostensibly seeks to gain a distance.[7] He accuses Rilke of participating in a movement of thought that produces "a monstrous humanization of the 'creature,' i.e., the animal, and a corresponding animalization of man," thereby perpetuating the popular biological metaphysics of the end of the nineteenth century that, in the wake of Schopenhauer and Nietzsche, posits the instinctual will of animal life as a primordial and uninhibited ease of movement through the elemental spheres of existence.[8] Because he identifies human life with the capacity for—and curse of—representational thought, "a consciousness of objects . . . that is conscious of itself and is reflected onto itself," Rilke is compelled to conflate the ostensible lack of self-consciousness of animal life with freedom.[9] To cite Pippin once more, what Rilke's conception seems to preclude is an understanding of "reflective absorption as *an intensification of such absorption,* not a thematizing and ultimately theatricalizing distancing." Pippin adds that this sort of "theatricalizing might be said to occur only when something like the normative structure of such mindedness begins to break down, fails to sustain allegiance, becomes a *reflected object of inquiry,* not a *mode of life.*"[10] I will return to this theme of breakdown and reification in due course; for the moment I would like to note very briefly some further aspects of Heidegger's critical engagement with Rilke's poem.

As Heidegger sees it, Rilke's "creaturely" understanding of the Open blinds him to the true ontological distinction of human being, one that cannot be captured by the language of consciousness, self-reflection, and subject-object relations. Grounded as it is in a forgetting of the ontological difference between Being and beings, Rilke's understanding of the Open as a locus of unimpeded motility forecloses

7. The following is much indebted to Giorgio Agamben's *The Open: Man and Animal,* trans. Kevin Attell (Stanford: Stanford University Press, 2004). I will return to Agamben's important essay later.

8. Martin Heidegger, *Parmedides,* trans. André Schuwer and Richar Rojcewicz (Bloomington: Indiana University Press, 1998), 152 (translation modified), 158.

9. Ibid., 158.

10. Pippin, "Authenticity," 592.

the possibility of thinking "the free of Being, and it is precisely this free that the 'creature' never sees; for the capacity to see it constitutes what is essentially distinct about man and consequently forms the insurmountable essential boundary between animal and man." As Heidegger continues, "'The open' in the sense of the unceasing advance of beings in the realm of beings [*im Sinne des unaufhörlichen Fortgangs des Seienden im Seienden*] and 'the open' in the sense of the free of the clearing of Being in distinction from all beings are verbally the same, but in what the words name they are so different that no oppositional formulation could suffice to indicate the gap between them."[11]

In Heidegger's "postmetaphysical" understanding, the Open is just the historical field of man's understanding of Being, the ultimate locus and archive of which is human speech. Put somewhat differently, only human being stands in a relation to *truth* understood as *unconcealedness,* as the emergence into presence of beings in their Being. For Heidegger, only human beings can be said to be "on to" things in a way that is responsive, indeed *beholden to,* what and how they are—in a way, that is, that necessarily includes the possibility of being right or wrong about them.[12] For Heidegger, then, the essence of human being can be captured neither by a focus on the "mental," on the structure and contents of the human mind, nor by turning to man's animal will or vitality (for Heidegger, *will* and *representation* form two sides of the same metaphysical picture of the world). Rather, human life unfolds in an articulated space of possibilities embodied in the forms of life into which one contingently comes to be initiated, the practices that define one's historical community. In this space of possibilities, things show themselves in various ways, *as* various sorts of entities: as hammers and nails, as nightingales and sunsets, as oil reserves and lumber, as symphonies and poems, as wine and wafer, as lovers, enemies, gods.

11. Heidegger, *Parmedides,* 152 (translation modified).
12. In *On Beauty and Being Just* (Princeton: Princeton University Press, 1999), Elaine Scarry provides a wonderful description of how these features—responsiveness to the otherness of entities, the capacity to be right or wrong, beholding as being beholden to—function in our relation to beautiful objects.

As fundamentally excluded from what he calls the "strife between unconcealedness and concealedness," the animal is, as Heidegger puts it elsewhere, *poor in world* (*weltarm*), while man is essentially *world-forming* (*weltbildend*); the stone, by contrast, is simply *weltlos,* without world.[13] It is against this background that Heidegger draws the distinction between animal behavior—his word is *sich benehmen*—and human comportment—*sich verhalten*. What Rilke privileges as uninhibited movement within the Open, Heidegger sees as a purely functional and instinctual captivation (*Benommenheit*) by an environment, as absorption in an *Umwelt* as opposed to an intentional comportment within the openness of a *Welt*. That is, after criticizing the picture Rilke inherits from the metaphysical tradition (in its post-Cartesian incarnation), in which man is seen to be somehow enclosed within the dimension of the mental, the mediations of consciousness (and only secondarily related to world), Heidegger is compelled to distinguish man's engaged absorption in a space of possibilities—in a historical form of life or *world*—from an animal's absorption in its *environment*. Heidegger is compelled, that is, to make a distinction between two ways of being in the midst of life, two sorts of relations to the otherness of entities, only one of which transpires, as it were, in—or better, *as*—the Open, the clearing of an understanding of Being:

The *captivation* [*Benommenheit*] of the animal therefore signifies . . . *having every apprehending* [*Vernehmen*] *of something as something withheld from it.* And furthermore: in having this withheld from it, the animal is precisely *taken by things* [*hingenommen durch* . . .]. Thus animal captivation characterizes the specific manner of being in which the animal relates itself to something else even while the possibility is withheld [*genommen*] from it—or is taken away [*benommen*] from the animal, as we might also say—of comporting and relating itself to something else *as* such and such at all, *as* something present at hand, *as* a being. And it is precisely because this possibility—apprehending *as*

---

13. Ibid., 160. Heidegger establishes these distinctions in *The Fundamental Concepts of Metaphysics: World, Finitude, Solitude*, trans. William McNeill and Nicholas Walker (Bloomington: Indiana University Press, 1995).

something that to which it relates—is withheld from it that the animal can find itself so utterly taken by something else.[14]

As Giorgio Agamben has suggested in his perspicacious commentary on these and related passages, Heidegger's argument forces us to contemplate a mode of openness and exposure that might be characterized as a *nonrelation to an opacity:* "For the animal, beings are open but not accessible; that is to say, they are open in an inaccessibility and an opacity—that is, in some way, in a nonrelation. This *openness without disconcealment* distinguishes the animal's poverty in world from the world-forming which characterizes man."[15]

Because Rilke failed to grasp the true nature of the animal/human divide—the difference between the animal's poverty in world and man's destiny as world-forming—his poetry fails to accede to the status of an *event* in the history at issue for Heidegger (unlike that of Heidegger's master poet, Hölderlin). Because he lacked the poeticophilosophical resources for imagining human mindedness beyond the frame of rational, representational thinking—the poetic "saying" of such a beyond would have been the "Rilke event"—he was compelled to elevate animal life to the status of superhuman exception (part of Heidegger's argument is that Rilke achieves poetically what Nietzsche achieves philosophically—*the passage to the limit of the metaphysical tradition*):

Since Rilke's poetry . . . neither experiences nor respects the essential boundary between the mystery [*Geheimnis*] of the living being (plant and animal) and the mystery of the historical being, i.e., man, his poetical words never attain the true height of a historically foundational decision. It is almost as if in this poetry there is operative an unlimited and groundless humanization

---

14. Ibid., 247–48. Heidegger adds that such captivation "should not be interpreted . . . as a kind of rigid fixation on the part of the animal as if it were somehow spellbound. Rather this captivation makes possible and prescribes an appropriate leeway for its behavior, i.e., a purely instinctual redirecting of the animal's driven activity in accordance with certain instincts in each case" (248). Indeed, it is really only man who is capable of rigid fixation, of becoming stuck or spellbound in his doings in the world.
15. Agamben, *Open,* 55.

of the animal, by which the animal, with respect to the original experience of beings as a whole [*des Seienden im Ganzen*], is even raised above man and becomes in a certain way a "super-man" [*Über-Menschen*].[16]

III

Agamben's crucial contribution to this "debate" between Rilke and Heidegger as to the meaning of "the Open" in animal and human life has been to underline a profound ambiguity in Heidegger's own position. Agamben points to the ways Heidegger's very insistence on the radical ontological distinction between animal and human life— one conceived, precisely, in opposition to Rilke's still "metaphysical" understanding of the animal/human divide—brings the two kinds of life into an uncanny proximity, one duly noted by Heidegger himself. That is to say, for Heidegger man's freedom and destiny as "world-forming" include a dimension—I am tempted to say a traumatic dimension—that brings him into proximity to the animal, that renders him, in a certain sense, creaturely.

Interestingly, one of the points at which this proximity begins to register in Heidegger's argument is where he refers to the Pauline conception of a longing for redemption immanent in creaturely life itself, in the haunting vision of creation groaning in travail (Romans 8:18–22). Paul's words suggest to Heidegger that the "*animal's poverty in world [is] a problem intrinsic to animality itself*."[17] In its captivation by a narrowly delimited functional environment, the animal "finds itself essentially exposed to something other than itself, something that can indeed never be manifest to the animal either as a being or as a non-being." But precisely such exposure, writes Heidegger, "brings an *essential disruption* [*wesenhafte Erschütterung*] into the essence of the animal."[18]

16. Ibid., 160–61 (translation modified).
17. Heidegger, *Fundamental Concepts*, 273.
18. Ibid., 273. Here Heidegger actually comes very close to those passages in the Eighth Elegy—one thinks, above all, of the image of the bat in flight—where Rilke qualifies his vision of creaturely absorption, where he suggests that "in the alert, warm animal there lies / the pain and burden of an enormous sadness."

For Heidegger, it is this disruptive dimension of animal captivation that stands behind Paul's evocation of suffering creation (the word Heidegger uses, *Benommenheit,* translated here as "captivation," already registers a dimension of shock and thus could just as easily be translated as "benumbedness"). Heidegger furthermore suggests that the phenomenology of profound boredom—a mood Heidegger posits as that of contemporary *Dasein*—provides a crucial site for the elaboration of the proximity of animal and human forms of exposure to alterity. In both animal captivation and human boredom, which Heidegger characterizes as an "*entrancement [Gebanntheit]*" of Dasein within beings as a whole," the being in question is delivered over to an *arresting opacity.*[19] "*In becoming bored,*" as Agamben summarizes Heidegger's claim (one that the latter unfolds over the course of some two hundred pages),

*Dasein is delivered over* (ausgeliefert) *to something that refuses itself, exactly as the animal, in its captivation, is exposed* (hinausgesetzt) *in something unrevealed.* . . . In being left empty by profound boredom, something vibrates like an echo of that "essential disruption" that arises in the animal from its being exposed and taken in an "other" that is, however, never revealed to it as such. For this reason the man who becomes bored finds himself in the "closest proximity"—even if it is only apparent—to animal captivation. Both are, in their most proper gesture, *open to a closedness;* they are totally delivered over to something that obstinately refuses itself.[20]

The conclusion to be drawn from this proximity of animal *Benommenheit* and the human *Gebanntheit* that registers itself above all in the fundamental mood of boredom is in its own way quite stunning: "The jewel set at the center of the human world and its *Lichtung,*" Agamben writes, "is nothing but animal captivation; the wonder 'that beings *are*' is nothing but the grasping of the 'essential disruption' that occurs in the living being from its *being exposed in a nonrevelation*

---

19. Heidegger, *Fundamental Concepts,* 282.
20. Agamben, *Open,* 65.

[my emphasis].” But this means, Agamben continues, that “Dasein is simply an animal that has learned to become bored; it has awakened *from* its own captivation *to* its own captivation. This awakening of the living being to its own being-captivated, this anxious and resolute opening to a not-open, is the human.”[21]

IV

What we have tracked with the help of Agamben’s careful reading of Heidegger is, I suggest, the beginning of a shift in the notion of the “creature” and the “creaturely” that leads us from Rilke’s conception, as elaborated in his eighth *Duino Elegy,* to one that belongs more firmly in a tradition I would like to characterize as “German-Jewish.” We have arrived, that is, at a peculiar point of (near) contact between a dimension of Heidegger’s thought and that of a series of German-Jewish writers who in one way or another have placed the notion of the creaturely at the center of their literary and philosophical elaborations of *human* life under conditions of modernity. I am thinking, above all, of Franz Kafka, Franz Rosenzweig, Gershom Scholem, Walter Benjamin, Paul Celan, and, though he belongs to a somewhat different lineage, Sigmund Freud. For these writers, however, creaturely life—the peculiar proximity of the human to the animal at the very point of their radical difference—is a product not simply of man’s thrownness into the (enigmatic) “openness of Being” but of his exposure to a traumatic dimension of political power and social bonds whose structures have undergone radical transformations in modernity. The “essential disruption” that renders man “creaturely” for these writers has, that is, a distinctly political—or better, *biopolitical*—aspect; it names the threshold where life becomes a matter of politics and politics comes to inform the very matter and materiality of life. The “strife between unconcealedness and concealedness,” the antagonism that, according to Heidegger, runs through the very core

---

21. Ibid., 68, 70. We should note that in *Sein und Zeit* Heidegger regularly uses the word *benommen* to characterize Dasein’s “fallen” mode of absorption in its world.

of human existence, is conceived in this tradition as the traumatic kernel of man's inscription into the space of political contestation broadly conceived.[22]

To put a name on it, the tradition of thought that I am calling "German-Jewish" is one that takes as its point of departure some form of the "decisionist" logic of sovereignty articulated by Carl Schmitt, according to which the very constitution of a space of juridical normativity—a space where the rule of law is in effect—always includes an immanent reference to a state of exception. According to this logic, the sovereign agency enjoys the power to suspend the law—the decision on the state of exception—in the name of protecting the security of the state or of reestablishing the stability to which law can then apply. As Schmitt later emphasizes, sovereign power and authority are fundamentally linked to the constitution of the field of the political as an agonistic space defined by friend/enemy distinctions.[23] For Schmitt, that is, the boundary between "us" and "them"—and for him the decision on this boundary is the political decision as such, the one that first introduces the dimension of politics into human life—is established on the basis of a more complex topology that positions the sovereign within a zone of *extralegal authority within the law.* The

22. In his difficult lecture course on Parmenides from 1942 to 1943, Heidegger too has indicated that the "strife between unconcealedness and concealedness" is at the core of political life; indeed, it defines the very space of the polis. Agamben has suggested that for Heidegger "the originary political conflict between unconcealedness and concealedness will be, at the same time and to the same degree, that between the humanity and the animality of man" (*Open,* 73). By contrast, I am proposing that the emergence of the political *generates* a uniquely human form of animality or *creatureliness.*

23. See Carl Schmitt, *The Concept of the Political,* trans. George Schwab (Chicago: University of Chicago Press, 1996). There Schmitt writes, for example, that "the specific political distinction to which political actions and motives can be reduced is that between friend and enemy" and adds that "the distinction of friend and enemy denotes the utmost degree of intensity of a union or separation, of an association or dissociation" (27). As Schmitt sees it, without the possibility of the extreme case of actual conflict, the very space of politics disappears: "For only in real combat is revealed the most extreme consequence of the political grouping of friend and enemy. From this most extreme possibility human life derives its specifically political tension. . . . A world in which the possibility of war is utterly eliminated, a completely pacified globe, would be a world without the distinction of friend and enemy and hence a world without politics" (35).

*external* boundary with respect to the other declared to be the "enemy" presupposes a kind of *internal* boundary between law and its immanent "outside." In a recent attempt to characterize this peculiar internal boundary, Giorgio Agamben has put it this way: *"Being-outside, and yet belonging:* this is the topological structure of the state of exception, and only because the sovereign, who decides on the exception, is, in truth, logically defined in his being by the exception, can he too be defined by the oxymoron *ecstasy-belonging."* [24]

In his own account of these topological paradoxes, Schmitt underlines the specific "creativity" associated with such *ecstasy-belonging:*

The exception is that which cannot be subsumed; it defies general codification, but it simultaneously reveals a specifically juridical formal element: the decision in absolute purity. The exception appears in its absolute form when it is a question of creating a situation in which juridical rules can be valid. Every general rule demands a regular, everyday frame of life to which it can be factually applied and which is submitted to its regulations. The rule requires a homogeneous medium. This factual regularity is not merely an "external presupposition" that the jurist can ignore; it belongs, rather, to the rule's immanent validity. There is no rule that is applicable to chaos. Order must be established for juridical order to make sense. A regular situation must be created, and sovereign is he who definitely decides if this situation is actually effective. All law is "situational law." The sovereign creates and guarantees the situation as a whole in its totality. . . . The decision reveals the essence of State authority most clearly. Here the decision must be distinguished from the juridical regulation, and (to formulate it paradoxically) authority proves itself not to need law to create law [*daß sie, um Recht zu schaffen, nicht Recht zu haben braucht*]." [25]

24. Giorgio Agamben, *The State of Exception,* trans. Kevin Attell (Chicago: University of Chicago Press, 2005), 12.
25. Carl Schmitt, *Politische Theologie: Vier Kapitel zur Lehre von der Souveränität* (Berlin: Duncker und Humblot, 1993), 19. Translation cited in Giorgio Agamben, *Homo Sacer: Sovereign Power and Bare Life,* trans. Daniel Heller-Roazen (Stanford: Stanford University Press, 1998), 15–16.

What I am calling creaturely life is the life that is, so to speak, called into being, *ex-cited,* by exposure to the peculiar "creativity" associated with this threshold of law and nonlaw; it is the life that has been delivered over to the space of the sovereign's "ecstasy-belonging," or what we might simply call "sovereign jouissance."[26]

There is a corollary to this point that is equally important. Schmitt famously claims that the crucial concepts of all modern theories of government are secularized theological concepts. More specifically, he argues that the concept of the state of exception is, in jurisprudence, strictly analogous to the concept of *miracle* in theology. And indeed, he suggests that the attenuation of the notion of the state of exception has impoverished the liberal theory of the state to the same degree that the devaluation of the notion of miracle has impoverished liberal theology:

For the idea of the modern constitutional state [*Rechtsstaat*] attains predominance along with deism, with a theology and metaphysics, that is, that just as much banishes miracle from the world (along with any sort of interruption of natural laws—the exception that belongs to the very concept of miracle) as it does the direct intervention of the sovereign into the governing rule of law. The rationalism of the Enlightenment repudiates the state of exception in every form.[27]

For the tradition of thought I am invoking here, however, if one can speak of a dimension of the miraculous (in the ethicopolitical realm), it will pertain not to a repetition, not to a new instantiation of the topology of the sovereign exception, but to some form of its suspension, some way of *uncoupling from the mode of subjectivity/subjectivization*

---

26. As Agamben has put it, "He who has been banned is not, in fact, simply set outside the law and made indifferent to it but rather *abandoned* by it, that is, exposed and threatened on the threshold in which life and law, outside and inside, become indistinguishable. It is literally not possible to say whether the one who has been banned is outside or inside the juridical order." Agamben, *Homo Sacer,* 28–29.

27. Schmitt, *Politische Theologie,* 43.

*proper to it.* It will involve, in a word, an intervention into the realm of "creaturely life" and the processes of its production.[28]

V

In Benjamin's writings, which provide an especially rich archive for thinking about these issues, creaturely life is often associated with a mood closely linked to that of boredom, namely melancholia. In his *Origin of German Tragic Drama,* Benjamin argues that the melancholy affect "emerges from the depths of the creaturely realm" and "is the most genuinely creaturely of the contemplative impulses."[29] The background for these remarks is his idiosyncratic concept of natural history. In Benjamin's parlance, *Naturgeschichte* has to do with what Pippin referred to as the breakdown and reification of the normative structures of human life and mindedness. It refers, that is, not to the fact that nature also has a history but to the fact that the artifacts of human history tend to acquire an aspect of mute, natural being at the point where they begin to lose their place in a viable form of life (think of the process whereby architectural ruins are reclaimed by

28. For an extended discussion of the concept of miracle in Rosenzweig and Benjamin, among others, see Eric Santner, "Miracles Happen: Benjamin, Rosenzweig, Freud, and the Matter of the Neighbor," in *The Neighbor: Three Inquiries in Political Theology,* by Slavoj Žižek, Eric Santner, and Kenneth Reinhard (Chicago: University of Chicago Press, 2005). In a discussion of the Israeli-Palestinian impasse, Žižek has suggested that such a miraculous dimension opened up with the gesture of the so-called refuseniks, those Israeli soldiers who refused to serve in the occupied territories. By way of such a gesture, the creaturely aspect of those subject to the ongoing state of exception that characterizes so much of life in the occupied territories is transformed into that of the *neighbor.* And as Žižek adds, "We should note the difference between this Judaeo-Christian love for a neighbor and, say, the Buddhist compassion with suffering: this compassion does not refer to the 'neighbor' in the sense of the anxiety-provoking abyss of the Other's desire, but ultimately to the suffering which we, humans, share with animals (this is why, according to the doctrine of reincarnation, a human can be reborn as an animal)." See Slavoj Žižek, *Welcome to the Desert of the Real* (London: Verso, 2002), 116. I am suggesting, of course, that this Lacanian figure of the "anxiety-provoking abyss of the Other's desire" needs to be understood in conjunction with the theory of the state of exception.
29. Walter Benjamin, *The Origin of German Tragic Drama,* trans. John Osborne (London: NLB, 1977), 146. Subsequent references will be made in the text.

nature). This paradoxical exchange of properties between nature and history that constitutes the material density of natural historical being can be thought of in exactly the opposite way as well. Because human beings have not only natures but also *second natures,* when an artifact loses its place in a historical form of life—when that form of life decays, becomes exhausted, or dies—we experience it as something that has been *denaturalized,* transformed into a mere relic of historical being. To put it yet another way, natural history is born out of the dual possibilities that life can persist beyond the death of the symbolic forms that gave it meaning and that symbolic forms can persist beyond the death of the form of life that gave them human vitality. Natural history transpires against the background of this space between real and symbolic death, this space of the "undead."[30]

Natural history, as Benjamin understands it, thus points to a fundamental feature of human life, namely that the symbolic forms in and through which this life is structured can be hollowed out, lose their vitality, break up into a series of enigmatic signifiers, "hieroglyphs" that in some way continue to address us—get under our psychic skin—though we no longer possess the key to their meaning. For Benjamin, natural history ultimately names the ceaseless repetition of such cycles of emergence and decay of human orders of meaning, cycles that are, for him—and this is where the Schmittian background can be felt—always connected to violence.[31] It furthermore

30. In his essay "The Idea of Natural History," Theodor Adorno makes use of Lukacs's notion of "second nature" to help clarify Benjamin's understanding of natural history. The crucial phenomenon is, as Adorno puts it, "this fact of the world of historically produced conventions, of things that have become alien to us, that can't be decoded but that we encounter as ciphers." Theodor W. Adorno, "Die Idee der Naturgeschichte," in *Philosophische Frühschriften,* ed. Rolf Tiedemann (Frankfurt a.M.: Suhrkamp, 1973), 356.

31. In his early essay "The Critique of Violence," Benjamin characterizes the violence, the *Gewalt,* that he later associates with natural history and that Schmitt analyzes as the agonistic, decisionist logic of sovereignty, as *mythic.* Agamben has recently argued that Schmitt developed his own understanding of this logic through a reading of Benjamin's essay. See Agamben, *State of Exception,* 52–54. Benjamin, as we now know, wrote to Schmitt in 1930 that his own study of baroque drama was deeply indebted to the latter's presentation of the doctrine of sovereignty in the seventeenth century.

provides the key to the symbolic mode privileged by the baroque dramatists who experienced life in seventeenth-century Germany as one of irremediable exposure to the violence of natural historical temporality: *allegory*. Allegory is the symbolic mode that most vividly engages with man's thrownness into the "bad infinity" of natural historical "progression" (think here of Benjamin's own allegory of the angel of history staring helplessly at the wreckage of such "progress"). The great achievement of the allegorical mode of representation was, as Benjamin put it in one of the most famous passages from the book, that it rendered a sense of life bereft of any secure reference to transcendence, of life utterly exposed to the implacable rhythms of *natural history:*

Whereas in the symbol destruction is idealized and the transfigured face of nature is fleetingly revealed in the light of redemption, in allegory the observer is confronted with the *facies hippocratica* of history as a petrified, primordial landscape. Everything about history that, from the very beginning, has been untimely, sorrowful, unsuccessful is expressed in a face—or rather in a skull. (166; translation modified)

Allegory, he continues, is "the form in which man's subjection to nature is most obvious" (166). And in language that directly anticipates Sebald's gaze on human affairs, Benjamin writes that human history has meaning for the baroque poets "solely in the stations of its decline" (166). Allegory, a symbolic mode in which the link between figure and meaning is experienced as a human construct, is the proper mode of representation of *Naturgeschichte* because, as Benjamin continues,

the greater the significance, the greater the subjection to death, because death digs most deeply the jagged line of demarcation between physical nature and significance. But if nature has always been subject to the power of death, it is also true that it has always been allegorical. Significance and death both come to fruition in historical development, just as they are closely linked as seeds in the creature's graceless state of sin. (166)

One might think, in this context, of the first lines of Paul Celan's remarkable poem *Engführung* ("The Straitening"), in which this allegorical sensibility is pushed to a point of extreme of self-reference:

Verbracht ins
Gelände
mit der untrüglichen Spur:
Gras, auseinandergeschrieben. Die Steine, weiß,
mit den Schatten der Halme.

[Driven into the
terrain
with the unmistakable track:
grass, written asunder. The stones, white,
with the shadows of grass blades.][32]

It is not simply that gravestones — if that is indeed what they are — push aside blades of grass; it is that nature becomes divided from itself, becomes "written asunder," through exposure to the violence of human history. For Benjamin, such exposure provides access to a new aesthetic dimension, one that can no longer be captured by the notion of beauty:

The word "history" stands written on the countenance of nature in the characters of transience. The allegorical physiognomy of the nature-history, which is put on stage in the *Trauerspiel,* is present in reality in the form of the ruin. In the ruin history has physically merged into the setting. And in this guise history does not assume the form of the process of an eternal life so much as that of irresistible decay. Allegory thereby declares itself to be beyond beauty. Allegories are, in the realm of thoughts, what ruins are in the realm of things. (178)

32. Celan was, of course, a dedicated reader of Benjamin. The translation of the poem was done by Michael Hamburger, whose connections to Sebald are developed at length in *The Rings of Saturn.* See *Poems of Paul Celan,* trans. Michael Hamburger (New York: Persea Books, 1988).

Allegory is, on this view, the symbolic mode proper to the experience of irremediable exposure to the violence of history, the rise and fall of empires and orders of meaning, the endless cycle of struggles for hegemony; it is, furthermore, what defines the posture of melancholy, the affect so intimately linked to the dimension we have been calling "the creaturely." One should add that the "posture of melancholy" had, both for Benjamin and for the cultural tradition at issue, a quite literal meaning. The allegorical sensibility associated with the melancholic disposition and "immersion in the life of creaturely things" bent the back forward, drew the gaze earthward: "Everything saturnine points down into the depths of the earth. . . . Here the downward gaze is characteristic of the saturnine man, who bores into the ground with his eyes" (152). For Benjamin, Dürer's famous woodcut *Melancholia I* provides the ultimate emblem of this posture and of the allegorical sensibility as one that arises from a condition of radical designification, of an emptying out of (conventional) meaning:

The deadening of the emotions, and the ebbing away of the waves of life which are the source of these emotions in the body, can increase the distance between the self and the surrounding world to the point of alienation from the body. As soon as this symptom of depersonalization was seen as an intense degree of mournfulness, the concept of the pathological state, in which the most simple object appears to be a symbol of some enigmatic wisdom because it lacks any natural, creative relationship to us, was set in an incomparably productive context. It accords with this that in the proximity of Albrecht Dürer's figure, *Melencholia,* the utensils of active life are lying around unused on the floor, as objects of contemplation. (140) [33]

33. Recalling the image of the bat in Rilke's Eighth Elegy, one might note that in Dürer's allegory of melancholy it is a bat that holds the scroll bearing the inscription "Melencholia I." As Giorgio Agamben has noted, "This can be considered an authentic minor emblem that holds the key to the larger emblem that contains it. In the *Hieroglyphica* of Horapollo, the bat in flight is interpreted as representing man's attempt to boldly transcend the misery of his condition by daring the impossible: 'For this creature, although lacking wings, attempts to fly.'" Giorgio Agamben, *Stanzas: Word and Phantasm in Western Culture,* trans. Ronald L. Martinez (Minneapolis: University of Minnesota Press, 1993), 27.

Finally, perhaps alluding to his own earlier essay "The Critique of Violence," Benjamin suggests that the experience of natural historical temporality is nowhere more unnerving than in the realm of *law*. As he puts in the work on baroque drama, "The most obvious catastrophes did not perhaps impress this experience on men any more bitterly than the changes in legal norms, with their claims to eternal validity, which were particularly evident at those historical turning-points. Allegory established itself most permanently where transitoriness and eternity confronted each other most closely" (224).[34]

VI

Given this last claim, it should come as no surprise that for Benjamin it is Kafka's writings that provide the greatest single resource for understanding the dimension of creaturely life in its modern incarnations. In Kafka's universe, the "natural historical" dimension of law that gives rise to the allegorical sensibility comes to be registered as a chronic state of agitation and disorientation, a perpetual state of exception/emergency in which the boundaries of the law become undecidable. There the dimension of creaturely life is an index of an

---

34. In the study of baroque drama, Benjamin focuses on various figures in which the energies of such turning points seem to condense, among them the tyrant, the martyr, and the intriguer. In *The Notebooks of Malte Laurids Brigge,* Rilke presents the fourteenth and fifteenth centuries under the sign of such disorientation, as the "heavy, massive, desperate age" in which the proliferation and confusion of friend/enemy distinctions became insupportable: "Who in that age could be strong enough to refrain from murder? Who didn't know that the worst was inevitable? Here and there someone whose glance had during the day met the savoring glance of his murderer, would be overwhelmed by a strange foreboding. . . . The eyes of the dogs, as they looked up at him, were filled with doubt, and they grew less and less sure of his commands. From the motto that had served him all his life, a secondary meaning quietly emerged. Many long-established customs appeared antiquated, but there didn't seem to be any substitutes to take their place. . . . And then, before the late supper, this pensiveness over the hands in the silver washbasin. Your own hands. Could any coherence be brought into what they did? any order or continuity in their grasping and releasing? No. All men attempted both the thing and its opposite. All men canceled themselves out; there was no such thing as action." Rainer Maria Rilke, *The Notebooks of Malte Laurids Brigge,* trans. Stephen Mitchell (New York: Vintage, 1983), 228–29.

ongoing and passionate subjection not to a Creator God or even to a sovereign whose legitimacy is figured on the model of the Creator, but to an agency, a master's discourse, that has been attenuated and dispersed across a field of relays and points of contact that no longer cohere, even in fantasy, as a consistent "other" of possible address and redress. In Kafka, the law is everywhere and nowhere. The "psycho-theology of everyday life" in Kafka—the dimension that has called forth both psychoanalytic and theological readings of his work—is generated, I am suggesting, by a mutation in the logic of the sovereign function, by new modes of organization and dissemination of what I earlier characterized as sovereign jouissance (this mutation and dispersion of the master's authority was, of course, the great topic of Michel Foucault's mature work). The typical experience of Kafka's protagonists recalls Agamben's gloss on Heidegger's phenomenology of boredom, the mood where human and animal life enter into an uncanny proximity: "Dasein is delivered over to something that re-fuses itself, exactly as the animal, in its captivation, is exposed in something unrevealed."[35] In Kafka, the dimension of the "unre-vealed"—a dimension condensed in the objects that seize the allegor-ical imagination—pertains not to man's destiny in the openness of Be-ing but to the status of law in its (now dispersed, now chronic) state of exception. When, at his execution at the end of *The Trial,* Josef K. exclaims, "like a dog," Kafka is thus referring not only to the pathetic scene of K.'s execution but also to the larger structure of K.'s experi-ence with the law, one that renders him, precisely, "creaturely." To bring it to a formula, creaturely life is just life abandoned to the state of exception/emergency, that paradoxical domain in which law has been suspended in the name of preserving law. And once again, what is included in the state of exception is not simply outside the law but inside an *outlaw dimension internal to the law,* subject not to law but rather to sovereign jouissance.

Creatureliness is also at issue in the reference to *shame* that imme-diately follows upon Josef K.'s exclamation ("like a dog") and provides the last words of the novel as we know it: "It was as if the

35. Agamben, *Open,* 65.

shame would outlive him."[36] In a 1935 essay on shame recently published under the title *On Escape,* Emmanuel Levinas has suggested (in a still Heideggerian vein) that shame does not simply refer to one's reduction to one's animal nakedness but pertains to the dimension where one is, as Levinas puts it, *riveted to oneself,* placed in that (non)relation to an opacity that is one's own being: "Nakedness is shameful when it is the sheer visibility of our being, of its ultimate intimacy. And the nakedness of our body is not that of a material thing, antithesis of spirit, but the nakedness of our total being in all its fullness and solidity of its most brutal expression of which we could not fail to take note."[37] To flesh out the nature of the "solidity" at issue in this abandonment to oneself, Levinas refers to the famous scene in *City Lights* in which Chaplin's tramp swallows a whistle at a party given by his benefactor; every time he hiccups, a whistle emanates from his body. As Levinas puts it, the whistle "works like a recording device, which betrays the discrete manifestations of a presence that Charlie's legendary tramp costume barely dissimulates. . . . It is . . . our intimacy, that is, our presence to ourselves, that is shameful."[38]

What Levinas gets right here—and that is what is so perfect about the example from *City Lights*—is that shame pertains not merely to the body but to an uncanny, somehow material, excess experienced as both intimate and foreign to oneself (Jacques Lacan coined the phrase *extimacy (extimité)* to capture this dimension). In his efforts to deepen Levinas's analysis—to move it beyond its still overly Heideggerian frame—Agamben comes much closer, I think, to what is at issue in the final words of Kafka's *Trial:*

To be ashamed means to be consigned to something that cannot be assumed. But what cannot be assumed is not something external. Rather, it originates in our own intimacy; it is what is most intimate in us (for example, our own physiological life). Here the "I" is thus overcome by its own passivity, its

---

36. The following reflections are indebted to various presentations Joan Copjec has given on the topic of shame.

37. Emmanuel Levinas, *On Escape* [*De l'évasion*], trans. Bettina Bergo (Stanford: Stanford University Press, 2003), 65.

38. Ibid.

ownmost sensibility; yet this expropriation and desubjectification is also an extreme and irreducible presence of the "I" to itself. It is as if our consciousness collapsed and, seeking to flee in all directions, were simultaneously summoned by an irrefutable order to be present at its own defacement. . . . This double movement, which is both subjectification and desubjectification, is shame.[39]

My one reservation concerning Agamben's otherwise compelling formulation is that it appears to occlude the paradoxical—the *extimate*—status of the occasion of shame (again, think of Chaplin's whistle). What is impossible to assume is not an intimacy that is already constituted but one that is, if I may put it that way, ex-cited into existence by the very summons that ostensibly turns us toward it (recall the meaning of *excitare:* to call or summon out). The creaturely life that Benjamin found everywhere in Kafka's writings is, in a word, a piece not of nature, there to be assumed or not assumed, but of natural history; in Kafka's work—and this is, I think, what gives it its particular force—creatureliness is a by-product of exposure to what we might call the *excitations of power,* those enigmatic bits of address and interpellation that disturb the social space—and bodies—of his protagonists.

In one of his many attempts at characterizing the process and effects of being rendered creaturely by such exposure, Benjamin focuses quite explicitly on the bodies of Kafka's figures, so many of whom are bent over, contracted, distorted (Benjamin's word is *entstellt*). The prototype of the cringed body is, Benjamin suggests, a figure who appears nowhere in Kafka's work but haunts it nonetheless, *das bucklicht Männlein,* or the hunchback: "Among the images in Kafka's stories, none is more frequent than that of the man who bows his head far down on his chest: the fatigue of the court officials, the noise affecting the doormen in the hotel, the low ceiling facing the visitors in the

---

39. Giorgio Agamben, *Remnants of Auschwitz: The Witness and the Archive,* trans. Daniel Heller-Roazen (Cambridge: MIT Press, 1999), 105–6. Speaking of the shame announced at the end of *The Trial,* Agamben refers to the creaturely life K. is compelled to assume as "*a new ethical material* . . . in the living being" (104; my emphasis). I will argue that Sebald's work brings this new ethical material into focus in an original and sustained way.

gallery. In the *Penal Colony* those in power use an archaic apparatus which engraves letters with curlicues on the backs of guilty men."[40] The image is crucial for Benjamin, for he also suggests that redemption can be understood as a passage through and beyond the creaturely life materialized in these cringed bodies. The hunchback, Benjamin writes, "will disappear with the coming of the Messiah, who (a great rabbi once said) will not wish to change the world by force but will merely make a slight adjustment in it [*nur um ein Geringes sie zurechtstellen werde*]."[41]

VII

In this context I might note the crucial difference between my "biopolitical" approach to creaturely life and that of Beatrice Hanssen, who also places this notion at the center of her work on Walter Benjamin and the German-Jewish tradition more generally.[42] Hanssen's exemplary project is to excavate in this tradition the resources for a new

40. Benjamin, "Franz Kafka: On the Tenth Anniversary of His Death," trans. Harry Zohn, in *Walter Benjamin: Selected Writings*, vol. 2, *1927–1934*, ed. Michael Jennings, Howard Eiland, and Gary Smith (Cambridge: Harvard University Press, 1999), 810–11. Benjamin's evocation of the hunchback strongly resonates with Primo Levi's description of the so-called Muselmann, the figure who represents, for Levi, the paradox of the complete—and impossible—*witness* to the truth of the death camps: "They crowd my memory with their faceless presence, and if I could enclose all the evil of our time in one image, I would choose this image which is familiar to me: an emaciated man, with head dropped and shoulders curved, on whose face and in whose eyes not a trace of thought is to be seen." Primo Levi, *Survival in Auschwitz: The Nazi Assault on Humanity*, trans. Stuart Wolf (New York: Touchstone, 1996), 90. The Muselmann is, it seems, the figure whose being has been fully reduced to the substance of a "cringe," whose existence has been reduced to its pure, "protocosmic" being, who is *there* yet no longer "in the world." What remains, that is, at this zero degree of social existence, in this zone between symbolic and real death, is not pure biological (animal or vegetable) life but rather something like the direct embodiment of creaturely life. We might say that the Muselmann is *the human in the neighborhood of zero*.
41. Benjamin, "Kafka," 811. Benjamin cites the song, "Das buckliche Männlein," from the famous collection *Des Knaben Wunderhorn: Alte deutsche Lieder*, edited by Achim von Arnim and Clemens Brentano.
42. In the following I will be referring to Beatrice Hanssen's *Walter Benjamin's Other History: Of Stones, Animals, Human Beings, and Angels* (Berkeley: University of California Press, 2000). Subsequent references will be made in the text.

"ethico-theological response to the creatural" (162), a capacious form of openness to "infra-human" forms of life that would help to break down the boundaries between the human and the nonhuman. By contrast, I have emphasized the paradoxes of the "political theology" of creaturely life as a distinctly human dimension. To put it somewhat differently, human beings are not just creatures among other creatures but are in some sense *more creaturely* than other creatures by virtue of an excess that is produced in the space of the political and that, paradoxically, accounts for their "humanity."

Hanssen compellingly argues that Benjamin's understanding of creaturely life underwent significant changes over the course of his career. She suggests that the fate of the concept in his work largely took shape around the "inherent duplicity or ambiguity of the term *Kreatur* . . . [signaling] the lowliest form of animality as well as human depravity" (104). Among the texts that seem to document Benjamin's deep commitment to an "ethico-theological response to the creatural," perhaps none is more passionate than his famous essay on Nikolai Leskov, "The Storyteller." There Benjamin writes, for example, that "the righteous man is the advocate of all creatures [*der Fürsprech der Kreatur*], and at the same time he is their highest embodiment." And further, "The hierarchy of the creaturely world, which has its apex in the righteous man, reaches down into the abyss of the inanimate through many gradations."[43] But as Benjamin makes very clear, the compassion, caring, and righteousness at issue here are deployed not simply on behalf of the suffering of bare life or in the name of the protection of nature against instrumental reason, but in the service of what he refers to as the work of *disenchantment:* "In keeping with Russian folk belief, [Leskov] interpreted the Resurrection less as a transfiguration than as a disenchantment, in a sense akin to that found in fairy tales."[44] As I understand it, the enchantment at issue here can be understood only in conjunction with, indeed as a

43. Walter Benjamin, "The Storyteller," trans. Harry Zohn, in *Selected Writings,* vol. 3, *1935–1938,* ed. Howard Eiland and Michael Jennings (Cambridge: Harvard University Press, 2002), 158–59.
44. Ibid., 158.

by-product of, what I have referred to as sovereign jouissance. Disenchantment means, then, a deanimation of creaturely life or, better, of the "undeadness" proper to this dimension.[45]

Indeed, Hanssen seems to suggest as much when she turns to Benjamin's writings about Kafka and comes very close to the biopolitical conception of creaturely life I have been developing. As she puts it, "Much like 'Critique of Violence,' whose argument unmistakably formed the background of Benjamin's Kafka interpretation, the Kafka essay sought to uncover the mythical origins of the power exerted by secular law" (143). She then goes on to note the deep affinities between Benjamin's project and Freud's, emphasizing the central importance of *Totem and Taboo* for understanding both Kafka and Benjamin: "In the same way, Benjamin's Kafka essay retraced the presence and persistence of primeval history (*Urgeschichte*) in the historical present, a Freudian project also central to *The Arcades Project*. Indeed, the encounter or collision between the present and primeval beginnings (*Uranfänge*) accounted for the new form of experience Kafka's work depicted" (107). It should, however, be clear that Freud's account of totemism emerges not on the basis of some sort of intuition about human-animal similarities or an ethical sense of solidarity with animal life; it addresses, rather, one thing only: the afterlife of the sovereign jouissance embodied in the figure Freud so famously portrayed as the primal father. I will return to Freud's myth of the primal father and murder—this myth concerning the *Aufhebung* of myth—in chapter 2; for the moment I hope these remarks clarify the centrality of the biopolitical conception of creaturely life for the thinkers in question.

VIII

In a brilliant essay on Shakespeare's *The Tempest*, Julia Lupton has referred to the same German-Jewish tradition I have been invoking here to capture the structural and historical specificity of that most famous incarnation of creaturely life in the Western tradition, the figure of

---

45. I will return to the topic of the "undead" in the following chapters.

Caliban. It is precisely the concept of creaturely life she develops there that allows her to chart a new course of interpretive possibilities beyond the binary opposition that has framed so much of the scholarship on the play; that is, humanist universalization on the one hand and culturalist particularization/postcolonial historicization on the other. I would like to dwell for a moment on her essay because there are so many fruitful resonances between her project and the concerns of this book.

In her essay, Lupton emphasizes a dimension of creaturely life that will be central to my discussion. Noting the derivation of the word "creature" from the future-active participle of the Latin *creare,* Lupton writes that the *"creatura* is a thing always in the process of undergoing creation; the creature is actively passive or, better, *passionate,* perpetually becoming created, subject to transformations at the behest of the arbitrary commands of an Other."[46] "Creature" is not so much the name of a determinate state of being as the signifier of an ongoing *exposure,* of being caught up in the process of *becoming creature* through the dictates of divine alterity. This dimension of radical subjection—of created thing to creator—has induced, in the history of the concept, a series of further articulations, ultimately becoming generalized to signify "anyone or anything that is produced or controlled by an agent, author, master, or tyrant" (1). At the end of such a trajectory—and here we return to the duplicity inherent in the term noted by Hanssen—it makes some sense that the word that had, in its original theological context, denoted the entire domain of *nature* qua God's creation comes to signify what "borders on the monstrous and unnatural," comes to be "increasingly applied to those created things that warp the proper canon of creation" (1).[47]

<hr>

46. Julia Lupton, "Creature Caliban," *Shakespeare Quarterly* 51, no. 1 (Spring 2000): 1. Subsequent references will be made in the text.
47. It is difficult, in this context, not to think of Kafka's Gregor Samsa. As Stanley Corngold has reminded us, the etymology of the words Kafka uses to introduce Gregor's transformation in the famous first sentence of the story underlines this disturbance in the canon of creation: "'*Ungeheuer*' connotes the creature who has no place in the family; '*Ungeziefer*,' the unclean animal unsuited for sacrifice, the creature without a place in God's order." See "Introduction," in *"The Metamorphosis," by Franz Kafka,* trans. and ed. Stanley Corngold (New York: Bantam, 1986), xix.

In the conceptual history Lupton sketches, what ultimately under-writes this paradoxical passage from the natural to the unnatural in the semantic field of creaturely life is that feature of the "master" that was central to the theory of sovereignty elaborated by Schmitt and taken up by Benjamin and, most recently, Agamben. As Lupton puts it,

Creature represents the flip side of the political theology of absolute sover-eignty developed in the late-sixteenth and early-seventeenth centuries. In Schmitt's analysis the king is like God in the creative-destructive potential of his decisive word, his juris-diction. By extension, his subjects are his creatures, the objects of his continual sovereign activity, which is *a power that comes to the forefront during states of emergency,* when the normal functioning of positive law is lifted in favor of the king's executive decisions. (5; my emphasis)

Once again, it is not the mere fact of being in a relation of subject to sovereign that generates creaturely "non-nature," but the exposure to an "outlaw" dimension of law internal to sovereign authority. The state of exception/emergency is that aspect of law that marks a thresh-old of undecidability proper to the functioning of law/sovereign authority: the "master's discourse" in the state of exception marks a *sanctioned suspension of law,* an outside of law included within the law. Creaturely life emerges precisely at such impossible thresholds. In the course of her discussion of the play and the ways this dynamic cou-pling of sovereignty and creatureliness is elaborated in the relation-ship between Prospero and Caliban, Lupton sheds further—we might say "Nietzschean"—light on what Benjamin characterized, apropos of Kafka's figures, as the *cringe* of creaturely life:

The institution of sovereignty through the enforced establishment of differ-ence creates the conditions for resentment. . . . Resentment brings Caliban to speech at the level of the symptom, a psychosomatic phenomenon that artic-ulates and inflames the creaturely edges of his being. The pinches and cramps that Prospero visits upon Caliban need have no magical or physical source at all; they may simply manifest the passion born of enforced service, the sting-ing nettles of resentment as it flowers on the body of the creature inhabiting the edge of symbolization. . . . The aches and pains caused by Prospero's ınands are . . . a passionate inscription on the body of Caliban of his ᴧaster's rule. . . . "Thou shalt have cramps, / Side-stitches that shall pen thy breath up": the phenomenology of the cramp that pens up breath with its suturing side-stitches describes the suffocating, claustrophobic response, the oppressive sense of internal constraint, that occurs in reaction to Prospero's archaic, noncontractual rule over Caliban. . . . Caliban . . . suffers not under the law but outside the law. Lacking access to legal types of accounting, the Creature keeps track of servitude in the only writing available to him: the cramped script, the tattooing side-stitches of the symptom. (11)

In the course of her reflections, Lupton suggests that the very thing that constrains, that cringes the body of Caliban with creaturely excess, might become a resource for new kinds of social links. "Caliban's loneliness," she writes, "is a further sign of his imprisonment, of his exile *from* the island *on* the island, but it may also represent the possibility of another type of subjectivization, another model of humanity resident in the motif of the creature, that exists somewhere just beyond the conceptual limits of the play" (13). I understand the twentieth-century thinkers and writers discussed in this volume—and W. G. Sebald stands in as my central "witness" here—as all being dedicated to exploring just such possibilities.

IX

Though psychoanalytic thought will not play the dominant role in the following discussion, I nonetheless propose that the Freudian project can and should be understood as an attempt to get clear about the laws by which creaturely life is called—is *ex-cited*—into being and finds expression. The so-called formations of the unconscious can be understood, in other words, as the specific modes of expressivity of creaturely life. To put it somewhat differently, understanding what is at stake in psychoanalysis comes down to grasping Freud's crucial distinction between animal and human sexuality, between *instinct* and *drive*. One of Freud's great insights was that human sexuality, precisely that dimension of human life where we seem to be utterly reduced to animality, is actually the point at which our difference from animals is in some ways most radical. Human sexuality, in Freud's account, is fundamentally perverse, fundamentally swerves from any teleological orientation provided by instinctual endowment.[48] To return to Heidegger's distinction, what Freud discovers is that human sexuality conforms *neither* to animal behavior *nor* to intentional comportment in the world. Human sexuality is, for Freud, a *natural historical* phenomenon in Benjamin's sense: it is called into being by, it gets organized around, enigmatic signifiers—what Benjamin, in the context of his analysis of allegory, has referred to as the *erregende Schrift*—emanating from the locus of the other. As I will argue in detail in chapter 4, a good deal of Sebald's work is engaged with the problem of sexuality as a dimension of creaturely life.

Freud's discovery of the creaturely laws of human sexuality famously began with a false start. According to his first theory of the etiology of hysteria, symptoms are produced through the repression of a determinate and ultimately datable experience of premature "sexualization" in childhood—the *trauma* of sexual abuse at the hands of an adult (and thus the trauma of one's own, if I might put it that way, overwhelming passivity). Freud would revise this theory to allow for the etiology of neurotic symptoms based on not simply external events intruding on an essentially passive subject but *psychic events* connected to the birth of sexuality in the human child. These events pertain ultimately—and here I am reading Freud in light of Lacanian and post-Lacanian theory—to the encounter with the enigma of parental desire. The revised theory shares with the first the notion that what is traumatic is ultimately the overproximity to the mysterious desire of the other. The difference is that in the later theory such

48. Jonathan Lear has provided a concise summary of this point: "It seems more accurate to see Freud as subverting the category of rational animal altogether. For if we had to place our sexuality anywhere, it would be on the 'animal' side of this divide, but Freud shows us that it is precisely in our sexuality that we radically separate ourselves from the rest of the animal kingdom. It is only a slight exaggeration to say that there is nothing about human life we hold less in common with animals than our sexuality. We can imagine a bird happening to make a nest out of a lady's shoe; we cannot imagine her getting excited about it. The shoe-as-nest holds onto a biological function; the shoe-as-fetish leaves that behind." Lear, *Therapeutic Action: An Earnest Plea for Irony* (New York: Other Press, 2003), 150.

overproximity assumes a certain structural value and need not have been acted out in any egregious manner; the fundamentally disorienting encounter with the other's desire is now seen to be *constitutive* of what we understand as human subjectivity. What must be kept in mind here is that the shift to a more structural perspective on the emergence of the *Triebschicksal* or drive destiny that both opens and constrains the life of human desire does not supersede but complicates the event-structure at issue in the concepts of trauma and seduction. The encounter with the desire of the other remains, in a word, *eventful* (indeed, it is this very tension between structure and event, essence and contingency that one tries to capture with the notion of the *primal scene*).

According to this revised notion of seduction, the human child is *ex-cited* by enigmatic messages emanating from the parental other, messages indicating something profoundly amiss, something fundamentally lacking, in the other. As Lacan has put it,

A lack is encountered by the subject in the Other, in the very intimation that the Other makes to him by his discourse. In the intervals of the discourse of the Other, there emerges in the experience of the child something that is radically mappable, namely, *He is saying this to me, but what does he want?* . . . The desire of the Other is apprehended by the subject in that which does not work, in the lacks of the discourse of the Other, and all the child's *whys* reveal not so much an avidity for the reason of things, as a testing of the adult, a *Why are you telling me this?* ever-resuscitated from its base, which is the enigma of the adult's desire.[49]

According to this theory, the child works at translating this enigma into more or less determinate demands—demands one can comply with, reject, fail at fulfilling, feel guilty about, and so on. As Jean Laplanche, the student of Lacan who has most systematically elaborated this notion of the enigmatic message (and the *general theory of seduction* it implies), has written, the fundamental situation that gives rise to unconscious formations

49. Jacques Lacan, *The Four Fundamental Concepts of Psychoanalysis,* trans. Alan Sheridan (New York: W. W. Norton, 1981), 214.

is an encounter between an individual whose psycho-somatic structures are situated predominantly at the level of need, and signifiers emanating from an adult. Those signifiers pertain to the satisfaction of the child's needs, but they also convey the purely interrogative potential of other messages—and those other messages are sexual. These enigmatic messages set the child the difficult, or even impossible, task of mastery and symbolization and the attempt to perform it inevitably leaves behind unconscious residues. . . . I refer to them as the source-objects of the drives.[50]

It is this never-ceasing work of symbolization and failure at symbolization, translation, and failure at translation, that constitutes the *signifying stress* at the core of creaturely life.[51] We have here, then, something of a tragic cycle: my signifying stress is called forth—*ex-cited*—by my efforts to translate the signifying stress emanating from the other, indicating in its turn the other's "addiction" to his or her own enigmas. Or as Laplanche has put it, "Internal alien-ness maintained, held in place by external alien-ness; external alien-ness, in turn, held in place by the enigmatic relation of the other to his own internal alien."[52]

I would like to emphasize that at the heart of this conception of the birth of the unconscious and its formations is a fundamentally *natural historical* understanding of human being. The point of departure of the allegorical imagination as understood by Benjamin—one's "thrownness" into a dense matrix of natural historical signification— is, on this view, recapitulated at the genesis of every unconscious formation. To understand this one must bear in mind the difference between a "signifier of something" and a "signifier to someone" and so of an address that can never be fully "subjectivized," integrated into the texture of one's ego-life. As Laplanche has put it,

What comes to the fore at certain moments is that aspect of the signifier which signifies to someone, which interpellates someone, in the sense that

---

50. Jean Laplanche, *New Foundations for Psychoanalysis,* trans. David Macey (Oxford: Basil Blackwell, 1989), 130.
51. I first encountered this locution of "signifying" or "significant stress" in discussions with Irad Kimhi.
52. Jean Laplanche, *Essays on Otherness,* ed. John Fletcher (London: Routledge, 1999), 80.

we can speak of an official signifying a court decision, or issuing a . . . prefectoral decree. This foregrounding of "signifying to" is extremely important, as a signifier can signify *to* without its addressee necessarily knowing *what* it signifies. We know *that* it signifies, but not what it signifies. . . . Lacan suggests the image of hieroglyphs in the desert, or of cuneiform characters carved on a tablet of stone. . . . It . . . means that the signifier may be *designified,* or lose what it signifies, without thereby losing its power to signify *to.*[53]

Unconscious mental life gets mobilized around such enigmatic signifiers that can never be fully metabolized, translated into the projects that make up the life of the ego. They persist as loci of signifying stress, excitations linked to but not absorbed by our life in the space of meaning. It is the excess of pressure that emerges at such sites—really a kind of life in excess both of our merely biological life and of our life in the space of meaning—that I am calling *creaturely.*[54]

The signifiers that become "master" signifiers of unconscious mental life are, I would argue, precisely those that sustain a link to the threshold where life assumes its biopolitical intensity. To put it somewhat differently, the signifiers that pertain to the emergence—and emergency—of creaturely life are those that enter into the formation of the superego (a topic I will return to in chapter 2). For the moment, it is worth recalling a series of remarks Laplanche made on these connections. Their immediate concern is with the links between Kant's conception of the categorical imperative, Freud's myth of the primal father, and the agency of the superego. A true categorical

53. Laplanche, *New Foundations,* 44–45.

54. I think this is the ultimate intuition behind Lacan's claim about the Freudian "reality principle" as first adumbrated in the correspondence with Fliess. Lacan writes that "the reality principle has a secret that . . . is paradoxical. If Freud speaks of the reality principle, it is in order to reveal to us that from a certain point of view it is always defeated; it only manages to affirm itself at the margin. And this is so by reason of a kind of pressure that . . . Freud calls not 'the vital needs' . . . but *die Not des Lebens* in the German text. An infinitely stronger phrase. Something that *wishes.* 'Need' and not 'needs.' Pressure, urgency. The state of *Not* is the state of emergency of life." Jacques Lacan, *The Seminar of Jacques Lacan. Book VII, The Ethics of Psychoanalysis: 1959–1960,* trans. Dennis Porter (New York: W. W. Norton, 1992), 46.

imperative, Laplanche suggests, would be "an implacable 'do this' which did not have to be justified at all." He continues,

In the context of an extreme form of religion, namely the Judaic religion to which Levinas refers, God hands down the Law, and the Law does not have to be justified. Freud too raises the issue of the categorical imperative by pointing out that the orders given by the superego are tyrannical and unjustifiable. Because of his mania for phylogenesis, Freud traces this arbitrariness back to the first two tenets of the Father of the Horde: he was himself invulnerable and his possession of women must not be challenged.

Laplanche goes on to endow the signifiers that enter into the formation of the superego with the quality of partial objects, bits of the real forming the kernel of "psychotic enclaves inside the human personality as such":

There are good grounds for looking very seriously into the notion that the categorical imperative is born of the superego, and for dwelling on one specific aspect of it: categorical imperatives cannot be justified; they are certainly enigmatic in the same way that other adult messages are enigmatic; but not only are they unjustified, it is possible that they are unjustifiable, or in other words non-metabolizable. This means that they cannot be diluted, and cannot be replaced by anything else. They exist, and they are immutable and cannot be symbolized.[55]

Laplanche ultimately admits his perplexity concerning these matters, suggesting that they frame future investigations of unconscious mental life. My wager in this book is that the site for such investigations is the threshold where life takes on its specific biopolitical intensity, where it assumes the cringed posture of the *creature*. My further wager is that such investigations are most productive when undertaken in the company of poets.

55. Laplanche, *New Foundations,* 138–39.

x

Let me conclude by recalling a few words of the last great representative of the German-Jewish tradition I have invoked here, Paul Celan.
In his famous speech when he received the Georg Büchner Prize in
1960, Celan offers an account of poetic discourse as one addressed,
precisely, from and to the creaturely dimension of human life. In the
speech, Celan develops his conception of the poet's task by way of a
reading of Büchner's prose and plays, which he locates within the field
of tensions between the high artificiality of art—of *Kunst*—and what
Celan refers to as "the angle of inclination"—the *Neigungswinkel*—of
man's creatureliness.[56] Celan makes use of Büchner's famous story,
"Lenz," to establish the link between this "angle of inclination" and
historical trauma. Recalling the opening line of the story—"On the
20th of January Lenz walked through the mountains"—Celan tenta-
tively asks, "Perhaps we may say that every poem has its '20th of January' inscribed? Perhaps what's new for poems written today is just
this: that here the attempt is clearest to remain mindful of such dates
[*solcher Daten eingedenk zu bleiben*]?"[57] Celan is clearly alluding,
among other things, to the date of the infamous Wannsee Conference
during which the "final solution" of the Jewish question in Europe was

---

56. Paul Celan, "The Meridian," in *Selected Poems and Prose of Paul Celan,* trans. John
Felstiner (New York: W. W. Norton, 2001), 409. Celan is very likely alluding here to
Benjamin's remarks about the bent backs—the constitutive cringe—of so many of
Kafka's figures. But toward the end of *Malte,* Rilke provides a scene that Celan may also
have had in mind when he wrote these words. In it Rilke's protagonist finally encounters the blind newspaper vendor he had worked so hard at avoiding. What he encounters is, we might say, a fellow creature: "Immediately I knew that my picture of him was
worthless. His absolute abandonment and wretchedness, unlimited by any precaution
or disguise, went far beyond what I had been able to imagine. I had understood neither
the angle of his face [*den Neigungswinkel seiner Haltung*] nor the terror which the inside
of his eyelids seemed to keep radiating into him." It is, of course, crucial that Malte experiences this moment as a kind of revelation, one that seems to involve the elevation of
the creature to the status of *neighbor:* "My God, I thought with sudden vehemence, so
you really *are.* There are proofs of your existence. I have forgotten them all and never
even wanted any, for what a huge obligation would lie in the certainty of you. And yet
that is what has just been shown to me." Rilke, *Malte Laurids Brigge,* 210–11.
57. Celan, "Meridian," 409.

administratively resolved, an operation that transpired, as Agamben has rightly emphasized, within the framework of a state of exception declared to be the norm. It is, Celan suggests, only on the basis of attentiveness to the *Neigungswinkel* in oneself and the other—cringes that have contracted around the impact of such "dates," such historical "primal scenes," and the multiple layers and structures of experience they stand in for—that poetry can achieve, perhaps, the miracle of what he refers to as a "breath's turn," an *Atemwende* (think of it as Celan's poetological figure for the "slight adjustment" in the realm of creaturely life envisioned by Benjamin). It is a turn that transpires, as he says, within the *"mystery of an encounter"*:

The poem wants to reach an Other, it needs this Other. . . . It seeks it out, speaks toward it. . . . The attentiveness a poem devotes to all it encounters, with its sharper sense of detail, outline, structure, color, but also of "quiverings" and "intimations"—all this, I think, is not attained by an eye vying (or conniving) with constantly more perfect instruments. Rather, it is a concentration that stays mindful of all our dates.[58]

It as at this point that Celan explicitly refers to Benjamin's 1934 essay on Kafka, comparing his own conception of a concentration that stays mindful of all our dates to the kind of attentiveness that Kafka brought to creaturely life. The passage in question is well known: "Even if Kafka did not pray—and this we do not know—he still possessed in the highest degree what Malebranche called 'the natural prayer of the soul': attentiveness [*Aufmerksamkeit*]. And in this attentiveness he included all living creatures, as saints include them in their prayers."[59] As I see it, the great challenge to all contemporary efforts to think through the nature of ethical and political life and action is

58. Ibid., 409–10.
59. Benjamin, "Kafka," 812. I am not sure whether Celan had Rilke's Eighth Elegy in mind, but it is, finally, worth noting that Celan posits such attentiveness to the creaturely as the key to the passage into *das Offene:* "And once, given the attentiveness devoted to things and creatures, we even got near something open and free [*in die Nähe eines Offenen und Freien*]. And at last near utopia" (411).

to sustain, in this thought, the energies and focus of just such attentiveness to the singular archive I have been calling creaturely life.

I would like to address very briefly the historical question of why the
sense of creaturely life I have been elaborating here became so important for the German-Jewish thinkers I have discussed in this introduction. Of course the first thing to note is that the resonances of the
terms I have been using—the creature, the creaturely, creaturely life—
extended well beyond this small cluster of writers into the larger intellectual and cultural milieu of interwar and postwar Germany more
generally (we have already seen the intensity of both Rilke's and
Heidegger's engagement with these terms). Of particular importance
in this context is the journal *Die Kreatur,* which appeared from 1926 to
1929. First conceived by Florens Christian Rang, the journal was edited by Martin Buber, Joseph Wittig, and Viktor von Weizsäcker (the
editorial team was programmatically composed of a Jew, a Catholic,
and a Protestant). The title Rang had originally planned was *Grüße
aus den Exilen,* greetings from the places of exile. In the introduction
to the first volume, the editors emphasize the shared messianic longings of their Jewish, Protestant, and Catholic constituents, longings
grounded not only in the figure of exile but also in a solidarity with all
creaturely life, "a Yes to the connectedness of the created world, the
world as creature."[60]

But as I argued in my brief discussion of Hanssen's work, my strong
sense is that for the writers I have discussed here the "creaturely"

---

60. *Die Kreatur* 1 (1926–27): 2. Paul Mendes-Flohr traces the origins of the journal to
discussions of the so-called Patmos Circle, a group of Jewish and Christian thinkers
around Franz Rosenzweig and Eugen Rosenstock. See Mendes-Flohr, "Apocalyptic and
Prophetic Eschatology: A Jewish Homage to St. John of Patmos," paper delivered at a
symposium on "Revelation and the Environment A.D. 95–1995," September 1995. The
journal contained articles on the most urgent philosophical, political, and social issues
of the day and included contributions by the three editors as well as, among others,
Franz Rosenzweig, Eugen Rosenstock, Hermann Herrigel, Rudolf Ehrenberg, Hans
Ehrenberg, Ernst Simon, Hugo Bergmann, Walter Benjamin, Ludwig Strauß, and
Margarete Susman.

pertains not primarily to a sense of a shared animality or a shared animal suffering but to a biopolitical *animation* that distinguishes the human from the animal. To put it again in psychoanalytic terms, what we share with animals is life lived along the spectrum of pleasure and pain. Where we diverge from the animal is in our peculiar capacity for that pleasure-in-pain that Lacan refers to as "jouissance." And as I have furthermore proposed, the psychoanalytic concept of jouissance needs to be correlated with the topology of the state of exception as a crucial dimension of politicosocial bonds, a dimension that is no doubt susceptible to considerable historical mutation.

The question of why these German-Jewish writers manifest a special concern with or sensitivity to this dimension can be answered, I think, in two ways. First, it seems that the process of assimilation that German Jews underwent over the course of the long nineteenth century occurred, in large measure, as a kind of double bind in which the Jews were in effect told: "Be like me! You can't be like me!" The demand for assimilation was at some level structured as an "impossible" interpellation; it involved an exposure to an arresting opacity that could be experienced only as a persistent disruption and disorientation—as a *wesenhafte Erschütterung*—in the self-understanding of those Jews who tried to assume the demand.

More interesting, however, was a second aspect of the process of assimilation that had more to do with issues of secularization. For secular Jews, that is, the laws of normative Judaism—the commandments of the Torah—were themselves experienced to a very large extent as a set of opaque rules—enigmatic signifiers—with which they could no longer identify even if they did not fully cease to feel addressed by them. It is against this background that we can understand Gershom Scholem's characterization, in his correspondence with his friend Walter Benjamin, of the status of Holy Writ for Kafka as the "nothingness of revelation." In a now famous letter to Benjamin, he writes,

You ask what I understand by the "nothingness of revelation"? I understand by it a state in which revelation appears to be without meaning, in which it still asserts itself, in which it has *validity* but *no significance* [*in dem sie gilt, aber nicht bedeutet*]. A state in which the wealth of meaning is lost and what is in the process of appearing (for revelation is such a process) still does not disappear, even though it is reduced to the zero point of its own content, so to speak.[61]

This understanding of the distinctive predicament of the secular Jew as an exposure to a "valid" yet empty revelation might be seen as a late variation of the Pauline trope of the distinction between letter and spirit; the Jew is exposed to the "dead" letter without spirit and thus "writes" the letter on the surface of his body in the form of circumcision (rather than taking it into the spiritual depths of his heart). Indeed, from the perspective of the secular mind, there may be no more powerful image of "validity without significance" than this cut on the body in the name of the Law.

Scholem's assumption of this Pauline figure should be seen against the backdrop of the Kantian and post-Kantian conception of Judaism as a religion of pure heteronomy or "positivity," one set against the ideal of the radical autonomy of practical reason as moral self-legislation.[62] If Scholem is right about Kafka, it seems that his insight depends at least to some extent on a certain identification with this post-Kantian view of Judaism as a legalistic religion of radical subjection to the pure heteronomy of divine jurisdiction.[63] One might

---

61. Gershom Scholem, *The Correspondence of Walter Benjamin and Gershom Scholem, 1932–1940*, trans. Gary Smith and Andre Lefevre (New York: Schocken, 1989), 142.

62. In one of the most stunning performances of Jewish self-hatred in modern letters, Otto Weininger famously defines both Jews and women as beings who fundamentally lack access to this dimension of practical reason as conceived by Kant: "It is this Kantian Reason, this spirit, which seems to be lacking in both Jew and woman." For this reason, Weininger continues, the Jews are incapable of ever entering into a true social contract, of ever forming a genuine state as a union of *vernünftige Wesen*, beings with reason. Otto Weininger, *Geschlecht und Charakter* (Munich: Matthes und Seitz, 1980), 411.

63. Franz Rosenzweig has suggested that such a view of the Jewish law was in different ways internalized by both liberal and orthodox Judaism in the nineteenth century. See his open letter to Martin Buber, "Die Bauleute," in *Franz Rosenzweig: Der Mensch und sein Werk. Gesammelte Schriften,* vol. 3, ed. Reinhold Mayer and Annamarie Mayer (Dordrecht: Martinus Nijhoff, 1984), 699–712. Rosenzweig's argument here and in *The Star of Redemption* is that such a view loses the distinction between commandment (*Gebot*) and law (*Gesetz*). For Rosenzweig, commandment is a dimension that exceeds the opposition between letter and spirit, law and life.

say, then, that there was, among at least some German Jews, a kind of heightened sensitivity to and preoccupation with the dimension of arresting opacity I have associated with sovereignty and the problem of the state of exception. It was as if secular German Jews had already, at some level, rehearsed the psychic—or better, creaturely—complexities of life abandoned to the validity or force of law beyond any meaning or signification.

# The Vicissitudes of Melancholy

It generally takes only one or two sentences for a reader to get a feel for the affective atmosphere, the deeply melancholic *Befindlichkeit,* of W. G. Sebald's remarkable work. And indeed it has become a standard gesture of the already rich critical literature on Sebald to marshal the semantic field of this resonant word, "melancholy," to capture the specificity of Sebald's voice and the stakes of his literary project. The unavoidability of the question of melancholy in the critical engagement with Sebald's fiction not only is a function of the relentlessly somber tonality of the work and the obsessive preoccupation with death, destruction, and decay that informs it (not to mention the endless procession of real and imagined melancholics that populate the books), it has been determined as well by explicit statements by the author himself both inside and outside the body of the major literary works. Here one might recall, among numerous possible examples, the autobiographical reflection in the third part of the book-length prose poem *After Nature,* where the narrator, no doubt alluding to the opening lines of Goethe's *Dichtung und Wahrheit,* notes the confluence of deadly historical events and astrological influences that marked the "constellation" of his birth:

> At the moment on Ascension Day
> of the year 'forty-four when I was born,
> the procession for the blessing of the fields
> was just passing our house to the sounds
> of the fire brigade band, on its way out
> to the flowering May meadows. Mother
> at first took this as a happy sign, unaware
> that the cold planet Saturn ruled this hour's
> constellation and that above the mountains
> already the storm was hanging which soon thereafter
> dispersed the supplicants and killed
> one of the four canopy bearers. (88/76)[1]

Sebald suggests, in a way, that the rest of his life—including, of course, his particular sort of literary productivity—was something like an elaboration of this original "birthmark."

To take just one extraliterary example, in the foreword to one of his two published collections of essays on Austrian literature, Sebald explicitly defends the posture of melancholy assumed by the authors represented in the volume (authors whose presence in Sebald's fiction is at times registered in the form of extensive verbatim citation). There he writes that

> melancholy, the contemplation of the movement of misfortune, has nothing in common with the wish to die. It is a form of resistance. And this is emphatically so at the level of art, where it is anything but reactive or reactionary. When, with rigid gaze, it [melancholy] goes over again just how things could

---

1. Goethe's famous autobiography begins with a report of the astrological conditions at the time of his birth, noting that the positive aspects of the constellation balanced out the incompetence of his midwife, thereby saving his life.

have happened, it becomes clear that the dynamic of inconsolability and that of knowledge are identical in their execution. The description of misfortune includes within itself the possibility of its own overcoming.[2]

Surely one of the things that make it so difficult to write about Sebald, to say anything genuinely new or revelatory about his work, is that he has done so much himself to frame the discourse of his own reception, to provide in advance the terms for critical engagement with the work; his fiction already practices a rather efficient sort of autoexegesis that leaves the critic feeling a certain irrelevance (the posture of awestruck adoration that one finds in so much of the critical literature is, I think, one of the guises such irrelevance assumes). With this in mind, I will nonetheless follow this well-beaten path and reflect on the nature and role of melancholy in Sebald's work.

## II

With the word *Befindlichkeit,* I have already indicated a debt to Heidegger's conceptualization of mood as a primordial mode in which our "being in the world," our existential implication in a concrete historical situation, is registered. For Heidegger—and here we return to our earlier reflections on boredom—mood in general is a sort of *virtual archive* in which are inscribed the traces of an originary—and at some level traumatic—opening or attunement to "otherness" below the level of intentional states and propositional attitudes. Heidegger develops his thinking about mood or *Stimmung* in the context of the larger question of what it means for a human being to be "in" or "open to" the world, where being-in is understood as an ontological determination rather than as pertaining to spatial disposition or location (thus Heidegger's use of the term "*Da*-sein" or "being-*there*" to characterize the being of human being). For Heidegger, mood registers our sense of "always already" finding ourselves stuck in a specific historical constellation, which means first and foremost

2. W. G. Sebald, *Die Beschreibung des Unglücks: Zur österreichischen Literatur von Stifter bis Handke* (Frankfurt a.M.: Fischer, 1994), 12.

being stuck with, being riveted to, ourselves. "In being in a mood," as Heidegger puts it in his inimitable fashion, "Da-sein is always already disclosed in accordance with its mood as *that* being to which Da-sein was *delivered over* in its being as the being which it, existing, has to be."[3] Heidegger continues: "We shall call this character of being of Da-sein which is veiled in its whence and whither, but in itself all the more openly disclosed, this 'that it is,' the *thrownness* of this being into its there; it is thrown in such a way that it is the there as being-in-the-world. The expression thrownness is meant to suggest the *facticity of its being delivered over*" (127). And as Heidegger is quick to add, such facticity must be distinguished from the objective presence or givenness of an item in the world: "*Facticity is not the factuality of the* factum brutum *of something objectively present, but is a characteristic of the being of Da-sein taken on in existence, although initially thrust aside. The that of facticity is never to be found by looking*" (127). Heidegger furthermore emphasizes what he calls the *Lastcharakter des Daseins,* the burden proper to such facticity: "Mood does not disclose in the mode of looking at thrownness, but as turning toward and away from it. For the most part, mood does not turn toward the burdensome character of Da-sein revealed in it" (128). And as already noted, the disclosure proper to mood is to be distinguished from any sort of propositional attitude:

Phenomenally, *what* mood discloses and *how* it discloses would be completely misunderstood if what has been disclosed were conflated with that which . . . Da-sein "at the same time" is acquainted with, knows, and believes. Even when Da-sein is "sure" of its "whither" in faith or thinks it knows about its whence in rational enlightenment, all of this makes no difference in the face of the phenomenal fact that moods bring Da-sein before the that of its there, *which stares at it with the inexorability of an enigma.* (128; my emphasis)

The crucial thought in all of this is that of an originary *exposure* proper to human life, a vulnerability to the *mattering* of things before any

---

3. Martin Heidegger, *Being and Time,* trans. Joan Stambaugh (Albany: State University Press of New York, 1996), 127; my emphasis. Subsequent references are given in the text.

choice or decision on our part, before any reflection about value (Heidegger's word for this exposure is *Angänglichkeit*). To return to an earlier formulation, this mattering refers to our *ex-citation,* our being called out or addressed—our being *angegangen*—by that to which we are delivered over. Indeed, we might even say that we are delivered over *to an address* (rather than an inert otherness that might or might not address us). As Heidegger notes, it is only because things matter to us—"ex-cite us"—in this fundamental way that we are in a position to feel *threatened* by them:

> *In attunement lies existentially a disclosive submission to world out of which things that matter to us can be encountered.* Indeed, we must *ontologically* in principle leave the primary discovery of the world to "mere mood." Pure beholding, even if it penetrated into the innermost core of the being of something objectively present, would never be able to discover anything like what is threatening. (130)

III

In a series of lectures delivered in 1927, the year of the publication of *Being and Time,* Heidegger cited the work of Rainer Maria Rilke as offering crucial testimony regarding this primordial exposure to the mattering of things that characterizes human life.[4] Heidegger's turn to Rilke in his ongoing efforts to elaborate the specificity of this exposure or opening to otherness is especially important for us because the particular work he cites is one that, as I have already suggested, can be considered a crucial precursor text to all of Sebald's fiction: *The Notebooks of Malte Laurids Brigge.* Indeed, I suggest that in some ways *Malte* is more important for understanding Sebald's project than the work of many of the other writers whom critics have named in their efforts to locate Sebald in a literary tradition or genealogy (one thinks here of

---

4. Martin Heidegger, *Die Grundprobleme der Phänomenologie* (Frankfurt a.M.: Vittorio Klostermann, 1975 [*Gesamtausgabe,* vol. 24]), 244 ff. These lectures predate Heidegger's discussion of the eighth Duino Elegy cited in chapter 1 by some fifteen years.

Stifter, Borges, Nabakov, Kafka, and Bernhard, among others). The
parallels between Rilke's remarkable novel, published in 1910, and Sebald's work are far too extensive to elaborate here in any sort of detail;
let me note just a few features of *Malte* that return, in one incarnation
or another, in Sebald's writings. (For the moment, I will leave it to
readers to recall the specific parallels in Sebald's texts.)

In Rilke's autobiographical novel we have a first-person narrator in
self-imposed exile from his native country (in this case Denmark),
struggling to come to terms with the disorientations and dislocations
of modernity experienced on the streets of Paris. These struggles keep
the narrator, who strives to be a writer, hovering at the edge of mental collapse or even psychotic break (he exhibits, among other things,
symptoms of paranoia), and he eventually finds his way to the
Salpêtrière clinic for psychiatric evaluation and treatment. One of the
few places where Malte is able to find temporary respite from the as-
saults on his psychic integrity and residual aristocratic dignity is the
reading room of the Bibliothèque Nationale, where he communes
with like-minded poets. The novel is presented as a series of notebook
entries in which the narrator-hero explores a newly discovered dimension of interiority that is shown to correlate strictly with his capacity for (and extreme endangerment by) exposure to the shocks of
his urban surround and the kinds of suffering to which they bear witness. As he puts it early in the novel: "I am learning to see. I don't
know why it is, but everything enters me more deeply and doesn't
stop where it once used to. I have an interior that I never knew of.
Everything passes into it now. I don't know what happens there."[5]
Accompanying Malte's protocol of urban excitations and his increasing inability to parry or metabolize their onslaught, we find a series
of extended lyrical reflections on individual and anonymous death,
childhood, the spirit world, historical violence, the lives of artists and
kings, the mutation of the object world in capitalist modernity, works
of literature and art, and the possibility of human and divine love.
(The great exegetical challenge posed by *Malte* is of course that of

5. Rainer Maria Rilke, *The Notebooks of Malte Laurids Brigge,* trans. Stephen Mitchell
(New York: Vintage, 1990), 5.

correlating this series of lyrical reflections with the encounter with urban modernity.) Not unlike so many of the figures that populate Sebald's texts—including the central narrator figure, "W. G. Sebald"—Malte has been "expelled" from a closed universe (his aristocratic Danish society was, to be sure, in the midst of dissolution, a process that becomes manifest, above all, in the alienation of objects from their use-values and the mutations of the experience of death and dying) and thrust into one whose "openness" is more often than not experienced as entropy.[6] Yet it is one that, for better or worse, has radically transformed the conditions of perception, thinking, and writing (Malte repeatedly questions whether he is up to the challenges posed by such transformations). In his 1927 lectures, Heidegger cites a lengthy passage from the novel that captures this radical and disorienting sense of exposure at the very historical moment when, in the years before World War I, the fabric of social relations in Europe was coming undone. (Here one will recall Sebald's obsession with the year 1913, a year, as he suggests, of radical existential, moral, and political vertigo.) Certainly one of the fundamental questions raised by both Rilke's and Sebald's work is the specific nature of openness to world under the dual impact of historical violence and the structural dislocations generated by capitalist modernity. Indeed, both literary projects throw into relief the contradictory meanings of the word "exposure," meanings we have already touched on in chapter 1. On the one hand, it signifies what Heidegger refers to as being-in, being always already in the midst of a matrix of meaningful relations (a world, a "clearing" of an understanding of Being). On the other hand, it signifies the essential disruption—the *wesenhafte Erschütterung*—introduced by one's abandonment to an arresting opacity. I cite this rather lengthy passage as a way of introducing the "poetics of exposure" that would become the signature style and method of Sebald's fiction.

---

6. In the *Duino Elegies,* Rilke's resistance to the forces of modernization is marshaled not as resistance against loss but rather as mournful resistance against the disappearance of the space and symbolic resources in which loss could still be experienced and worked through. The *Duino Elegies* are, in a sense, second-order elegies: elegies for the passing of the space in which elegy is still possible.

The passage Heidegger cites in his 1927 lectures takes place during one of Malte's many restless peregrinations through Paris. As a flaneur on the verge of a nervous breakdown, Malte manifests the typical mental state of the Sebaldian narrator; in the course of his wanderings, he comes upon a scene that momentarily freezes him and the world in a shudder of *mutual exposure*:

Will people believe that there are houses like this? No, they'll say I am not telling the truth. But this time it *is* the truth; nothing has been left out, and of course nothing has been added. Where would I get it from? People know that I'm poor. People know that. Houses? But, to be exact, they were houses which no longer existed. Houses which had been demolished from top to bottom. It was the other houses that were there, the ones that had stood alongside them, tall neighboring houses. Apparently they were in danger of collapsing, since all support had been removed; a whole scaffolding of long, tarred poles had been rammed diagonally between the rubble-strewn ground and the bared wall. I don't know if I have already said that this is the wall I am talking about. It was, so to speak, not the first wall of the existing house (as you would have supposed), but the last of the ones that were no longer there. You could see its inside. You could see, at its various stories, bedroom walls with wallpaper still sticking to them; and here and there a piece of floor or ceiling. Near these bedroom walls there remained, along the entire length of the outer wall, a dirty-white space through which, in unspeakably nauseating, worm-soft digestive movements, the open, rust-spotted channel of the toilet pipe crawled. The gaslight jets had left dusty gray traces at the edges of the ceiling; they bent here and there, abruptly, ran along the walls, and plunged into the black, gaping holes that had been torn there. But the most unforgettable things were the walls themselves. The stubborn life of these rooms had not let itself be trampled out. It was still there; it clung to the nails that were left, stood on the narrow remnant of flooring, crouched under the corner beams where a bit of interior still remained. You could see it in the paint which it had changed, slowly, from year to year: blue into moldy green, green into gray, yellow into a faded, rotting white. But it was also in the places that had been kept fresher behind mirrors, paintings, and wardrobes; for it had traced their outlines over and over, and had been with cobwebs and dust even in these hidden places, which were now laid bare. It was in every flayed strip of surface; it was in the damp blisters on the lower edges of the wallpaper; it fluttered in the torn-off shreds, and oozed from the foul stains which had appeared long before. And from these walls, once blue, green, and yellow, and now framed by the broken tracks of the demolished partitions, the air of these lives issued, the stubborn, sluggish, musty air which no wind had yet scattered. There the noons lingered, and the illnesses, and the exhalations, and the smoke of many years, and the sweat that trickles down from armpits and makes clothing heavy, and the stale breath of mouths, and the oily smell of sweltering feet. There the pungent odor of urine lingered, and the odor of soot, the gray odor of potatoes, and the heavy, sickening stench of rancid grease. The sweet smell of neglected infants lingered there, the smell of frightened schoolchildren, and the stuffiness from the beds of pubescent boys. And all the vapors that had risen from the street below, or fallen down from above with the filthy urban rain. And many things brought there by the weak house-winds, which always stay in the same street; and much more whose origin would never be known. I said, didn't I, that all the outer walls had been demolished except the last one—? It is this wall that I have been talking about all along. You would think I had stood looking at it for a long time; but I swear that I began to run as soon as I recognized this wall. For that's what is horrible—that I did recognize it. I recognize everything here, and that's why it passes right into me; it is at home inside me.[7]

What is so striking about this passage is the way the narrator's own sense of exposure, of a certain *skinlessness* with respect to excitations from the outside—Freud would speak of a lack of *Reizschutz*—is correlated with the flayed surface of that outside; here one wounded interiority responds to, resonates with, another. More important, the excitations in question in this "attunement" pertain to something spectral, to traces of life no longer there, which for that very reason seems to have acquired a more radical and disturbing quality of "thereness" whose impact is experienced as traumatic. That everything Malte "sees" in the face of this urban ruin acquires its legibility in an *instant* brings this discourse of traumatic epiphany into proximity to the medium of photography. Indeed, one might think here of the anecdote Max Ferber tells to the narrator of the final story of *The*

7. Rilke, *Malte*, 46–48.

*Emigrants,* concerning a case of silver poisoning suffered by a lab assistant in a photography studio in Manchester. The man's body had
absorbed so much silver over the course of his professional life "that
he had become a kind of photographic plate, which was apparent in
the fact . . . that the man's face and hands turned blue in strong light,
or, as one might say, developed (165/244)."[8] Malte's sensorium becomes such a photographic plate not so much for what is there to be-
hold—as Heidegger suggested, "pure beholding, even if it penetrated
into the innermost core of the being of something objectively present,
would never be able to discover anything like what is threatening"—
but for the traces of past lives and lost possibilities. Malte becomes, in
a word, a *medium* in a double sense: photographic apparatus and
locus of communion with the dead. There is, then, a peculiar sort of
materialism at work here, one we might call "spectral." And it was
W. G. Sebald, I will argue, who became the true master of this "spectral materialism" that serves to register and archive a certain *real*
whose status is, paradoxically, *virtual.*[9]

8. Sebald changed the name of this figure from Max Aurach to Max Ferber in the English edition to spare the sensitivities of the London-based painter Frank Auerbach, on
whose life and work some features of the character were based.

9. In a recent book on photography and the Holocaust, Ulrich Baer coins the term "spectral evidence" to capture the nature of photographic work aimed at transmitting the impact of traumatic events. Baer, *Spectral Evidence: The Photography of Trauma* (Cambridge:
MIT Press, 2002). The book is informed by the "ethical turn" in deconstruction that took
shape around the debates on Paul de Man's wartime writings. In the course of those debates, a new sense of the stakes of deconstructive interpretive practices emerged. At first,
deconstruction came to be seen as a sort of *Trauerarbeit* with respect to the political violence wrought in the name of (aesthetic) "totalities" of one sort or another (the "aesthetic
ideology" of the German *Volksgemeinschaft* was the model here); then it became the site
of resistance to any full symbolic metabolization of loss, which was itself posited as being
in some fashion complicit with fantasies of totalization; finally, deconstructive reading
was itself posited as a form of testimony, as the ultimate act of bearing witness to a traumatic kernel of historical violence—the Holocaust being the key event in all of this—that
persisted as a remainder or remnant beyond all forms of contextualizing understanding.
Though I value this work considerably, I suggest that Baer's ambition, which aims at
thinking historically about the recalcitrance of (traumatic) experience to historical thinking, finds its true fulfillment not in the work he analyzes in his study but rather in Sebald's
prose fiction, which he curiously fails to mention. I also hope that a more psychoanalytic
approach to the "creaturely" residues of traumatic events can move beyond what I perceive as the limitations of work growing out of the ethical turn in deconstruction.

Sebald's post-Holocaust practice of this paradoxical form of materialism will, of course, include dimensions of historical experience and human suffering unknown to Rilke. If anything, the demands for and on this "method" will become radicalized, pushed to a limit, in the post-Holocaust setting. For the moment, we might note the distance traversed between the two bodies of work—which all the while remain in intimate proximity—by recalling a recent installation in Berlin by the French artist Christian Boltanski called "Missing House." In 1990, the artist mounted plaques on the wall of a house in the Grosse Hamburgerstrasse bearing the names of the residents who inhabited the (now missing) adjacent house in the years from 1930 to 1945 (the house had been destroyed during aerial bombardment of Berlin in 1945, leaving a vacant lot that was never filled). The plaques give the names, dates of birth and death, and occupation of the residents and are placed at the location corresponding to their dwelling in the missing house. The names include those of Jewish residents as well as those of the non-Jews who came to occupy the apartments once their Jewish neighbors were forced out or deported. At another location in the city, Boltanski set up archival boxes in which he placed photocopies of family photographs, letters, children's drawings, and rationing tickets, among other remnants of the lives of the former residents. We might think of this work as providing a kind of relay point between Malte's wall and the various ruined objects occasioning Sebald's post-Holocaust ruminations on absence. In Boltanski's archive of absence, the generalized pathos of Malte's gaze takes on a historical specificity without sacrificing the resources of affectivity. In Boltanski's work, the stunned melancholy of Malte's stance becomes infused with the curiosity and rigor of historical research, a mixture that, as we shall see, goes to the very heart of Sebald's project.

IV

Nearly all the terms I have used thus far to introduce this notion of "spectral materialism" suggest the relevance (for understanding Sebald) of not so much the work of Heidegger as that of one of his great antipodes in Weimar Germany, Walter Benjamin. The proximity of Sebald's work to the thought of Walter Benjamin has, of course, already been duly noted by critics, though few have done more than make a passing reference to a vague sort of "Benjaminian" quality of the work, a family resemblance to certain of Benjamin's interests and procedures. In an essay on Sebald and romanticism, for example, James Chandler, who notes the proliferation, in nearly all the literature on Sebald, of "terms such as *eerie, sublime, ghostly, spectral,* and above all *haunting,*" characterizes the figure of Jacques Austerlitz in the following way: "With his trademark rucksack, and his penchant for resituating history and memory over an analysis of built space, Austerlitz appears early on in the book as a kind of vagabond Walter Benjamin—vaguely suicidal, laboring away at an unfinished project, driven by passions created in historical conditions with which he eventually and obliquely manages to come to terms."[10]

The link between Benjamin and Austerlitz, and more specifically between Benjamin's *Arcades Project* and Austerlitz's own monumental work of architectural and cultural history, is sealed by the connection Austerlitz finally acknowledges between his research and the forces of political violence that would destroy his sense of home and of belonging (the very forces that, of course, pushed Benjamin to suicide). As Austerlitz puts it, "As far as I was concerned the world ended in the late nineteenth century. I dared go no further than that, although in fact the whole history of the architecture and civilization of the bourgeois age, the subject of my research, pointed in the direction of the catastrophic events already casting their shadows before them at the time" (139–40/201). The suggestion here is that the repressed— Austerlitz's childhood in Prague and all that followed from it—first returned in the guise of his particular research agenda (here, as Freud notes more generally, repression is manifest only as the return of the repressed). It returns as a sort of symptomatic fetish. Much as the classical Freudian fetishist will latch on to an object recalling the last impression before the encounter with the traumatic scene—the missing maternal penis—Austerlitz gets stuck at the prehistory of the

---

10. James Chandler, "About Loss: W. G. Sebald's Romantic Art of Memory," *South Atlantic Quarterly* 102, no. 1 (Winter 2003): 243, 253.

events that would engulf the life of his family. Certainly one of the crucial differences between Austerlitz's work and Benjamin's is that the latter made the connection between the two historical formations explicit and did so in part through an extensive analysis of the structure of (commodity) fetishism.

Earlier in the novel, the narrator had described Austerlitz's research as pertaining to

> the architectural style of the capitalist era, a subject which he said had fascinated him since his own student days, speaking in particular of the compulsive sense of order and the tendency towards monumentalism evident in law courts and penal institutions, railway stations and stock exchanges, opera houses and lunatic asylums, and the dwellings built to rectangular grid patterns for the labor force. (33/48) [11]

No doubt alluding to the impossible scope of Benjamin's great unfinished and idiosyncratic project, we learn that Austerlitz's investigations "had long outstripped their original purpose as a project for a dissertation, proliferating in his hands into endless preliminary sketches for a study, based entirely on his own views, of the family likeness between these buildings" (33/48). As we shall see in the course of this discussion, Sebald's own understanding of family likeness pertains not simply to a set of shared, positive features but also to the ways divergent objects, institutions, epochs, and destinies are *similarly distorted* by the pressures of traumatic events.[12]

---

11. In an earlier conversation in Antwerp, Austerlitz had said, apropos of such monumentalism—in this case, that of the Antwerp train station—that "when we step into the entrance hall we are seized by a sense of being beyond the profane, in a cathedral consecrated to international traffic and trade" (10/16). Another link between Austerlitz's project and Benjamin's is that the former cites as one of his key resources for his research on Paris in the nineteenth century one that Benjamin regularly uses in *The Arcades Project:* Maxime du Camp's six-volume history of Paris.

12. I will be suggesting, in a word, that one of the keys to understanding Walter Benjamin's conception of a distorted similarity—*entstellte Ähnlichkeit*—is to think of the inverse of this formulation, that is, of similar distortion. For an extended discussion of Benjamin's thinking about similarity, see Sigrid Weigel, *Entstellte Ähnlichkeit: Walter Benjamins theoretische Schreibweise* (Frankfurt a.M.: Fischer, 1997).

In a later description of the project in which we recognize both Benjaminian and Foucauldian aspects, Austerlitz notes again his feelings of inhibition in the face of the project's demands:

Even in Paris, said Austerlitz, I had thought of collecting my fragmentary studies in a book, although I constantly postponed writing it. The various ideas I entertained at different times ranged from the concept of a systematically descriptive work in several volumes to a series of essays on such subjects as hygiene and sanitation, the architecture of the penal system, secular temples, hydrotherapy, zoological gardens, departure and arrival, light and shade, steam and gas, and so forth. (120–21/174)

We sense early on, then, that something was amiss with this project, that it bears a certain *symptomatic* weight. Austerlitz himself admits a certain perplexity as to his own motivations for the project: "Why he had embarked on such a wide field . . . he did not know" (33/48). We then learn about his obsessive ruminations and research on railway stations whereby it appears that he had at some level avoided the Parisian station bearing his own name, the very one that, once he had opened to his personal memories, would be discovered to have deep connections not only to his own biography but to the history of fascism and the Holocaust in France more generally. Continuing his reflections on the motivations behind his research, Austerlitz notes that

it was also true that he was . . . obeying an impulse which he himself, to this day, did not really understand, but which was somehow linked to his early fascination with the idea of a network such as that of the entire railway system. At the very beginning of his studies, said Austerlitz, and later, when he was first living in Paris, he used to visit one of the main railway stations almost daily, usually the Gare du Nord or the Gare de l'Est. (33/48–49)[13]

13. After the Holocaust it is, of course, nearly impossible to avoid the association of railway networks and deportations, an association Sebald surely counted on. Readers of Sebald's work will no doubt also make the link between Austerlitz and Paul Bereyter, the hero of the second of Sebald's *Emigrants* stories, who, as if following the fateful pull of an oracular statement pronounced by an uncle that he would "end up on the railways," commits suicide on the railway tracks of his hometown.

At this point in the book readers may or may not register the curious absence of the Gare d'Austerlitz from this list; one is thereby seduced, in a sense, into participating in the repression that still constrains Austerlitz's awareness of his own implication in the very "network" to which he is so powerfully drawn. We later learn, of course, that the area around the Gare d'Austerlitz had been the site for the warehousing of goods appropriated from the deported Jews of Paris. And in the final pages of the novel, Austerlitz senses that his father had departed from this very station in his attempt to escape from the Nazis. At this point, we also learn that Austerlitz had, in his own way, been deeply drawn to the Gare d'Austerlitz all along—"that station, said Austerlitz, has always seemed to me the most mysterious of all the railway terminals of Paris" (292/408)—and that in his student days he had even contemplated writing something about its layout and history. He now recalls (some twenty years have passed since he first described his research to the narrator, in which no mention was made of the station) that the Gare d'Austerlitz had always produced a sense of unease in him. This feeling was somehow embodied in a set of bicycle racks that he remembers only as "a scaffolding reminiscent of a gallows with all kinds of rusty iron hooks" (292/408) as well as by a mass of pigeon feathers lying on the floor beneath the hooks. Together these impressions generated a sense "of being on the scene of some unexpiated crime" (292/409). These various impressions and recollections give us a first taste of Sebald's practice of spectral materialism. It involves, among other things, a capacity to register the persistence of past suffering that has in some sense been absorbed into the substance of lived space, into the "setting" of human history.[14] What

14. In Rilke's novel, Malte's spectral materialism takes on a decidedly psychosomatic quality: "The existence of the horrible in every atom of air. You breathe it in as something transparent; but inside you it condenses, hardens, takes on pointed, geometric shapes between your organs; for all the torments and agonies suffered on scaffolds, in torture-chambers, madhouses, operating rooms, under bridges in late autumn: all this has a stubborn permanence, all this endures in itself and, jealous of everything that is, clings to its own dreadful reality. People would like to forget much of it; sleep gently files down these grooves in the brain, but dreams drive it away and trace the designs again" (*Malte*, 73).

Hegel called "objective spirit," the institutional concretions of moral and political life across time, includes, in Sebald's work, the "spirits" of those whose suffering in some fashion underwrote that "objectivity." As we shall see, it is precisely the persistence of this "spirit world" that leads Sebald, in a thoroughly Benjaminian manner, to posit human history as a species of natural history, of *Naturgeschichte*.

The gaps in Austerlitz's discourse during his initial meetings with the narrator—gaps only partially filled in by the work of "recovered memory"—introduce us to yet another dimension of Sebald's spectral materialism. In Sebald's universe, one's subjective involvement with another human being is not simply a function of some sort of spiritual affinity; it depends, rather, on the degree to which one participates, at first often unknowingly, in what I have referred to as their "spirit world." We are, as it were, in proximity to the "neighbor" when we have entered the enigmatic space of his or her hauntedness. What is at issue in such proximity is, in other words, not empathy in the usual sense. One is not so much trying to see the world from someone else's point of view as trying to register the blind spots of that point of view and to unpack the stresses condensed in this blindness.[15]

The most extended effort thus far to read Sebald in light of Benjamin has been offered by Judith Ryan in a perspicacious essay on *Austerlitz,* in which Benjamin's reading of surrealism, along with related material from *The Arcades Project,* provides the key frame of

---

15. In the second story of *The Emigrants,* Sebald indicates that his own style of writing and mode of approach to his subject—in this case to a former schoolteacher, Paul Bereyter, in the wake of the latter's suicide—are designed specifically to forestall the pitfalls of empathic identification. After a series of efforts at imagining Paul at various moments in his life and in the moment of his death, the narrator writes, "Such endeavors to imagine his life and death did not, as I had to admit, bring me any closer to Paul, except at best for brief emotional moments of the kind that seemed presumptuous to me. It is in order to avoid this sort of wrongful trespass that I have written down what I know of Paul Bereyter" (29/44–45). As any reader of Sebald knows, there is nothing straightforward about such "writing down." Rather, it involves the paradox that already informs the *Aufschreibesystem,* the "discourse network," of psychoanalytic practice. The way to the truth of another human subject and destiny beyond the wrongful trespass of emotionally driven empathy is, in large measure, by way of one's own "dreamwork" that gets mobilized around the irritant of the other's alterity.

reference.[16] The essay largely focuses on a number of motifs that Sebald undoubtedly borrowed from Breton's *Nadja* (Ryan suggests that certain photographs as well as the omnipresence of pigeons and dovecotes in *Austerlitz* are allusions to Breton's novel). It is well known that Sebald's work is to a very large degree constructed out of extended and often unmarked textual citations and allusions, a practice that in itself indicates a certain proximity to Benjamin's conception of his *Arcades Project*.[17] However, Ryan's argument goes well beyond any sort of mapping of intertextuality in Sebald's oeuvre, a project that is, given Sebald's celebrity, no doubt keeping scores of literary scholars busy. What concerns her is the way Sebald's appropriation of both

16. Judith Ryan, "Fulgurations: Sebald and Surrealism," unpublished manuscript. I am grateful to the author for making her text available to me. As Ryan notes, Sebald cites Benjamin's surrealism essay in his own short essay on the work of the schizophrenic poet Ernst Herbeck. See "Eine kleine Traverse: Das poetische Werk Ernst Herbecks," in *Die Beschreibung des Unglücks*, 131–48.

17. Sebald, of course, is often quite explicit about his citations, as when he openly paraphrases the work of particular authors, often assuming their voice for long stretches. One thinks, for example, of his citations (in *Vertigo*) from Casanova's account of his escape from prison in Venice. But numerous citations are simply presented in the voice of the narrator, as when Sebald appropriates language from a story by Adalbert Stifter to describe his drug-induced visions of earth and sky during a hospital stay in the first section of *The Rings of Saturn* (17/28; here I am indebted to Mark McCulloh, *Understanding Sebald* [Columbia: University of South Carolina Press, 2003], 61), or when he cites the work of Peter Weiss in ostensibly autobiographical recollections about an early encounter with sexuality in the last section of Vertigo (238/271; here I am indebted to Jörg Drews, "Meisterhaft suggerierte Angstzustände," in *W. G. Sebald*, ed. Franz Loquai [Eggingen: Edition Isele, 1997]). Indeed, what Sebald says about Thomas Browne in the first section of *Vertigo* is clearly meant, too, as a self-description: "In common with other English writers of the seventeenth century, Browne wrote out of the fullness of his erudition, deploying a vast repertoire of quotations and names of authorities who had gone before, creating complex metaphors and analogies, and constructing labyrinthine sentences that sometimes extend over one or two pages, sentences that resemble processions or a funeral cortège in their sheer ceremonial lavishness" (19/30). The numerous allusions to and citations from Kafka's story, "The Hunter Gracchus," in *Vertigo* occupy an intermediate zone between attribution and nonattribution; although the passages are unmarked, Sebald makes it abundantly clear that he is working with Kafka's story. We will return to Kafka's presence in Sebald's work later in the discussion. For a focused treatment of the question of intertextuality in Sebald, see Marcel Atze, "Koinzidenz und Intertextualität: Der Einsatz von Prätexten in W. G. Sebalds Erzählung 'All' estero,'" in *W. G. Sebald*, 151–75.

surrealism and Benjamin's reflections about it (and related matters) marks a further stage—and perhaps even a dead end—in the trajectory Benjamin had already traced in the passage from surrealism to his own work. What is ultimately at stake is the possibility, after the Holocaust, of anything like what Benjamin had praised the surrealists for producing through their experiments, namely a new kind of relation to the material world generative of what he at this point in his thinking refers to as "profane illuminations."

Benjamin coins this term to characterize the kind of experience the surrealists were after in their efforts to overcome the autonomous work of art, in the intoxications they cultivated in their "dreamwork." Such illuminations were based on the new gaze the surrealists brought to material culture, and specifically to objects that had become outmoded, had acquired the status of detritus, in accordance with the accelerated rhythms of capitalist temporality. (Precisely as producer of junk, capitalism became, for Benjamin, the operator of a new, specifically modern dynamic of natural history.) Speaking in particular about Breton, Benjamin writes:

What are these things? Nothing could reveal more about Surrealism than their canon. . . . He can boast an extraordinary discovery: he was the first to perceive the revolutionary energies that appear in the "outmoded"—in the first iron constructions, the first factory buildings, the earliest photos, objects that have begun to be extinct, grand pianos, the dresses of five years ago, fashionable restaurants when the vogue has begun to ebb from them. The relation of these things to revolution—no one can have a more exact concept of it than these authors. No one before these visionaries and augurs perceived how destitution—not only social but architectonic, the poverty of interiors, enslaved and enslaving objects—can be suddenly transformed into revolutionary nihilism.[18]

18. Walter Benjamin, "Surrealism: The Last Snapshot of the European Intelligentsia," trans. Edmund Jephcott, in *Walter Benjamin: Selected Writings*, vol. 2, *1927–1934*, ed. Michael Jennings, Howard Eiland, and Gary Smith (Cambridge: Harvard University Press, 1999), 210.

The crucial point for Benjamin was that "histrionic or fanatical stress on the mysterious side of the mysterious takes us no further; we penetrate the mystery only to the degree that we recognize it in the everyday world, by virtue of a dialectical optic that perceives the everyday as impenetrable, the impenetrable as everyday."[19]

In *The Arcades Project*, Benjamin would retreat somewhat from his confidence in the surrealist project and suggest that rather than a dialectics of awakening and the concomitant release of the energies congealed in the "impenetrable," the surrealists in part succumbed to the intoxicating dream images they produced in their work. Ryan argues that Sebald's project marks yet a further retreat:

Sebald, in a second turn of the argument, engages with both the Surrealists' and Benjamin's optimistic view of illuminating moments, questioning their ability to perform in the post-Auschwitz period the transforming function with which, in their different ways, they had invested them. Illumination, in Sebald's novel, stands under the sinister signs of the darkness in the human psyche that enlightenment only superficially represses: imperialism, genocide, and war.[20]

The argument is, in some sense, that Sebald's work generates not so much profane illuminations as apocalyptic darkenings, moments where the last traces of light are, as it were, sucked back into black holes of despair and pain.

It is, of course, already somewhat problematic to associate Benjamin with any sort of optimism; indeed, in the surrealism essay he explicitly endorses a position of radical pessimism. Nonetheless, Ryan's point is well taken in that Benjamin's stance remains—at least according to a certain reading—resolutely political even and especially where his gaze turns toward the ruins and waste products of capitalism. To put it differently, for Benjamin the saturnine gaze on the detritus of the capitalist universe is sustained by a vision of

19. Ibid., 216. This is the sentence Sebald cites in his essay on Herbeck.
20. Ryan, "Fulgurations," 11.

political acts that would *interrupt* the course of history (understood as
that of capitalist globalization), whereas for Sebald it remains unclear
if there is any space left for such a vision.[21] The question is, then,
whether Sebald parts with Benjamin's efforts to perform a *political*
temporalization of historical experience; whether, that is, the "historical metaphysic" that the narrator so admires in Austerlitz's approach
to material culture, and that is no doubt based in large measure on a
reading of Benjamin's work, retains any sort of political orientation.
In *Austerlitz,* recall, the narrator notes "the way in which, in [Auster-
litz's] mind, the passing on of his knowledge seemed to become a
gradual approach to a kind of historical metaphysic, bringing remembered events back to life" (12–13/18–19). In Benjamin's view, this work
of reanimation can take place only based on and as a fundamental political decision and act; there can be no neutral place from which such
work intervenes into the past. That is the central point of Benjamin's
notion of *Jetztzeit*—the present situation of danger and crisis—in his
famous theses "On the Concept of History."[22] Our question with regard to Sebald will ultimately concern the nature of the relation between the saturnine gaze that informs his work and the dimension of
the act, between melancholic immersion into the past—his specific
form of *spectral materialism*—and the sphere of ethical and political
agency and production. How might we understand the ethical and
political ramifications of the memory work performed in Sebald's aesthetic practice? Does it *already* have the status of an ethical and political orientation and even intervention? To put it another way, why do
so many readers find Sebaldian melancholy so *pleasurable,* and how

21. Susan Buck-Morss has offered a nice formulation of the problematic relation of optimism and pessimism in Benjamin's work, one that takes into account his often affirmative stance with respect to new media technologies, something utterly foreign to Sebald:
"Extreme optimism concerning the promise of the 'new' nature of technology, and total pessimism concerning the course of history, which without proletarian revolution
would never leave the stage of prehistory." Susan Buck-Morss, *The Dialectics of Seeing:
Walter Benjamin and the Arcades Project* (Cambridge: MIT Press, 1991), 64.
22. Walter Benjamin, "On the Concept of History," trans. Harry Zohn, in *Walter
Benjamin: Selected Writings,* vol. 4, *1938–40,* ed. Howard Eiland and Michael W. Jennings (Cambridge: Harvard University Press, 2003). The text is, of course, better
known as the "Theses on the Philosophy of History."

might one imagine the ethical and political dimensions of this pleasure? Is the kind of dark beauty that Sebald so wondrously perfected an invitation toward self-extension into the world in all its brutal and often disastrous complexity, or does it offer the seductions of a kind of quietist complacency in the guise of morally charged sentiment and "memory work"?

v

Sebald inscribed his elective affinity with Benjamin in the title of his third volume of prose fiction, which, given the benefit of the hindsight provided by *Austerlitz,* suggests an allusion to an early sketch from *The Arcades Project* that Benjamin called *The Ring of Saturn, or Some Remarks on Iron Construction.* But in Sebald's *Rings of Saturn,* the key Benjaminian component is not so much the focus on the architectural styles of the bourgeois age that would become Austerlitz's primary object of research; it is the concept of historical life that Benjamin elaborated in his study of baroque drama and that no doubt influenced Sebald in his choice of the English title of his last published work, "natural history."[23] And indeed, at the end of the original set of lectures that make up *On the Natural History of Destruction* (the German title was *Luftkrieg und Literatur* [Aerial War and Literature]), Sebald quotes what may very well be the most famous passage in all of Benjamin's writings, the long "caption" he composed to a painting by Paul Klee that he owned for a time. The passage lays out Benjamin's own bleak vision of human history as a natural history of destruction. As familiar as the passage is, it is worth quoting in full:

There is a picture by Klee called *Angelus Novus.* It shows an angel who seems about to move away from something he stares at. His eyes are wide, his

23. In his 1982 essay "Zwischen Geschichte und Naturgeschichte," Sebald also notes that Lord Solly Zuckerman, once scientific adviser to the British military on matters of aerial bombing, had carried around the plan to publish a study on the bombing under the title "The Natural History of Destruction." See Sebald, *Campo Santo,* ed. Sven Meyer (Munich: Hanser, 2003), 255–56.

mouth is open, his wings are spread. This is how the angel of history must look. His face is turned toward the past. Where a chain of events appears before *us, he* sees one single catastrophe, which keeps piling wreckage upon wreckage and hurls it at his feet. The angel would like to stay, awaken the dead, and make whole what has been smashed. But a storm is blowing from Paradise and has got caught in his wings; it is so strong that the angel can no longer close them. This storm drives him irresistibly into the future, to which his back is turned, while the pile of debris before him grows toward the sky. What we call progress is *this* storm.[24]

There is an element of uncertainty in this allegory with respect to the status of progress, an uncertainty that, I think, informs both Benjamin's and Sebald's work: Is progress—understood first and foremost as the modern *faith* in progress in and through history and human agency—the force that keeps the angel from *attending* to the dead, from *tarrying with the negative* of human history, or is it more emphatically the force that *generates* that very violence? Even more important, is the task suggested by the allegory the awakening from an intoxicating faith in progress to a sober vision of history understood as a single, unmitigated disaster? In that case, the open mouth and wide-eyed stare of the angel would represent an effort at *agape,* a love that would bear witness to human suffering. But one cannot exclude the possibility that the vision of history fixed by the angel's stare is itself a kind of mythic dream or nightmare image—in Benjamin's terms, a species of *phantasmagoria*—that makes the angel ever more subject to the storm blowing from Paradise. Here one might recall Benjamin's critique of Auguste Blanqui, who in his final cosmological speculations conceived of history as an infernal and eternal recurrence of the same written across the heavens. As Benjamin puts it in a late, unpublished text on Blanqui's *L'éternité par les astres,* the "unconscious irony of Blanqui's elaborate enterprise is that the terrible accusation he directs against society takes on the form of unconditional

24. Benjamin, "On the Concept of History," 392. See *On the Natural History of Destruction,* trans. Anthea Bell (New York: Random House, 2003), 67–68; *Luftkrieg und Literatur* (Frankfurt a.M.: Fischer, 2002), 73–74.

acquiescence to its tendencies. The book proclaims the idea of the eternal return ten years before Nietzsche's *Zarathustra*, with hardly less pathos and with truly hallucinatory power."[25] In light of the title of Blanqui's last work, Benjamin seems to suggest that the crucial *disaster* has not yet occurred—the one that would also suspend the hallucinatory power of such astral visions that bind the subject ever more rigidly to the social tendencies at issue, tendencies that foreclose the imagination of alternative futures.[26]

The complexity of Benjamin's views on these matters is palpable in the following aphorism from *Central Park*:

The course of history, seen in terms of the concept of catastrophe, can actually claim no more attention from thinkers than a child's kaleidoscope, which with every turn of the hand dissolves the established order into a new array. There is profound truth in this image. The concepts of the ruling class have always been the mirrors that enabled an image of "order" to prevail.—The kaleidoscope must be smashed.[27]

I understand this aphorism at least in part as a condensation of Benjamin's reflections on the concept of "mythic violence" from his early essay "Critique of Violence." For Benjamin, what makes violence *mythic* is in large measure its entanglement in the repetition compulsions of political power, of the rise and fall of empires, states, rulers, and ideologies, the homogeneous time of an endless chain of succession in which one sovereign power–structure after another finds its momentary place in the sun of world history. As Austerlitz

---

25. Walter Benjamin, "Blanqui," trans. Edmund Jephcott, in *Selected Writings*, 4:93. A link to the hallucinatory power of Sebald's own saturnine vision of human history is perhaps suggested by the fact that in Sebald's last novel the narrator meets with Austerlitz in Paris at Le Havane bistro bar in the Boulevard Auguste Blanqui.

26. As Buck-Morss has put it, figures like Blanqui, Baudelaire, and Nietzsche manifest a tendency to ontologize "the emptiness of the historical experience of the commodity, the new as the always-the-same." Benjamin's work aimed at demonstrating "that far more violence . . . was required in order to redeem the material world" (Buck-Morss, *Dialectics*, 201).

27. Walter Benjamin, *Central Park*, trans. Edmund Jephcott and Howard Eiland, in *Selected Writings*, 4:166.

puts it in one of his early conversations with the narrator, this natural historical rhythm is precisely what is registered in the face of any of the great monuments of the bourgeois age: "At the most we gaze at it in wonder, a kind of wonder which in itself is a form of dawning horror, for somehow we know by instinct that outsize buildings cast the shadow of their own destruction before them, and are designed from the first with an eye to their later existence as ruins" (19/28).

In *The Star of Redemption,* Rosenzweig refers to this form of temporality organized around the rise and fall of sovereign power and authority as *kriegerische Zeitlichkeit,* "martial temporality."[28] Sovereignty is, for Rosenzweig, a political-theological "solution" to the problem of positing meaningful units within and against the forward rush of time. For Rosenzweig, sovereignty is thus ultimately a mode of temporalization:

The world's people as such are without orbits [*Kreislauf*]; their life cascades downhill in a broad stream. If the state is to provide them with eternity, this stream must be halted and dammed up to form a lake. The state must seek to turn into an orbit that pure sequence of time to which the peoples as such are committed. It must transform the constant alternation of their life into preservation and renewal and thus introduce an orbit capable, in itself, of being eternal. (332)

"History," Rosenzweig continues, "seems to fade away in unobstructed alternation and transformation. But the state steps in and imposes its law on the change. Now of a sudden there exists something that endures. Indeed at first sight it now seems as if everything is decreed [*fest-gesetzt*], everything enduring" (332–33). Rosenzweig is playing here, of course, with the German word for law, *Gesetz;* to be *fest-gesetzt* means to be posited, decreed, established as a stable and firm *precedent* that binds the future, that the future is obliged to repeat or iterate. But because of the fundamental tension between law and

---

28. Franz Rosenzweig, *Der Stern der Erlösung* (Frankfurt a.M.: Suhrkamp, 1990), 368; *The Star of Redemption,* trans. William W. Hallo (Notre Dame, IN: University of Notre Dame Press, 1985), 332.

life, principle and contingency, precedent and novelty, this very process of iteration is internally unstable. Thus, as Rosenzweig puts it, "The state reveals its true face. Law was only its first word. It cannot assert itself against the alternations of life. Now . . . the state speaks its second word: the word of coercion [*Gewalt*]" (333). The repetition of juridical precedent is, in other words, in a quite literal sense the *compulsion to repeat*.[29] It is precisely this dimension of repetition compulsion that defines, for Benjamin, the sphere of "mythic violence." Again, Rosenzweig's elaboration of this concept emphasizes, above all, its temporal dimension:

Coercion [*Gewalt*] provides life with legal redress against law. By being coercive itself, and not just legal, the state remains hard on the heels of life. *The point of all coercion is to institute new law.* It is not the denial of law as one might think under the spell of its cataclysmic behavior; on the contrary, it lays the basis for law. But a paradox lurks in the idea of new law. Law is essentially old law. And now it is clear what coercion is: the renewer of old law. In the coercive act, the law constantly becomes new law. And the state is thus equally both lawful and coercive, refuge of the old law and source of the new. . . . At every moment the state is forcibly deciding the contradiction between conservation and renovation, between old law and new. It thus constantly resolves the contradiction, while the course of the people's life only delays the solution perpetually through the onward flow of time. The state attacks the problem, indeed the *state is itself nothing but the constantly undertaken resolution of this contradiction.* (333; my emphasis)

The consequence of this "being and time" of the state, of its specific mode of "capturing" temporal life, is "that war and revolution is the only reality known to the state; it would cease to be a state the moment where neither the one nor the other were to take place—even if it be only in the form of a thought of war or revolution. The state can

29. Rosenzweig is no doubt influenced here by Nietzsche's *Genealogy of Morals,* the second essay of which begins with the problem of inducting human beings into a life that includes the concept of promises, that is, the notion that the future can be bound by a pledge made in the past.

at no moment lay down the sword" (333–34). Finally, Rosenzweig characterizes this intervention of sovereign authority into the temporal flow of life—let's call it "sovereign temporalization"—as a form of ban (*Bann*), which can mean, among other things: sovereign authority; the prohibition or punishment decreed by sovereign authority; spell; banishment; abandonment. As Rosenzweig puts it,

For the new, which otherwise always gets beyond the old, is momentarily confined in its sphere of influence [*Bannbereich*]. It takes the new moment to break the power of the old and to threaten to let life flow on once more as a free river. But at once the state raises its sword again and again condemns the river to a standstill [*bannt den Fluß aufs neue zum Stehenden*], the onward motion to a circle. . . . [I]t is the state which first introduces standstills, stations, epochs into the ceaseless sweep of this life. Epochs are the hours of universal history [*Weltgeschichte*], and only the state introduces them through its martial spell [*seinen kriegerischen Bannspruch*] which makes the sun of time stand still until on any given day "the people shall have prevailed over its enemies." . . . Only the state drops into the current of time those reflections of true eternity which, as epochs, form the building blocks of universal history. (334)[30]

In a sense, Rosenzweig's theory of the state comes down to a meditation on the two meanings of the word "succession." In its efforts

---

30. Both Jean-Luc Nancy and Giorgio Agamben have invoked the concept of the ban to characterize the "event" of life's capture by the political. In Nancy's words, "To abandon is to remit, entrust, or turn over to . . . a sovereign power, and to remit, entrust, or turn over to its ban, that is, to its proclaiming, to its convening, and to its sentencing. . . . One always abandons to a law. The destitution of abandoned Being is measured by the limitless severity of the law to which it finds itself exposed. Abandonment does not constitute a subpoena to present oneself before this or that court of law. It is a compulsion to appear absolutely under the law, under the law as such and in its totality. In the same way—it is the same thing—to be banished amounts not to coming under a provision of the law but rather to coming under the entirety of the law. Turned over to the absolute of the law, the abandoned one is thereby abandoned completely outside its jurisdiction. . . . Abandonment respects the law; it cannot do otherwise." Nancy, "Abandoned Being," cited in Agamben, *Homo Sacer: Sovereign Power and Bare Life,* trans. Daniel Heller-Roazen (Stanford: Stanford University Press, 1998), 58–59.

to overcome the meaningless succession of one moment after the other, the state introduces "standstills, stations, epochs." This mode of overcoming, however, merely transposes the homogeneity of "natural," temporal succession into the ceaseless violence of *hegemonic succession*: the *naturgeschichtlich* succession of sovereign power-structures figured in the image of the child's kaleidoscope, "which with every turn of the hand dissolves the established order into a new array."

VI

One might get a better sense of the "mythic" dimension of this sovereign temporalization by noting its structural similarities with the myth that Freud posited as articulating the origins of civilization out of the prehistoric pattern of the social life of humankind—the infamous *primal horde*. In *Totem and Taboo,* Freud argued that the libidinal economy of social life in the present requires us to posit a prehistory in which the fundamental capacity for entering into nonviolent, contractual relations of reciprocity and mutual recognition was still undeveloped. According to the myth that Freud pieced together from speculations by Charles Darwin and Robertson Smith, humankind originally lived in small hordes that each stood under the rule of a powerful senior male—the "primal father"—who governed the junior males with brute force and appropriated the females for his own, absolute enjoyment. According to the logic of life in the horde, each generation would inaugurate new struggles for the position of senior male/primal father. As Freud saw it, the "eternal recurrence" of the primal horde pattern can be suspended only when the junior males topple and murder the senior male *in solidarity with one another.* As Freud suggests, it is really only on the basis of this deed—one that had to be repeated innumerable times before it assumed structural significance—that *patriarchy,* the organization of social life sustained by the father qua *symbolic* agency, could arise. The junior males, as Freud writes, "hated their father, who presented such a formidable obstacle to their craving for power and their sexual desires; but they loved and admired him too." The symbolic father is, Freud suggests, born out of the dynamic tensions of just such ambivalence:

After they had got rid of him, had satisfied their hatred and had put into effect their wish to identify themselves with him, the affection which had all this time been pushed under was bound to make itself felt. It did so in the form of remorse. A sense of guilt made its appearance, which in this instance coincided with the remorse felt by the whole group. *The dead father became stronger than the living father had been* [my emphasis]. . . . What had up to then been prevented by his actual existence was thenceforward prohibited by the sons themselves, in accordance with the psychological procedure so familiar to us in psychoanalyses under the name of "deferred obedience."

The first fruit of this peculiar form of obedience was, Freud argues, the cultural practice of totemism, one that included the institution of the core taboos that continue to animate the oedipal scenario:

They revoked their deed by forbidding the killing of the totem [animal], the substitute for their father; and they renounced its fruits by resigning their claims to the women who had now been set free. They thus created out of their filial sense of guilt the two fundamental taboos of totemism, which for that very reason inevitably corresponded to the two repressed wishes of the Oedipus complex.[31]

But as Freud also argues, a cultural shift of this magnitude had to be consolidated by way of a ritualized repetition of the drama of its emergence, in this case the murder and consumption of the to-tem animal that stands in as the mediator between the primal father and his symbolic representation: "The totem meal, which is per-haps mankind's earliest festival, would thus be a repetition and a

31. Sigmund Freud, *Totem and Taboo,* trans. James Strachey (New York: W. W. Norton, 1989), 177–78.

commemoration of this memorable and criminal deed, which was the beginning of so many things—of social organization, of moral restrictions, and of religion."[32] When he returns, in *Moses and Monotheism*, to the importance of this mythic complex for his thinking about culture, society, and religion, Freud emphasizes once again that the ambivalence at the core of a cultural achievement of this order required some form of performative elaboration, one that includes the dimension of *obligatory excess*:

In order to be able to live in peace with one another the victorious brothers renounced the women for whose sake they had killed the father, and agreed to practice exogamy. . . . The ambivalence of the sons towards the father remained in force during the whole further development. Instead of the father a certain animal was declared the totem; it stood for their ancestor and protecting spirit, and no one was allowed to hurt or kill it. Once a year, however, the whole clan assembled for a feast at which the otherwise revered totem was torn to pieces and eaten. No one was permitted to abstain from this feast; it was the solemn repetition of the father-murder, in which social order, moral laws, and religion had had their beginnings.[33]

The crucial paradox at the heart of this condensed story of the birth of the capacity for self-regulation and legislation out of totemic identification—the procedure for the appropriation and internalization of paternal attributes—is that the *renunciation* of the parricidal impulse (along with the fantasy of absolute jouissance entailed by the yearned-for position of the primal father) can be fully sustained only by a *compulsion to enjoy* that same impulse, though at the significant symbolic remove of ritual performance (the totem meal). And as Freud would later emphasize, it is the psychic agency he called the

32. Ibid., 176. One of the contemporary phenomena that led Freud to his theory of totemism was, of course, the practice of the Christian sacraments, which for Freud represented a peculiar persistence of a cannibalistic imaginary into modernity.
33. Sigmund Freud, *Moses and Monotheism*, trans. Katherine Jones (New York: Vintage, 1967), 168.

*superego* that would become the intrapsychic locus of this paradox at the heart of the capacity for self-regulation/legislation.[34]

For the moment, the point to emphasize is the closeness of Freud's myth of the primal father to Carl Schmitt's conception of the sovereign who retains the paradoxical right to suspend the law, to decide on the state of exception. Sovereign authority in the state of exception/emergency is structurally homologous with that of the primal father in Freud's account of human prehistory. In each case, a monstrous paternal agency *immediately speaks the law* without being subject to any law himself (what I have been calling creaturely life is, so to speak, the agitation introduced into human life by way of such a voice/vocal object).[35] Now, it was Freud's argument in *Moses and*

---

34. In *Civilization and Its Discontents,* Freud offers a more structural interpretation of the myth of the primal father as the fantasy—born of the eternal conflict of the drives—that sustains the vitality of the superego. The first part of the story is familiar: "After their [the band of brothers'] hatred had been satisfied by their act of aggression, their love came to the fore in their remorse for the deed. It set up the super-ego by identification with the father; it gave that agency the father's power, as though as a punishment for the deed of aggression they had carried out against him, and it created the restrictions which were intended to prevent a repetition of the deed." But now Freud adds the following: "Whether one has killed one's father or has abstained from doing so is not really the decisive thing. One is bound to feel guilty in either case, for the sense of guilt is an expression of the conflict due to ambivalence, of the eternal struggle between Eros and the instinct of destruction or death. This conflict is set going as soon as men are faced with the task of living together." Freud, *Civilization and Its Discontents,* trans. James Strachey (New York: W. W. Norton, 1989), 95.
35. In a discussion of Freud's famous case of the "Rat Man," Jonathan Lear has offered the following rather more mundane scenario for the formation of a punishing superegoic voice, a process that nonetheless produces another hunchbacked creature: "Melanie Klein has argued that the earliest internalizations occur via phantasies of physical incorporation. In good-enough circumstances, the comfort, reassurance, and satisfaction which the child receives at the breast is taken in with the mother's milk. That is, the milk itself becomes a concrete vehicle of meaning. Goodness is the meaning of the milk. . . . Similarly, the child may begin to form a superego around a prohibitive utterance: for the Rat Child, it may have been the voice of the father saying, 'Don't do that!' The utterance is itself the physical movement of meaning. The father's tongue has set the air around it vibrating, and a prohibitive meaning informs that vibrating air. That meaning reaches the Rat Child's ear via its concrete vehicle and triggers a chain of neurological reactions. One outcome is that the Rat Child can hear his father; another is that he can hear the prohibitive voice over and over 'inside his head.' The Rat Child

*Monotheism* that the Exodus story—this founding myth of Jewish ethnogenesis—recapitulates and thus newly actualizes the (proto)cultural labor of suspending and superseding the primal horde pattern of generational succession embodied in the world of pharaonic kingship.[36] For Freud as well as for Benjamin, the great conceptual, ethical, and political problem was to grasp the special nature of the violence at work in the event of such a suspension and to understand the

---

experiences his own rage as tremendously powerful; and one way to deal with the anxiety it arouses is, in phantasy, to move it over to invest the father's voice. This isn't a thought or a judgment; it is the nonrational, phantastic movement of content. However, though the phantasy-movement of content is not itself rational, it may acquire a dynamic, intrapsychic function. Rage gains some expression, phantastically expressed over there, in the voice of the father, and it is used intrapsychically to inhibit outbursts of rage. And so the movement of meaning in phantasy helps to shape intrapsychic structure. The Rat Child begins to live a life which is to be understood in significant part as an extended cringe before the voice of the Rat Dad." Jonathan Lear, *Open Minded: Working Out the Logic of the Soul* (Cambridge: Harvard University Press, 1998), 99; my emphasis.

36. In his brilliant interpretation of Freud's *Moses,* Robert Paul has emphasized the ways the mythic schema of pharaonic succession closely cleaves to the primal horde pattern. According to the mythic paradigm, the living pharaoh embodies the position of the god Horus, who replaces his father, Osiris, as husband of Isis once Osiris has been castrated and killed by Seth, Osiris's evil younger brother. In the myth, the role of the rebellious junior male is split into Seth/Horus; Horus accedes to the throne only after engaging in battle with Seth (Horus castrates Seth, Seth puts out one of Horus's eyes). "This," Paul writes, "is an elementary transformation of the horde pattern and can be interpreted to mean that the pharaoh is depicted as an oedipal victor: that is, as a son who has succeeded his father and become senior male. By virtue of having accomplished this momentous feat, the son is seen as fit to rule over his fellows." By contrast, the great cultural achievement performed by Moses—the break with the world of Egypt, with "paganism"—was to have established an entirely new conception of generational succession. As Paul succinctly puts it, "The pharaonic model can thus be seen as what happens when the junior male emerges victorious from a struggle for succession, as opposed to what happens when a junior male rebels to end the system of succession itself, as Moses does." Robert Paul, *Moses and Civilization: The Meaning Behind Freud's Myth* (New Haven: Yale University Press, 1996), 31–32. In all of this one should also keep in mind the myth of Saturn/Kronos, the god indirectly associated with the mood we have been exploring here. Saturn/Kronos murdered his father Uranus and tried unsuccessfully to prevent his own violent displacement by his offspring by eating them. We might say that melancholy—the saturnine disposition—involves a profound attunement to the resonances of this mythic pattern in the present.

*libidinal economy* of the form of life it inaugurates. In the language of Benjamin's essay "Critique of Violence," the problem pertains to the concept of "pure" or "divine violence," *göttliche Gewalt;* in the terms of Benjamin's aphorism on the concept of catastrophe from *Central Park,* the question pertains to the violence invoked by the demand that "the kaleidoscope must be smashed."

However, as I noted above, the great problem Freud introduced with his view of the emergence of civilization is that the superego, the psychic agency in and through which the subject becomes libidinally attached to the "civilizing process"—to the exodus from "Egypt"— also becomes the locus of a nearly impossible ambivalence, the site where the primal horde pattern and its "mythic violence" are in some sense both sustained and suspended *in the same stroke.* The passage beyond the primal horde pattern is undone, or at the very least profoundly endangered, by the psychic agency that seems to consolidate its success. The superego, as Freud conceptualized that psychic agency, represents the paradoxical persistence of the primal horde pattern in and through the very passage beyond it, for as we have seen, in order to sustain the energies of the superego one must, so to speak, guiltily enjoy the murder of the primal father—*over and over again.*[37]

---

37. According to Robert Paul's revision of Freud's argument in *Moses and Monotheism,* the trauma that haunts the Jewish tradition is not, as Freud posited, the murder of Moses by the ancient Israelites who could not tolerate the rigors of the cult he imposed, but rather the violence of the Mosaic break itself with "pagan" Egypt, violence that in light of the law instituted at Sinai becomes a criminal stain on the tradition opened by that law. As Paul summarizes this fundamental revision of Freud's argument, "The destruction of Egypt is . . . a crime on Moses's hands. . . . Moses's rebellion is at once a patricide, since Pharaoh is Moses's father; a deicide, since Pharaoh is a living god; a regicide, since Pharaoh is the ruler of the Egyptian empire; and a revolt of the servant against the master, since Moses leads the enslaved Israelites against their overlord and taskmaster. . . . Because of the guilt engendered by this deed the covenant on Mount Sinai is instituted, and from that guilt the Law gains its compulsory force. According to the Mosaic Law—which is, however, a statement of the more general human social principle of reciprocity—justice demands like for like: punishment, in talionic fashion, must match the crime. . . . Because this debt remains uncollected, the Israelites are violators of the Law by virtue of the very events that led to its promulgation. The Law itself, no matter how restrictive it may seem, protec-

What Freud was unable to grasp, I suggest, is that it is precisely in the commandment to love one's neighbor as oneself that one finds the resources for intervening in and supplementing the superego bind that can so easily support the very sorts of violent patterns of succession Freud had thought it would suspend. Love of neighbor is the "miraculous" opening of a social link based on the creaturely deposits left by the state of exception that, as Freud indicates, *structurally haunts* the subject in and through the formation of the superego.[38] And as Sebald's work seems to argue, such "miracles" depend on the performance of acts of witnessing, that is, of transforming such creaturely *deposits* into a form of *deposition*.

To return to the point of departure for this long excursus, the thing to keep in mind is that the word "myth" needs to be understood not simply as the effort to distort the truth of history, to cover up its catastrophic aspect;[39] it also names a dimension of immobilizing fantasy at work in that very image of history. Our question then continues to be the degree to which Benjamin and, especially, Sebald remain under the spell—within the *Bannbereich*—of mythic violence when they evoke, with such hallucinatory power, the vision of history as a singular catastrophe.

---

tively wards off the as-yet unexecuted and dreaded talionic punishment for the original crime" (210). In this view, Moses introduces into the Jewish tradition a dynamic we might call "last cannibal syndrome" according to the witticism, "There are no more cannibals; I ate the last one." Moses is such a "last cannibal" in that the deeds he performs in God's name leading to the revelation at Sinai are transgressions in the context of that same revelation. Freud's argument is that the psychic agency he called the superego is forever agitated by the structure of this profoundly conflicted narrative of exodus/ emergence.

38. For a brilliant analysis of the ways love of neighbor can come to supplement the superego dynamic that remains attached to the structuring force of the sovereign exception, see Kenneth Reinhard, "Toward a Political Theology of the Neighbor," in *The Neighbor: Three Inquiries in Political Theology,* by Slavoj Žižek, Eric Santner, and Kenneth Reinhard (Chicago: University of Chicago Press, 2005).

39. See, for example, Michael Jennings, *Dialectical Images: Walter Benjamin's Theory of Literary Criticism* (Ithaca: Cornell University Press, 1987): "Myth covers and distorts the intensely destructive, corrosive force of history; it is Benjamin's term, in other words, for what we would today call ideology" (78).

VII

As we have already seen, the vision of history as ceaseless catastrophe is most fully elaborated by Benjamin in his study of baroque drama. But Benjamin's work on the baroque and the concept of natural history he developed there in conjunction with the analysis of the allegorical mode of representation was never intended to be a free-standing piece of academic scholarship. It was, rather, composed as an intervention into a contemporary historical crisis, one he came to understand increasingly in Marxist terms. As far as I know, Benjamin himself offers no detailed justification for the translation of the categories of political theology—his work on the baroque sovereign and the state of exception—into those of Marxist social analysis, of categories developed apropos of the court and literary culture of seventeenth-century Europe into those relevant to the analysis of capitalist modernity. A few of the links between the project on the baroque and the new work on modernity, however, ought to be relatively clear. A first connection is manifest in what Marx characterized as the revolutionary energies of capitalism itself. The capitalist mode of production converts into its own structural principle the natural historical rhythms proper to the reason of states. Mythic violence, the natural-historical cycles of the rise and fall of empires and states—of the establishment, augmentation, and decay of institutions—under conditions of modern capitalism, all this had at some level penetrated the fabric of daily life, had become part of the "life cycle" of capitalist production itself.

There is no better—or more poetic—elaboration of this process whereby what I have called "sovereign temporalization" mutates into the temporalization proper to the rhythms of commodity production and consumption than the *Communist Manifesto*. The monuments and ruins left by empires and states—and again, this is the very stuff of natural history for Benjamin—have been superseded by those of the bourgeoisie: "It has been the first to show what man's activity can bring about. It has accomplished wonders far surpassing Egyptian pyramids, Roman aqueducts, and Gothic cathedrals; it has conducted expeditions that put in the shade all former Exoduses of nations and crusades."[40] And in what has become one of the most celebrated passages in all of Marx's writings, we read these crucial lines:

The bourgeoisie cannot exist without constantly revolutionizing the instruments of production, and thereby the relations of production, and with them the whole relations of society. Conservation of the old modes of production in unaltered form, was, on the contrary, the first condition of existence for all earlier industrial classes. Constant revolutionizing of production, uninterrupted disturbance of all social conditions, everlasting uncertainty and agitation distinguish the bourgeois epoch from all earlier ones. All fixed, fast-frozen relations, with their train of ancient and venerable prejudices and opinions, are swept away, all new-formed ones become antiquated before they can ossify. All that is solid melts into air.[41]

40. *The Communist Manifesto,* in Karl Marx, *Selected Writings,* ed. David McLellan (Oxford: Oxford University Press, 1985), 224. Both Rosenzweig and Benjamin had a conception of the Exodus of the Israelites different from Marx's. This event did not, in their view, belong simply within the order of (natural) historical time but rather prefigured a mode of unplugging from it. It is such an unplugging that counts for both thinkers as the core of messianism (here we should also recall Freud's paradoxical position somewhere between Marx and Rosenzweig/Benjamin on the status of the Exodus).

41. Ibid., 224. This last famous phrase provided the title for what is still one of the best available discussions of the relations between the forces of modernization and the responses of aesthetic modernism, Marshall Berman's *All That Is Solid Melts into Air: The Experience of Modernity* (New York: Simon and Schuster, 1982). Berman's concise summary of the multiple dimensions of modernization is extremely helpful; it serves, too, as a kind of catalog of the occasions for Sebaldian melancholy: "The maelstrom of modern life has been fed from many sources: great discoveries in the physical sciences, changing our images of the universe and our place in it; the industrialization of production, which transforms scientific knowledge into technology, creates new human environments and destroys old ones, speeds up the whole tempo of life, generates new forms of corporate power and class struggle; immense demographic upheavals, severing millions of people from their ancestral habitats, hurtling them halfway across the world into new lives; rapid and often cataclysmic urban growth; systems of mass communication, dynamic in their development, enveloping and binding together the most diverse people and societies; increasingly powerful national states, bureaucratically structured and operated, constantly striving to expand their powers; mass social movements of people, and peoples, challenging their political and economic rulers, striving to gain some control over their lives; *finally, bearing and driving all these people and institutions along, an ever-expanding, drastically fluctuating capitalist world market*" (16; my emphasis).

Benjamin's *Arcades Project* was, of course, dedicated to document-ing in microscopic detail the ramifications of this "everlasting uncer-tainty and agitation"—this natural historical nihilism proper to capi-tal itself—in the physiognomy of the modern metropolis and in the everyday life of modern urban dwellers. But for Marx as well as for Benjamin, this nihilism was nowhere more concentrated and potent than in the phenomenon of the commodity itself. That is to say, it was as if the laws of natural history evoked by both Benjamin and Rosen-zweig had entered into the very substance of material objects, had be-come merged with their materiality. The object world itself became, in a word, a primary locus of what Rosenzweig characterized as mar-tial or agonistic temporality.

The self-splitting of the object qua commodity into use-value and exchange-value and the rapidity with which both aspects of value de-composed under pressures from the market—for Benjamin, fashion was the ultimate emblem of this acceleration—was for Benjamin a radicalization of a process already fixed by the gaze of melancholy (think of his commentary on Dürer's famous woodcut, *Melancholia I*). Benjamin's thought here is grounded in the experience of objects that have survived the form of life in which they had their meaning, in which their concept was still alive. (From this perspective, all those natural history museums where artifacts of past civilizations are put on display and where explanatory texts attempt to reinsert these stranded objects back into the context of their original life-worlds are so many duplications of Dürer's woodcut.) As Benjamin notes in his study of the baroque, the Christianization of Europe meant that the objects of pagan civilizations—above all their "naturalist" representa-tions of deities—became remainders in this sense, hieroglyphs of a past life to which full access was no longer possible. And precisely as such they could be and were indeed hypercathected, invested with an excess of signification.[42] For Benjamin, capitalism was at some level a

---

42. As Benjamin writes in his *Trauerspiel* book: "The attire of the Olympians is left be-hind, and in the course of time the emblems collect around it. And this attire is as crea-turely as a devil's body. . . . Alongside the emblems and the attire, the words and the names remain behind, and, as the living contexts of their birth disappear, so they become the origins of concepts in which these words acquire a new content, which is

vast machinery for the production of just such remainders, objects that assume the status of enigmatic signifiers, what Benjamin refers to as "dry rebuses" or "stirring writing."[43] As he puts it in response to a letter in which Adorno addressed his friend's notion of the dialectical image as "constellated between alienated things and incoming and disappearing meaning," as figures "instantiated in the moment of in-difference between death and meaning," Benjamin writes: "With re-gard to these reflections, it should be kept in mind that, in the nine-teenth century, the number of 'hollowed-out' things increases at a rate and on a scale that was previously unknown, for technical progress is continually withdrawing newly introduced objects from circulation."[44] Or as he puts it in a famous aphorism in *Central Park,* "The devaluation of the world of things in allegory is surpassed within the world of things itself by the commodity."[45]

One of Benjamin's primary concerns pertains to the ways the dis-tress that in early modernity had been to a very large extent *localizable,* concentrated within the sphere of the traditional master or sover-eign—the realm of *Haupt- und Staatsaktionen* and the charged, yet fragile charisma of the "king's body"—becomes "deterritorialized," leaks into the texture of the social space at large and indeed, *into the very soul* of the modern urban dweller. The zones of distress pertain-ing to issues of sovereign power and authority—the creaturely cor-relative of political theology—become dispersed into the sources of the "psychopathology of everyday life." As Benjamin puts it apropos of the concept of the "souvenir," or *Andenken,*

---

predisposed to allegorical representation. . . . The deadness of the figures and the ab-straction of the concepts are therefore the precondition for the allegorical metamor-phosis of the pantheon into a world of magical, conceptual creatures." Walter Benjamin, *The Origin of German Tragic Drama,* trans. John Osborne (London: NLB, 1977), 225–26.

43. Ibid., 176.

44. Walter Benjamin, *The Arcades Project,* trans. Howard Eiland and Kevin McLaugh-lin (Cambridge: Harvard University Press, 1999), 466 (N5, 2).

45. Benjamin, *Selected Writings,* 4:164. For Benjamin, Baudelaire's great distinction among nineteenth-century poets was that he was the one to have developed a poetic practice and persona around such a dynamic of debasement; as such he is the modern heir of the baroque allegorists.

The souvenir is the complement to "isolated experience" [*des "Erlebnisses"*]. In it is precipitated the increasing self-estrangement of human beings, whose past is inventoried as dead effects. In the nineteenth century, *allegory withdrew from the world around us to settle in the inner world.* The relic comes from the cadaver; the souvenir comes from the defunct experience [*Erfahrung*] which thinks of itself, euphemistically, as living [*Erlebnis*].⁴⁶

Social space, and above all psychic space, becomes crowded with such enigmatic signifiers, these new source-objects of drive in everyday life under capitalism. One might thus speak of the birth of (the subject of) psychoanalysis out of the "spirit" of the commodity.

VIII

These last remarks point to a fundamental ambiguity underlying Benjamin's discourse of natural history both in his analysis of the baroque and in its extension to the universe of the commodity. The ambiguity pertains to the notion of "deadening" and indeed to the entire semantic field of death and decay that Benjamin deploys throughout his work (as we shall see, this same ambiguity is at work in Sebald). What is often missed in the correlation of melancholy with death, deadening, and coldness is, we might say, the *manic* side of this state. As Benjamin emphasizes time and again, what distinguishes the allegorical sensibility is precisely its restlessness, its extravagant pomp, its excess of animation in the face of historical violence and destruction—the boneyard of history. The "petrified landscape" of natural history is, in a word, a locus of extreme excitation and agitation; the allegorical intention is, Benjamin argues, in constant motion, following a trajectory "from emblem to emblem down into the dizziness [*Schwindel*] of bottomless depths."⁴⁷ This excess of animation becomes, for him, the norm in the culture of modern capitalism. The landscape of urban life is, in this view, experienced as phantasmagoric, as a source of ceaseless and vertigo-inducing excitations and shocks—what Freud

46. Ibid., 183; my emphasis.
47. Benjamin, *Origin*, 232.

called *Reizüberflutung,* a flooding of the mind by stimulation. As I have already proposed, this paradoxical mixture of deadness and excitation, stuckness and agitation, might best by captured by the term "undeadness." This suggests, in turn, that the psychoanalytic cure (as well as ethical and political acts informed by Freud's discoveries) ought to be understood as a practice by means of which such nihilistic vitality would be deanimated.[48] Benjamin aims at the same uncanny admixture constituting the *Schwindel* proper to life amid commodities—these allegorical fragments littering the modern urban landscape—with the locution *erstarrte Unruhe,* petrified unrest, a phrase he takes from a poem by Gottfried Keller.[49] He uses the term to characterize the dynamic at work in Blanqui's cosmological phantasmagoria as well as Baudelaire's image of life that, as Benjamin puts it, knows no development.[50] As becomes especially clear in light of the remarks I have already cited about Blanqui, what Benjamin refers to as petrified unrest pertains to the dynamic of the *repetition compulsion,* the psychic aspect of the eternal recurrence of the same that for Benjamin defined the world of commodity production and consumption. The political theology of the seventeenth century with its always endangered sovereigns was, Benjamin argues, already a product of a process of secularization; the long nineteenth century represented the next, more radical stage in this process of "immanentization" whereby the divine charisma that had still stuck to the sovereign becomes disseminated throughout the social space as an "exciting" phantasmagorical presence—as a dimension of *surplus value*—attaching to objects and bodies that thereby become the focal points of ceaseless economic,

48. Recall my remarks in chapter 1 concerning Benjamin's discussion of disenchantment in "On the Storyteller." See also Eric Santner, *On the Psychotheology of Everyday Life: Reflections on Freud and Rosenzweig* (Chicago: University of Chicago Press, 2001), as well as my essay "Miracles Happen: Benjamin, Rosenzweig, Freud and the Matter of the Neighbor," in *The Neighbor: Three Inquiries in Political Theology,* by Slavoj Žižek, Eric Santner, and Kenneth Reinhard (Chicago: University of Chicago Press, 2005).
49. The relevant passage from Keller's "Verlorenes Recht, verlorenes Glück" is, "War wie ein Medusenschild / der erstarrten Unruh Bild" ("Was like a Medusa-shield, / image of petrified unrest"). See notes to Benjamin, *Central Park,* in *Selected Writings,* 4:195.
50. Benjamin, *Arcades Project,* 329 (J55a, 3, 5).

cultural, and political administration. What Michel Foucault (and later Agamben) called "biopolitics" and what one understands as modern industrial capitalism and commodity production emerge together in or, rather, as the field of this dissemination.[51]

The "manic" side of modern melancholy can thus be understood at least in part as a mode of response to what Marx characterized as the spectral dimension of our life with commodities. Recall a few of Marx's well-known formulations for this dimension. He speaks, for example, of the "phantom-like objectivity," *die gespenstige Gegenständlichkeit,* of the commodity as a congealed unit of human labor power invested with value; of the "metaphysical subtleties and theological niceties" of the commodity; of the "mystical character of the commodity"; of the fact that value "transforms every product of labor into a social hieroglyph." These formulations are ultimately so many ways of approximating what for Marx constitutes the *fetish* quality of the commodity, a term itself appropriated from "the misty realm of religion":

There the products of the human brain appear as autonomous figures endowed with a life of their own, which enter into relations both with each

---

51. As I noted earlier, this shift from the space of the court—the realm of the traditional master—to the multiple sites of economic and political administration/discipline was the main focus of Foucault's historiography of modernity, though there is little in Foucault's work on the status of capitalism as such in this shift. I have discussed this shift at length in Eric Santner, *My Own Private Germany: Daniel Paul Schreber's Secret History of Modernity* (Princeton: Princeton University Press, 1996). It was, as I have suggested, also crucial to Lacan's theorization of the status of symbolic power and authority in modernity. In his seventeenth seminar, Lacan posited the emergence, in the long nineteenth century, of a new social bond and discourse, the "discourse of the university," one that displaced the dominance of the "discourse of the master." What is suggested by Lacan's formula for the discourse of the university is that the biopolitical relation (what the Frankfurt school criticized as the totally administrated society) whereby knowledge aims at controlling the "real" of the human body and material world is directly correlated with a generalized investiture crisis in society at large. That is, there is a crisis whereby the symbolic authority regulating status and social roles—one's *dignitas*—no longer functions, where the distribution of symbolic authority is no longer grounded in the figure and charisma of a master. The new "master" is the one who can claim expert knowledge (a claim that could, however, never be fully grounded in an unbroken chain of reasons). Both Foucault and Lacan no doubt owe a certain debt to Max Weber's theorization of the mutation of authority in modernity.

other and with the human race. So it is in the world of commodities with the products of men's hands. I call this the fetishism which attaches itself to the products of labor as soon as they are produced as commodities, and is therefore inseparable from the production of commodities.[52]

Another crucial site where we encounter the manic aspect of the melancholy that was of such primary concern to Benjamin is in the work of Friedrich Nietzsche. In Nietzsche's writings, the withdrawal from life that characterizes the posture of melancholy is analyzed more broadly under the heading of the *ascetic ideal*. As Alenka Zupancic has emphasized in a recent study, the crucial point in Nietzsche's analysis is that this apparent withdrawal from the midst of life correlates strictly with a strange intensification of psychic and somatic being. As Zupancic has put it,

For Nietzsche, the asceticism involved in the ascetic ideal does not simply involve a renouncement of enjoyment; it involves, above all, a specific mode or articulation of enjoyment. Moreover, one could even say that the ascetic ideal coincides with the very "invention" of enjoyment: enjoyment as different from pleasure, as something which lies—to use Freud's term—beyond the pleasure principle.[53]

For Nietzsche, the primary locus of such "enjoyment" was conscience, "the cruel wheel of a restless, morbidly lascivious conscience"

---

52. Karl Marx, *Capital,* vol. 1, trans. Ben Fowler (New York: Vintage, 1977), 128, 163, 164, 167, 165. In his discussion of Marx's theorization of the fetishism of the commodity, Jacques Derrida has argued that Marx's strategy here should itself be understood as a kind of exorcism, as an attempt, that is, to localize in space and time the traumatic emergence of a spectrality that, for Derrida, has a far more general significance. Whereas for Marx there is something like a datable primal scene that marks the emergence—the "birthday"—of the specter, for Derrida the historical truth of spectrality cannot be so easily circumscribed, for it pertains more broadly to our capacity to use concepts and valuations and to inhabit the space of meaning. For Derrida, there is no ontology without "hauntology." See Jacques Derrida, *Specters of Marx: The State of the Debt, the Work of Mourning, and the New International,* trans. Peggy Kamuf (New York: Routledge, 1994), esp. 161. As I have been arguing, Benjamin's own position was something of a hybrid, namely that of introducing historical inflections into this general hauntology.
53. Alenka Zupancic, *The Shortest Shadow: Nietzsche's Philosophy of the Two* (Cambridge: MIT Press, 2003), 47.

producing "convulsions of an unknown happiness" and keeping the subject "awake, everlastingly awake, sleepless, glowing, charred, spent and yet not weary."[54] As Zupancic puts it, religion qua ascetic ideal, far from being an "opium of the people" that allows them to escape from a harsh reality, functions more as a stimulant, "an 'excitation-raiser' which binds us to this reality by activating some mortifying passion. Discomfort is soothed (or silenced) by crises and states of emergency in which a subject feels *alive*. But this 'alive' is nothing other than 'undeadness,' the petrifying grip of surplus excitation and agitation."[55]

This point leads Zupancic to reflections pertaining to the shift of focus I have emphasized in Benjamin's work from the political theology of the baroque to the theological niceties of the commodity, from early modern to properly modern "natural history": "With the term 'ascetic ideal,' Nietzsche names the passage from one logic of law to another, a passage from the law that forbids and regulates enjoyment to the law that commands (not pleasure but) enjoyment, confronting us with an imperative of enjoyment."[56] She goes on to clarify this position by recasting it as a shift of dominance within a persistent structural tension:

Actually, it would be more accurate to say that the two sides of the law—the prohibition of enjoyment and the surplus of enjoyment—were always linked, mutually supporting each other. (Surplus-) enjoyment is not simply something that is suppressed or repressed by the law. The prohibition of enjoyment equals the creation of a "beyond" where surplus-enjoyment (although forbidden) finds its place. This "beyond" is the very thing from which the law draws its power to *attach* us, since the law really functions not when it manages to hold us simply by fear of its authority, but when we adhere to it through a specific mode of (our) enjoyment. The "shift" mentioned above concerns the fact that this other side of the law (its "back side") becomes its front side. Or, perhaps more precisely: (surplus-) enjoyment is no longer a hidden support

54. Friedrich Nietzsche, *On the Genealogy of Morals/Ecce Homo,* trans. W. Kaufmann and R. J. Hollingdale (New York: Vintage, 1989), 141.
55. Zupancic, *Shortest Shadow,* 49.
56. Ibid., 50.

of the law; rather it becomes one with the law, as if a kind of short circuit between the two had been established.[57]

Although Zupancic does not mention the deep resonances of this view with Foucault's efforts to overcome what he referred to as the "repressive hypothesis"—the notion that power works only by way of prohibition, by saying *no*—she does make the connection to Agamben's work on biopolitics, which represents, in turn, the most powerful effort in recent years to develop Foucault's important insights on the shift from juridical power to biopower/disciplinary power. Zupancic suggests that her claims concerning the changing status of "enjoyment" in the libidinal economy of the modern subject's relation to law could be formulated in the terms that Agamben develops at the level of political theology: "Modern politics [according to Agamben] is characterized by the fact that the 'state of emergency' (the state that is, at one and the same time, the exception to as well as the support of the rule of law) is itself becoming a rule of law."[58]

What I am proposing here is that the mode of attention, analysis, and presentation practiced by Benjamin must be understood as a peculiar form of materialism—or even empiricism—whose "spectral object" is just this shifting locus of the state of emergency in modern life. In his *Little History of Photography,* Benjamin quotes a remark by Goethe: "There is a delicate empiricism which so intimately involves itself with the object that it becomes true theory."[59] In Benjamin's

57. Ibid., 51.
58. Ibid., 51. Zupancic's thesis concerning the problem of nihilism in Nietzsche's work is more complex than may at first appear in her presentation of the "active" form of nihilism qua ascetic ideal. If active nihilism is marked by a radical willing of nothingness, then there is a complementary form that is equally of concern to Nietzsche, a "passive" form defined "as the name of the configuration where men *will not to will rather than will nothingness*" (64). Especially interesting in the present context is Zupancic's claim that this double face of nihilism congeals into the very form of a whole series of "postmodern" commodities that combine the exciting imperative, "Enjoy!" with its equally formidable warning, "Enjoyment can kill you!" "What are these products? Coffee without caffeine, sweets without sugar, cigarettes without nicotine (i.e. 'substances deprived of their substance'). Perhaps these products should not be conceived of so much in terms of substances that lack the very thing that defines them, but, rather, as being composed of two substances, one neutralizing the exciting effect of the other" (68).
59. Benjamin, *Selected Writings,* 2:520.

work, such intimacy places the subject in relation to the state of emergency running through the fabric of everyday life. In Benjamin's materialism, the "real" is thus on the side of the "virtual/spectral." The exposure involved in such intimacy is of course a mediated one, one that passes through the filter of contemplation, analysis, and aesthetic production; it is one that must be *constructed*. The "bent" posture of melancholy stands in relation to, though it is not identical with, the "cringe" that bends the back of the *creature,* that figure of pure exposure to the state of exception immanent to law.

Benjamin's thought, developed from the early metaphysical writings through the study of the baroque and on into *The Arcades Project,* represents a constant effort at bringing into relief precisely this dimension of "creaturely" life and the various and changing ways it comes to be transmitted and disseminated through the political, economic, and cultural institutions of modernity, becomes embodied in its objects, enters the texture of their materiality, becomes the very substance of their "mattering." Benjamin's messianism, which was a constant throughout his career, must in turn be understood in direct relation to this figure of the creaturely, of life captured at the (ever shifting and mutating) threshold of the juridicopolitical order. For Benjamin, the only possibility for genuinely new social, political, and ethical relations in human life—for genuine creativity in these domains—emerges where this capture/captivation can be interrupted.

IX

Such an interruption is the key to Benjamin's conception of redemption. His study of baroque drama culminates in a remarkable set of passages in which he takes the baroque poets to task for their betrayal of the (natural historical) conception of creaturely life that had been their greatest poetic resource and achievement. Benjamin anticipates this criticism early on in his study: "That which lies here in ruins, the highly significant fragment, the remnant, is, in fact, the finest material in baroque creation. For it is common practice in the literature of the baroque to pile up fragments ceaselessly, without any strict idea of a goal, and, in the unremitting expectation of a miracle, to take the repetition of stereotypes for a process of intensification."[60] At the end of the book, such a miracle is correlated with the dissolution of the vertigo generated by such a piling up of fragments: "As those who lose their footing turn somersaults in their fall, so would the allegorical intention fall from emblem to emblem down into the dizziness of its bottomless depths, were it not that, even in the most extreme of them, it had so to turn about that all its darkness, vainglory, and godlessness seems to be nothing but self-delusion."[61] The baroque vision of natural history that sustains the allegorical sensibility turns out itself to be *mere allegory*:

The bleak confusion of Golgotha, which can be recognized as the schema underlying the allegorical figures in hundreds of the engravings and descriptions of the period, is not just a symbol of the desolation of human existence. In it transitoriness is not signified or allegorically represented, so much as, in its own significance, displayed as allegory. As the allegory of the resurrection. Ultimately in the death-signs of the baroque the direction of allegorical reflection is reversed; on the second part of its wide arc it returns, to redeem.

But Benjamin is quick to add: "Allegory, of course, thereby loses everything that was most peculiar to it."[62] It is just such a conversion of utter loss into absolute gain, of radical immanence into total transcendence, that for Benjamin is one of the great seductions of the melancholic immersion in creaturely life; it is the sign of a paradoxical loss of faith emerging at its very core: "And this is the essence of melancholy immersion: that its ultimate objects, in which it believes it can most fully secure for itself that which is vile, turn into allegories, and that these allegories fill out and deny the void in which they are represented, just as, ultimately, the intention does not faithfully rest in the contemplation of bones, but *faithlessly leaps forward to the idea of resurrection*."[63]

60. Benjamin, *Origin,* 178.
61. Ibid., 232.
62. Ibid.
63. Ibid., 232–33; my emphasis.

If I understand Benjamin correctly, the messianic dimension is to be distinguished from such faithlessness; it cannot be understood on the model of an exchange, of a simple conversion of loss into gain, death into life. To use one of Benjamin's favorite formulations, the *awakening* at issue in the messianic advent should be understood not as a resurrection, an animation of the dead, but, as I have suggested, as *a deanimation of the undead,* an interruption of the "ban," the captivation at work in the spectral fixations—the petrified unrest—that cringes/curves the psychic space of human subjects.

In this context, it might be helpful to juxtapose two important passages from Benjamin's work. In the study of baroque drama, Benjamin speaks of the importance of *night* in the poetry of the period:

> There is good reason for associating the dramatic action with night, especially midnight. It lies in the widespread notion that at this hour time stands still like the tongue of a scale. Now since fate, itself the true order of eternal recurrence, can only be described as temporal in an indirect, that is parasitical sense, its manifestations seek out the temporal dimension. They stand in the narrow frame of midnight, an opening in the passage of time, in which the same ghostly image constantly reappears.[64]

To this must be juxtaposed, as a kind of delayed commentary and intervention, Benjamin's famous remarks on the status of futurity in Judaism from the theses "On the Concept of History":

> We know that the Jews were prohibited from inquiring into the future: the Torah and the prayers instructed them in remembrance [*Eingedenken*], however. This disenchanted the future, which holds sway over all those who turn to soothsayers for enlightenment. This does not imply, however, that for the Jews the future became homogeneous, empty time. For every second was the small gateway in time through which the Messiah might enter.[65]

The messianic dimension involves a shift within the melancholic fixation on (the ghosts of) the past, a fixation or stuckness that can

64. Ibid., 135.
65. Benjamin, *Selected Writings,* 4:397.

actually inhibit the work of remembrance/*Eingedenken*. For what is ultimately at issue in Benjamin's thought is the preparation of a form of remembrance that has passed over into the ethical and political dimension of *act*. This is what it means, I think, for the narrow frame of midnight—this opening for the traffic with ghosts—to become the narrow gate through which the Messiah can enter. But as we have also seen, the dimension of the act is one that requires, as part of the construction of its site, the very spectral materialism that can, Benjamin suggests, be mobilized only in and through the gaze of melancholy. It is, I suggest, this peculiar and fragile tension and alliance between the melancholic immersion in creaturely life and the realm of action and practice that defines Benjamin's thinking from beginning to end. We might say that his thinking demands that any ethicopolitical act be oriented by, be performed on behalf of, creaturely life, the isolation and elaboration of which takes place under the saturnine gaze of melancholy.

I am trying to argue here for a middle position between two competing claims about the ethical status of melancholy. On the one hand there is the claim made by the partisans of the "ethical turn" in deconstruction that melancholy is the only affective posture that can maintain fidelity to those losses that the reigning ideological formation would like to disavow. Whereas mourning, which culminates in a reattachment of libido to new objects of desire (or idealization) proves to be an ultimately adaptive strategy to the governing reality principle and the demand "to get on with life," melancholy retards adaptation, attaches itself *to* loss; it says no! to life without the object (or ideal) and thereby—so it is claimed—holds open the possibility of alternative frameworks of what counts as reality (i.e., the possibility of a reality that would not demand such losses). And no doubt it is this view of melancholy that has attracted so many intellectuals to the work of Benjamin, who is often seen as the ultimate embodiment of such a stance.[66]

66. The first chapter of Eric Santner, *Stranded Objects: Mourning, Memory, and Film in Postwar Germany* (Ithaca: Cornell University Press, 1990), dealt with this view at some length. Slavoj Žižek has underlined the "politically correct" dimension of such a view of melancholy (and appropriation of Benjamin): "Mourning is a kind of betrayal, the second killing of the (lost) object, while the melancholic subject remains

On the other hand we find the competing claim that melancholy is really a mode of defense, that it involves a fundamental misunderstanding of the occasion of its affective disposition, in effect conflating an impossible possession (or structural lack) with a determinate loss (that need not have occurred). Taking Freud's puzzlement about melancholy as a point of departure—Freud had noted that it was often difficult to identify the loss the melancholic seems to be endlessly grieving for—Giorgio Agamben has suggested that in melancholy the withdrawal of libido represents the original datum rather than any determinate loss. "We ought to say," he writes, "that melancholia offers the paradox of an intention to mourn that precedes and anticipates the loss of the object." The melancholic disposition is caught up in a

desperate attempt to protect itself from the loss of that object and to adhere to it at least in its absence, so it might be said that the withdrawal of melancholic libido has no other purpose than to make viable an appropriation in a situation in which none is really possible. From this point of view, melancholy would be not so much the regressive reaction to the loss of the love object as the imaginative capacity to make an unobtainable object appear as if lost. If the libido behaves *as if* a loss had occurred although *nothing* has in fact been lost this is because the libido stages a simulation where what cannot be lost because it has never been possessed appears as lost, and what could never be possessed because it had never perhaps existed may be appropriated insofar as it is lost.[67]

---

faithful to the lost object, refusing to renounce his or her attachment to it. This story can be given a multitude of twists, from the queer one, which holds that homosexuals are those who retain fidelity to the lost or repressed identification with the same-sex libidinal object, or the post-colonial/ethnic one, which holds that when ethnic groups enter capitalist processes of modernization and are under the threat that their specific legacy will be swallowed up by the new global culture, they should not renounce their tradition through mourning, but retain the melancholic attachment to their lost roots." Žižek, "Melancholy and the Act," *Critical Inquiry* 26, no. 4 (Summer 2000): 658.

67. Giorgio Agamben, *Stanzas: Word and Phantasm in Western Culture,* trans. Ronald Martinez (Minneapolis: University of Minnesota Press, 1993), 20.

In this way melancholy comes very close to the modality of perversion that Freud called fetishism, that ingenious strategy of unconscious mental life that both avows and disavows a perception (of the missing maternal phallus) in a single symptomatic act or formation. "Similarly," Agamben writes, "in melancholia the object is neither appropriated nor lost, but both possessed and lost at the same time."[68] According to this view, melancholy proves to be the ultimate adaptive strategy, that is, a way of affirming the governing reality principle. By converting an impossible possession or, more important, a fundamental impasse, an antagonism tearing at the social substance, into a contingent or local loss or malfunction—one that does not fundamentally call into question the coordinates of reality—the melancholic loses the possibility of a radical ethical act, one that would take this impasse as the very ground of his or her intervention.

I have been arguing, however, for a third alternative, for the view, that is, that such an intervention must itself "learn" from melancholy how to home in on the agitations of creaturely life that materialize the persistence of deep structural stresses in the social body. I take it to be one of the fundamental lessons of what Franz Rosenzweig called the "new thinking" to sustain the *conjunction,* the "and" at issue here: melancholic immersion in creaturely life *and* ethicopolitical intervention into that very dimension; the saturnine gaze *and* the awakening to the answerability to the neighbor, to acts of neighbor-love.

x

It is, I think, this same tension between melancholic immersion and the dimension of action that informs Benjamin's remarks on the structure of reversal in Kafka's work, a reversal that, I suggest, stands in stark contrast to the reversal/conversion Benjamin calls "faithless" in the *Trauerspiel* book. And once more, it is a question of the unburdening of hunched backs. Toward the end of his 1934 essay on Kafka,

---

68. Ibid., 62. For another, extremely powerful reading of the ambiguities of melancholy, see Rebecca Comay, "Perverse History: Benjamin's Losses," in *Walter Benjamin Studies,* ed. Beatrice Hanssen and Andrew Benjamin (forthcoming).

Benjamin addresses the nature of the exertion at issue in Kafka's literary project. He refers to it as a kind of study (*Studium*) whose objects are the dispersed fragments of one's own alienated being:

The invention of motion pictures and the phonograph came in an age of maximum alienation of men from one another, of unpredictably intervening relationships which have become their only ones. Experiments have proved that a man does not recognize his own gait on film or his own voice on the phonograph. The situation of the subject in such experiments is Kafka's situation; this is what leads him to study, where he may encounter fragments of his own existence. . . . He might understand himself, but what an enormous effort would be required! It is a tempest that blows from forgetting, and *study is a cavalry attack against it.*[69]

It is this same wind, Benjamin suggests, that "so often blows from the prehistoric world [*aus der Vorwelt*] in Kafka's works and that also propels the boat of the hunter Gracchus" (815). But once again Benjamin insists that study offers a kind of counterforce. Referring to Kafka's short prose piece "The New Advocate," he writes,

Reversal is the direction of study which transforms existence into script. Its teacher is Bucephalus, "the new advocate," who takes the road back without the powerful Alexander—which means, rid of the onrushing conqueror. "His flanks free and unhampered by the thighs of a rider, under a quiet lamp far from the din of Alexander's battles, he reads and turns the pages of our old books." (815)

Noting an interpretation by Werner Kraft, who apparently saw in this text the most powerful and penetrating critique of myth ever offered in literature, a critique marshaled, ultimately, in the name of justice, Benjamin writes,

But once we have reached this point, we are in danger of missing Kafka by stopping here. Is it really the law which could thus be invoked against myth

---

69. Benjamin, *Selected Writings*, 2:814; my emphasis. Subsequent references will be made in the text. This storm will, of course, return in the famous allegorical reading of Klee's *Angelus Novus* in the theses "On the Concept of History."

in the name of justice? No, as a legal scholar Bucephalus remains true to his origins, except that he does not seem to be practicing law — and this is probably something new, in Kafka's sense, for both Bucephalus and the bar. *The law which is studied but no longer practiced is the gate to justice.* (815; my emphasis)

Underlining the radical modernity of Kafka's position, Benjamin notes that Kafka "doesn't dare attach to this study the promises which tradition has attached to the study of the Torah. His assistants are sextons who have lost their house of prayer; his students are pupils who have lost the Holy Writ [*Schrift*]. Now there is nothing to support them on their 'untrammeled, happy journey'" (815). Nonetheless, it is precisely in a law no longer practiced but studied that Benjamin locates Kafka's great innovation, the "law of his journey" (815). As Benjamin saw it, Kafka was able to formulate the trajectory of this journey most forcefully in his short prose piece — one that is itself presented as a commentary — "The Truth of Sancho Panza." As Benjamin concludes his essay, "Sancho Panza, a sedate fool and a clumsy assistant, sent his rider on ahead; Bucephalus outlived his. Whether it is a man or a horse is no longer so important, *if only the burden is taken off the back*" (816; my emphasis).

Not surprisingly, these remarks have themselves been the occasion of rather intense exegetical study and speculation. In a discussion of these same passages from Benjamin's Kafka essay, Sigrid Weigel has emphasized the proximity of the turn at issue in the notion of *Studium* to the mode of attention, listening, and reading developed by Freud:

The turn [*Umkehr*], which is characterized as a direction of study, marks an attitude of reading [*Lektüre-Haltung*] with regard to what is past. . . . It is precisely that attitude of reading that applies itself, in the Arcades project, to the topography of the city and the picture puzzles of the banal in modernity, whereby the legibility and decipherability of this writing is conceptualized in analogy with the language of the unconscious in psychoanalysis.[70]

---

70. Weigel, *Entstellte Ähnlichkeit*, 81. Weigel is thinking here of, among other passages, Benjamin's remark in *The Arcades Project* concerning the decoding of material culture: "Picture puzzles [*Vexierbilder*], as schemata of dreamwork, were long ago discovered by psychoanalysis. We, however, with a similar conviction, are less on the trail of the psyche than on the track of things. We seek the totemic tree of objects within the thicket of primal history." Benjamin, *Arcades Project*, 212 (I1,4).

When she returns to the notion of the "turn" in Benjamin's reading of Kafka, she suggests that the crucial precursor text for Benjamin's conception of what is ultimately at stake in this figure is Hölderlin's commentary on (his translation of) *Antigone*. There Hölderlin speaks of a "reversal of all modes and forms of representation" (*Umkehr aller Vorstellungsarten und Formen*).[71] Hölderlin's reflections here are at least in part concerned with the question of a revolutionary violence that would suspend the fateful violence that founds and amplifies the power and authority of states (we might speak of "antigonal" as opposed to "oedipal" violence).

This may make less surprising Giorgio Agamben's recent proposal that we read Benjamin's remarks on reversal in the Kafka essay as a late supplement to his earlier text "Critique of Violence." As I have noted, one of the goals of that essay was to articulate the nature of the violence—he called it "pure" or "divine" violence—that would interrupt the repetitive, "mythic" violence of the state and its institutions. Noting that all of Kafka's figures are confronted in some fashion with the spectral form of law in its state of exception, Agamben suggests that "study" is the key point of passage to radically new possibilities of life with the law:

In the Kafka essay, the enigmatic image of a law that is studied but no longer practiced corresponds, as a sort of remnant, to the unmasking of mythico-juridical violence effected by pure violence. There is, therefore, still a possible figure of law after its nexus with violence and power has been deposed, but it is a law that no longer has force or application, like the one in which the "new attorney," leafing through "our old books," buries himself in study, or like the one that Foucault may have had in mind when he spoke of a "new law" that has been freed from all discipline and all relation to sovereignty.[72]

Agamben denies that this vision has anything to do with some sort of endless transitional phase or never-ending deconstruction. What is

---

71. Cited in Weigel, *Entstellte Ähnlichkeit,* 103.

72. Giorgio Agamben, *The State of Exception,* trans. Kevin Attell (Chicago: University of Chicago Press, 2005), 63.

decisive, he claims, is that the law that is no longer practiced but only studied is not yet justice, "but only the gate that leads to it." In one fashion or another, Kafka's figures all try to study and to deactivate the (spectral excess of) law, to "play" with it.[73] The path to justice is opened, in other words, not through the elimination of law as such but through the suspension of that dimension of law that "cringes" the subject, renders him or her "creaturely." As Agamben concludes this set of reflections, "This liberation is the task of study, or of play. And this studious play is the passage that allows us to arrive at that justice that one of Benjamin's posthumous fragments defines as state of the world in which the world appears as a good that absolutely cannot be appropriated or made juridical."[74]

How we ultimately understand this series of enigmatic remarks will largely depend on the way we grasp the relations between some of the key words of this discussion: *deposit* (as in "creaturely deposits"), *depose* (as in "deposing the law"), and *deposition* (in the sense of giving testimony, bearing witness). The wager of the remaining chapters is that further immersion into the decidedly "learned play" of W. G. Sebald's remarkable prose may be our best hope of advancing this project.

---

73. Agamben, *State of Exception,* 64. In a recent text, Slavoj Žižek has proposed that it is precisely as such "play" that one should understand the discussion between Josef K. and the priest apropos of the parable of the gate to the law, that is, as displaying a figure of the law "deprived of the force of normativity, the law with which one can play freely." The crucial aspect of the exegetical exchange between Josef K. and the priest is, Žižek suggests, "the totally non-initiatic, non-mystical, purely 'external,' pedantically legal nature of this discussion. . . . There is no mystical Secret that we are approaching here, no Grail to be uncovered, just dry bureaucratic haggling—which, of course, makes the whole procedure all the more uncanny and enigmatic." Slavoj Žižek, *Iraq: The Borrowed Kettle* (London: Verso, 2004), 160–61.

74. Agamben, *State of Exception,* 64.

# 3

# Toward a Natural History of the Present

## I

One can begin almost anywhere in Sebald's work to find expressions of the utter fallenness of nature and human history, that view of creatureliness we have explored in the context of Benjamin's concept of *Naturgeschichte*. In his first published work of fiction, the prose poem *After Nature,* Sebald engages in one of the numerous efforts at ekphrasis that fill his writings; it is a description of Matthias Grünewald's most famous creation, the Isenheim altarpiece. The work is a complex, layered structure involving two folding wings enclosing a central altarpiece. The third wing, when opened, includes a rendering of the temptation of St. Anthony. Sebald presents the "unreal and demented thronging" that characterizes this section as offering Grünewald's vision of "life as such, as it unfolds, dreadfully, / everywhere and at all times" (25/22–23). The panel is filled with fantastic and horrific beasts, a body covered with syphilitic chancres, "excrescences of an entire life, / in the air, on land and in water" (26/23). To Grünewald, the author writes,

this is creation,
image of our insane presence
on the surface of the earth,
the regeneration proceeding
in downward orbits
whose parasitical shapes
intertwine, and, growing into
and out of one another, surge
as a demonic swarm. (26/23–24)

In Grünewald's art, one even finds a variation on the cringe that Benjamin identified as the signature posture of Kafka's creatures (perhaps more accurately, a mixture of a cringe and Josef K.'s posture at his execution): a "panic-stricken / kink in the neck . . . exposing the throat and often turning / the face towards a blinding light" (27/24). This, Sebald writes,

is the extreme response of our bodies
to the absence of balance in nature
which blindly makes one experiment after another
and like a senseless botcher
undoes the thing it has only just achieved. (27/24)

Sebald concludes his "reading" of the panel by alluding to another apocalyptic vision in which darkness finally comes upon burning city and boiling sea and "with it a yellow dust / that covers the land" (28/25).

In *The Emigrants,* Sebald has the painter Max Ferber visit the Isenheim altarpiece, one of the only trips he ever makes after he settles in Manchester. The visit proves to be the relay point of a metonymic chain that is quite typical for Sebald's work. Recalling his impressions of the Grünewald paintings to the narrator, Ferber speaks of the "monstrosity of that suffering, which, emanating from the figures depicted, spread to cover the whole of Nature, only to flood back from

the lifeless landscape to the humans marked by death" (170/253). Here
Sebald underlines the ambiguity at the heart of the natural historical
vision: the extreme response of our bodies to an absence of balance in
nature presupposes a nature already thrown off its tracks, a nature already "written asunder" by human history, by "our insane presence
on the surface of the earth." More important in the present context,
Ferber notes that his encounter with Grünewald's vision was the occasion of a series of memories that culminate in the figure of a cringe,
the trace of creaturely life registered in the limbs:

> When I was in Colmar, said Ferber, I beheld all of this in precise detail, how
> one thing led to another and how it had been afterwards. The flood of mem-
> ory, little of which remains with me now, began with my recalling a Friday
> morning some years ago when I was suddenly struck by the paroxysm of pain
> that a slipped disc can occasion. . . . At that moment, all I knew was that I
> mustn't move even a fraction of an inch, that my whole life had shrunk to that
> one tiny point of absolute pain. . . . Through it all I felt that being utterly crip-
> pled by pain in this way was related, in the most precise manner conceivable,
> to the inner constitution I had acquired over the years. I also remember that
> the crooked position [*krumme Stellung*] I was forced to stand in reminded me,
> even in my pain, of a photograph my father had taken of me in the second
> form at school, bent over my writing. (171–72/254–55) [1]

Ferber adds that it was the recollection of that cringe (before the Isenheim altarpiece) that sent him off to Lake Geneva to retrace memories of his father from the years before the war.

But it is with the *dust* of that apocalyptic vision from *After Nature*
that we touch upon what may well be Sebald's most privileged, most
emblematic object; it is everywhere present in the work and, along
with ash, serves as the single most poignant embodiment of death,

---

1. At the very beginning of *The Rings of Saturn,* the narrator is hospitalized with what
appears to be the same sort of back injury Ferber recalls. Here it becomes the occasion
of a deep identification with that most creaturely of creatures, Gregor Samsa: "In the
tortured position of a creature that has raised itself erect for the first time I stood leaning against the glass. I could not help thinking of the scene in which poor Gregor Samsa,
his little legs trembling, climbs the armchair and looks out of his room" (5/13).

decay, and transience in his writings. We might even say it is Sebald's emblem for materiality as such. One thinks, for example, of one of the epigraphs Sebald chooses to begin his *Rings of Saturn,* an entry from the *Brockhaus Encyclopaedia* that describes those rings as a combination of ice crystals and dust particles left over from a former moon. But there is in Sebald's fiction no more poignant evocation of the thinglike nothingness that is dust than the narrator's description of Ferber's working method in the *Emigrants.*[2] Recall that the narrator discovers Ferber's studio by accident during one of his Sunday peregrinations through the ruined industrial landscape of Manchester, itself a powerful embodiment of the rhythms of natural history in the "bourgeois age," as Austerlitz would have put it. The overall impression of the city is that of a ghost town in which even the grandest structures appeared "empty and abandoned" (the more evocative German word Sebald uses here is *verwaist,* orphaned; a related word the author uses elsewhere to characterize objects that have survived the form of life in which they had meaning is *herrenlos,* without a master). As if anticipating the later revelations of Ferber's biography, the narrator stumbles upon what had at one time been a Jewish part of the city, its remnants still legible on a few remaining brass plates of offices "bearing names that had a legendary ring to my ear: Glickmann, Grunwald and Gottgetreu" (157/232).[3] But such remnants are rare; for the most part, as the

---

2. As I have indicated, Sebald based his description of Ferber's art on the work of the German-born, London-based artist Frank Auerbach, whose parents perished in the Holocaust and who escaped Germany by the Kindertransport. Changes made to the English translation of the Max Ferber story—including the change of name from Aurach to Ferber and the deletion of a reproduction of Auerbach's work—were made at the request of the artist. See Maya Jaggi, "Recovered Memories," *Guardian,* September 22, 2001. The name change is especially unfortunate. The letters of the name Aurach "contain," among other things, *Rauch,* the German word for smoke, *ruach,* the Hebrew word for the divine spirit, and *aura,* the term that so preoccupied Benjamin in his writings about modernity.

3. Jewish names are a leitmotif in this story. In the course of telling his life story, Ferber relates the irony of his discovery that Manchester had been an important city for German and Jewish immigrants. He gives a list of Sephardic names—immigrants of long standing in England—as well as of German and German-Jewish names he encountered in Manchester, concluding that "although I had intended to move in the opposite direction, when I arrived in Manchester I had come home, in a sense"

narrator notes, "once the demolition rubble had been removed, all that was left to recall the lives of thousands of people was the grid-like layout of the streets" (157/233). In the midst of this barren cityscape in which the narrator even imagines that he "could hear sighs in the abandoned depots and warehouses" (158/234), he comes across the sign that leads him to Ferber's studio.

Entering the studio and adjusting his eyes to the darkness that, as he puts it, "had gathered in the corners," the narrator gives a brief inventory of the objects he can pick out of the assemblage of tools and materials (one thinks of the stranded objects strewn about the figure of Melancholy in Dürer's woodcut); he then notices Ferber himself, his face lit by light entering "through a high north-facing window layered with the dust of decades" (161/237). At this point the narrator introduces us to what he later gets to know as Ferber's modus operandi as an artist: "Since he applied the paint thickly, and then repeatedly scratched it off the canvas as his work proceeded, the floor was covered with a largely hardened and encrusted deposit of droppings, mixed with coal dust, several centimeters thick at the centre and thinning out towards the outer edges, in places resembling the flow of lava" (161/237). Ferber tells the narrator that he rigorously avoided changing anything at his place of work and "that nothing further should be added but the debris generated by painting and the dust that continuously fell and which, as he was coming to realize, he loved more than anything else in the world. He felt closer to dust, he said, than to light, air or water" (161/238). Ferber's very sense of being at home in the world was, as the narrator learns, dependent on this peculiar material, "the grey, velvety sinter left when matter dissolved, little by little, into nothingness" (161/238). Indeed, the narrator

---

(192/287). He then adds the ominous remark, linking the age of industrialization to the death camps he escaped through emigration, "and with every year I have spent since then in this birthplace of industrialization, amidst the black facades, I have realized more clearly than ever that I am here, as they used to say, to serve under the chimney" (192/287). Toward the end of the story, the narrator visits the Jewish cemetery in Bad Kissingen, the site of the Ferber family plot. After reading the names off various stones, he writes that it "made me think that perhaps there was nothing the Germans begrudged the Jews so much as their beautiful names, so intimately bound up with the country they lived in and with its language" (224/335).

concludes that Ferber's "prime concern was to increase the dust," that his entire artistic project "amounted to nothing but a steady production of dust, which never ceased except at night" (161–62/238–39). Finally, speaking about the repetitive labor of sketching and erasure that went into each of Ferber's portraits, the narrator suggests that "an onlooker might well feel that it had evolved from a long lineage of grey, ancestral faces, rendered unto ash but still there, as ghostly presences, on the harried paper" (162/239–40).[4] Sebald's entire project is, we might say, an effort to tease out the testimony of dust and ash, to see in such material deposits the very "matter" of historical depositions.

In an interview in 1998, Sebald addressed his obsession with these materials: "I'm very taken with the whole business of ashes and dust. You'll find them again and again in my writing; they're always there in some form or another."[5] In this context, Sebald recalls his admiration for the Swiss writer Robert Walser, whose short prose piece "Ash, Needle, Pencil, and Match" no doubt informed Sebald's own relationship with these materials that, as Walser puts it, demand to be attended to with fervor and care.[6] Paraphrasing Walser on the subject of ash, Sebald continues, "It's the most humble substance there is! The very last product of combustion, with no resistance in it. . . . The borderline between being and nothingness. Ash is a redeemed substance, like dust."[7] This last remark is especially curious in the larger context of Sebald's writings. There is, first of all, no suggestion of redemption in Walser's text, and the idea of redemption seems generally quite foreign to Sebald's natural historical vision of the world. And in an essay on Walser in which Sebald discusses this prose piece

4. In this context one might recall Benjamin's reference to the Catholic poet Charles Péguy (cited in a study by Daniel Halevy): "Péguy used to speak of that irredeemability of things, that recalcitrance, that heaviness of things, indeed of beings, which in the end allows a little ash to survive from the efforts of heroes and saints." Walter Benjamin, *The Origin of German Tragic Drama,* trans. John Osborne (London: NLB, 1977), 157.
5. Cited in Sara Kafatou, "An Interview with W. G. Sebald," *Harvard Review,* no. 15 (Fall 1998): 32.
6. Robert Walser, *Träumen: Prosa aus der Bieler Zeit, 1913–1920,* ed. Jochen Greven (Frankfurt a.M.: Suhrkamp, 1985), 327–28.
7. Kafatou, "Interview," 32.

at length, the vision of redemption has disappeared entirely.[8] Indeed, Sebald characterizes this piece as one of Walser's saddest and goes on to identify the four substances whose humility Walser sincerely *and* ironically celebrates as instruments of torture associated with the impossible—and loveless—life of this writer. The sad, emotional intensity of Walser's prose, which Sebald places even above that of Kafka, derives from the fact that here, "in this offhanded little treatise on ash, needle, pencil, and match, the writer is in truth writing about his own martyrdom; the four things of concern to him are by no means linked together arbitrarily but are rather the author's instruments of torture, in a word, that which he needs in order to stage his own self-immolation and display what remains when the fires have gone out."[9]

8. W. G. Sebald, "Le promeneur solitaire: Zur Erinnerung an Robert Walser," in *Logis in einem Landhaus* (Munich: Hanser, 1998).

9. Sebald, *Logis,* 150. The idea that dust and ash are in some sense "redeemed substances" derives, perhaps, from a remark of Benjamin's in his short essay on Walser—a remark cited by Sebald—in which Benjamin writes, "If we were to attempt to sum up in a single phrase the delightful yet also uncanny element in them [Walser's figures], we would have to say: *they have all been healed.*" Walter Benjamin, "Robert Walser," trans. Rodney Livingstone, in *Walter Benjamin: Selected Writings,* vol. 2, *1927–1934,* ed. Michael Jennings, Howard Eiland, and Gary Smith (Cambridge: Harvard University Press, 1999), 259. In *The Coming Community,* trans. Michael Hardt (Minneapolis: University of Minnesota Press, 1993), Giorgio Agamben has added to Benjamin's enigmatic remark some equally enigmatic commentary that nonetheless opens a direction of thought with respect to our discussion. "The curtain rises on Robert Walser's world," Agamben writes, "when the very last demon of Gehenna has been escorted back to heaven, when the process of the history of salvation has been completed, leaving no residue" (31). This is a state, he continues, in "which evil in its traditional supreme expression, the demonic, has disappeared" (31). This means, for Agamben, that Walser's "creatures are irreparably astray, but in a region that is beyond perdition and salvation: Their nullity, of which they are so proud, is principally a neutrality with respect to salvation—the most radical objection that has ever been levied against the very idea of redemption" (6). I take Agamben to be claiming that Walser's figures have in some sense passed beyond the condition of creatureliness I have been elaborating, that their life is no longer "excited" by sovereign authority (and its state of exception), even and especially when it has been disseminated into the social body as a whole: "Like the freed convict in Kafka's *Penal Colony,* who has survived the destruction of the machine that was to have executed him, these beings have left the world of guilt and justice behind them: The light that rains down on them is that irreparable light of the dawn following the *novissima dies* of judgment. But the life that begins on earth after the last day is simply human life" (7).

In *The Rings of Saturn,* certainly the most concentrated evocation of *Naturgeschichte* in Sebald's oeuvre, the author pursues further the image of combustion—*Verbrennung*—characterizing it as "the hidden principle behind every artefact we create" (170/202). The context of this remark is a discussion of deforestation, "the steady and advancing destruction, over a period of many centuries and indeed millennia, of the dense forests that extended over the entire British Isles after the Ice Age" (169/201). "Our spread over the earth," this *promeneur soli-taire* writes, "was fuelled by reducing the higher species of vegetation to charcoal, by incessantly burning whatever would burn" (170/202; one thinks here, perhaps, of the further transformation of charcoal into art and dust in Ferber's studio). And finally, summing up this condensed natural history of combustion, the narrator concludes: "From the earliest times, human civilization has been no more than a strange luminescence growing more intense by the hour, of which no one can say when it will begin to wane and when it will fade away. For the time being, our cities still shine through the night, and the fires still spread" (170/203).[10]

Sebald briefly returns to the topic of heat and destruction in *Austerlitz.* On one of his visits to the Andromeda lodge, the home of his school chum Gerald, Austerlitz reports an outing with his friend and Gerald's great-uncle, Alphonso, himself an amateur naturalist who spends most of his days outdoors, registering the gradual destruction of nature by human encroachment.[11] During one of their outings

10. These lines recall the narrator's evening boat ride in Venice with an Italian astro-physicist he meets in a bar (second story of *Vertigo*). Watching the glowing city from the water, the narrator's companion and pilot speaks of "the miracle of life born of car-bon . . . going up in flames." He then directs the boat past the municipal incinerators: "A deathly silent concrete shell beneath a white pall of smoke. I asked whether the burn-ing went on throughout the night, and Malachio replied: *Si, di continuo. Brucia contin-uamente.* The fires never go out" (61/73–74).

11. Speaking of the wonders of the coastline at Devon and Cornwall, Alphonso says that "now . . . those glories [have] been almost entirely destroyed by our passion for collect-ing and by other imponderable disturbances and destructions" (90/131). Earlier, Alphonso is cited as having told Gerald and Austerlitz "that everything was fading before our eyes, and that many of the loveliest of colors had already disappeared" (88/130). The tradition of natural historical research and speculation in the Fitzpatrick clan—natural history in the more technical sense—was established by Gerald's great-grandfather, who was said to have had regular contact with Charles Darwin during the latter's preparation

together in which Alphonso initiates the two boys into "the mysterious world of moths," the former suggests that the balance of nature was ultimately thrown off by an excess of heat in the human animal:

[The moths'] body temperature will then be thirty-six degrees Celsius, like that of mammals, and of dolphins and tunny fish swimming at full speed. Thirty-six degrees, according to Alphonso, has always proved the best natural level, a kind of magical threshold, and it has sometimes occurred to him . . . that all mankind's misfortunes were connected with its departure at some point in time from that norm, and with the slightly feverish, overheated condition in which we constantly found ourselves. (92/134–35)[12]

The paradox I have been noting throughout this discussion is manifest here too. What ultimately subjects man, in an emphatic sense, to the destructive forces of natural history is precisely his aberrant place in the "great chain of being." Man's subordination to the course of natural history is a consequence of a spiritual supplement that separates man from animal while in some sense making him more animal than animal, this "more" being the very seal of his "creatureliness." This is exactly the paradox I noted earlier apropos of human sexuality. What ostensibly makes humans "beasts," "animal-like," a part of "fallen nature" is what radically distinguishes them from all of nature: the perverse dimension of their sexuality, the fact that the life of man is defined by *drive destiny* rather than *instinct*. (The "loss" of instinct and its substitution/overwriting by drive destiny is at least in part what is meant by the psychoanalytic concept of castration.) Put somewhat differently, what makes man creaturely is that he is not sim-

---

of *The Descent of Man*. Austerlitz, of course, also notes that the entire household had been turned into a "kind of natural history museum" filled with vitrines and cabinets full of specimens from the animal, vegetable, and mineral kingdoms.

12. Moths become a special obsession for Austerlitz, who relates that "of all creatures I still feel the greatest awe [*Ehrfurcht*] for them" (93/136). He tells the narrator of his habit of freeing the moths he finds each morning clinging to the wall of his house, as if stuck/propelled by a death drive, the urge to become dust: "If you do not put them out again carefully they will stay where they are, never moving, until the last breath is out of their bodies, and indeed they will remain in the place where they came to grief even after death, held fast by the tiny claws that stiffened in their last agony, until a draft of air detaches them and blows them into a dusty corner" (93–94/136–37).

ply alive but also excited/constrained by that dimension of surplus animation I have called "undeadness."

II

Although dust and ash clearly function in Sebald's oeuvre as the very
emblems of natural history, there is an entire series of privileged substances and objects that have a share in this status. Sebald's relation to
materiality, to matter, bears a family resemblance to that of his
German contemporary in the field of visual arts, Anselm Kiefer, who
has developed a whole set of allegorical materials—straw, lead, copper, sand, burlap, fern—to evoke the "natural history of destruction"
that has shaped so much of German history. The object that links
Sebald's work most closely to Benjamin's treatment of *Naturgeschichte*
is, no doubt, the skull (and bones more generally). As Benjamin famously puts it, "Everything about history that, from the very beginning, has been untimely, sorrowful, unsuccessful, is expressed in a
face—or rather in a skull."[13] The first section of *The Rings of Saturn*
features a prominent image of a human skull as well as the story of the
narrator's efforts to locate the skull of the seventeenth-century writer
Thomas Browne. Browne, the author of "Brief Discourse of the
Sepulchral Urns Lately Found in Norfolk" (1658), is in turn presented
as an eloquent representative of Benjamin's understanding of the
baroque and of melancholy more generally. In the course of his bio-
graphical sketch of Browne, the narrator introduces an additional
Benjaminian dimension, one underlining the political face of melancholy. The narrator speculates that Browne attended the public autopsy that Rembrandt immortalized in his famous painting of the
surgeons' guild. The painting shows the master surgeon spreading
strands of exposed muscle tissue and tendons on the forearm of the
corpse, who is, as the narrator tells us, one Aris Kindt, a common

---

13. Benjamin, *Origin*, 167. I have changed the translation of *Totenkopf* from death's-
head to skull. In *One-Way Street,* Benjamin writes of the skull that it manifests "total ex-
pressionlessness—the black of the eye-sockets—coupled with the most unbridled expression—the grinning rows of teeth." *Walter Benjamin: Selected Writings,* vol. 1,
1913–26, ed. Marcus Bullock and Michael W. Jennings (Cambridge: Harvard University
Press, 1996), 463.

thief who had been executed for his crimes. Noting the irregularity of the spatial representation of the body—"not only [is it] grotesquely out of proportion compared with the hand closer to us, but it is also anatomically the wrong way round"—the narrator suggests that "there was deliberate intent behind this flaw in the composition." "That unshapely hand," he continues, "signifies the violence that has been done to Aris Kindt. It is with him, the victim, and not the Guild that gave Rembrandt his commission, that the painter identifies" (16–17/26–27).

Noting that there is no evidence of Browne's attendance at the autopsy or from what or whose perspective he might have viewed it had he been there, the narrator returns to the more cosmic aspect of the writer's vision of creaturely life. Paraphrasing that vision, the narrator returns us to the now familiar rhythms of *Naturgeschichte,* understood both by Benjamin and by Sebald as the single most potent counterargument to the bourgeois faith in progress: "On every new thing there lies already the shadow of annihilation. For the history of every individual, of every social order, indeed of the whole world, does not describe an ever-widening, more and more wonderful arc, but rather follows a course which, once the meridian is reached, leads without fail down into the dark" (24/35–36). Here we might also recall the shifts in meaning of the word "creature" from denoting the entire domain of *nature* qua God's creation to what "borders on the monstrous and unnatural."[14] Browne, too, finds his gaze drawn to "the abnormalities of creation, be they the deformities produced by sickness or the grotesqueries with which Nature, with an inventiveness scarcely less diseased, fills every vacant space in her atlas" (21/32–33). The narrator understands Browne's vision to be rooted in his experience as a physician "who saw disease growing and raging in bodies" and for whom, therefore, time itself is the toxin for which there is no cure: "The winter sun shows how soon the light fades from the ash, how soon night enfolds us. Hour upon hour is added to the sum. Time itself grows old. Pyramids, arches and obelisks are melting pillars of snow" (24/36).

14. See once more Julia Lupton, "Creature Caliban," *Shakespeare Quarterly* 51, no. 1 (Spring 2000): 1.

The destruction of human dwellings and monuments as a result of natural processes and human violence is, of course, at the very heart of the vision of natural history that dominates Sebald's writings. The former processes are perhaps most vividly portrayed in the section on the ruins of Dunwich in *The Rings of Saturn*. Once a thriving port counting more than fifty churches, monasteries, and convents, bustling shipyards and fisheries, dozens of windmills, and a merchant fleet of eighty vessels, the town has for the most part succumbed to the eroding force of the sea and now lies "beneath alluvial sand and gravel, over an area of two or three square miles" (155/187). Sebald reproduces photographs of Eccles Church Tower, which until the end of the nineteenth century still stood on Dunwich beach, as well as of the ruin of All Saints. "In 1919 it, too, slipped over the cliff edge, together with the bones of those buried in the churchyard" (157/189). Here, too, Sebald points toward the essential paradox of natural history. It is not simply that the vast fortifications the people of Dunwich built to protect them "against attack from the landward side and against the force of the sea, which was ceaselessly eroding the coast" (157/189–90) failed to do so; it is also, as Sebald will emphasize with greater force in a series of disquisitions on fortifications in *Austerlitz,* that such structures inevitably *solicit* the force of violence upon them. As Austerlitz puts it, they "cast the shadow of their own destruction before them, and are designed from the first with an eye to their later existence as ruins" (19/28). Fortifications are, we might say, the very emblem of what Rosenzweig called *kriegerische Zeitlichkeit,* "martial temporality," and Benjamin called mythic violence.[15]

III

The reference to the bones of the churchyard of All Saints brings us back to this privileged object in Sebald's work. We find the richest and

---

15. In his discussion of the fate of Dunwich, the narrator provides a spatial, geopolitical translation of such temporality as the movement *west*. Noting the westward expansion of the town, the narrator writes that "the slowly dying town . . . followed . . . one of the fundamental patterns of human behaviour. A strikingly large number of our settlements are oriented to the west and, where circumstances permit, relocate in a westward direction. The east stands for lost causes" (159/191).

most overdetermined engagement with this emblem of human mortality in the long section introducing readers to the central importance of London's Liverpool Street Station in the life of Jacques Austerlitz. Recall that Austerlitz dramatically recovers bits of his childhood memories when he wanders into the Ladies' Waiting Room of that station, following an impulse he does not understand at the time. It is there that he begins to recall the traumatic past—his parting from home, family, and native language—that had at some level already been returning to him in the guise of his great research project on the architecture and culture of the "bourgeois age." Though the chronology is never fully clarified, it seems that Austerlitz's breakthrough visit to Liverpool Street Station took place shortly before the breakdown he suffered when his project began to falter after he took early retirement in 1991 (the return of his personal memories was indeed a likely catalyst for this breakdown). That crisis, which rapidly assumed the generalized form of a crisis of language in the manner described by Hugo von Hofmannsthal in his famous "Chandos letter," leads Austerlitz, after he decides to bury his writings in a compost heap "under layers of rotted leaves and spadefuls of earth" (125/180), to a series of compulsive and mostly nocturnal wanderings through the streets of London.[16] Although these wanderings manage to hold suicidal

---

16. The language of the Chandos letter is recognizable in passages such as this: "The entire structure of language, the syntactical arrangement of parts of speech, punctuation, conjunctions, and finally even the nouns denoting ordinary objects were all enveloped in impenetrable fog. . . . The very thing which may usually convey a sense of purposeful intelligence—the exposition of an idea by means of a certain stylistic facility—now seemed to me nothing but an entirely arbitrary or deluded enterprise. I could see no connections anymore, the sentences resolved themselves into a series of separate words, the words into random sets of letters, the letters into disjointed signs, and those signs into a blue-gray trail gleaming silver here and there, excreted and left behind it by some crawling creature, and the sight of it increasingly filled me with feelings of horror and shame" (124/179–80). Sebald alludes to the Chandos letter throughout his writings. The centrality of the Hofmannsthal story is a function not only of its canonical portrayal of a crisis of language, but also of its evocation of creaturely life as a realm of profound suffering and meaninglessness (as well as of unspeakable ecstasy and joy). The last lines of chapter 7 in *The Rings of Saturn* contains one such allusion to the Chandos letter; the themes of psychic distress and crisis of language are further heightened by the reference to Hölderlin (the chapter deals with the narrator's visit to Michael Hamburger, who is known, among other things, for his translations of Hölderlin's poetry): "We waited for the taxi beside the Hölderlin pump, and by the faint light that fell from the living-room

thoughts at bay, they end up leading him over and over again to the Liverpool Street Station and therewith back to the boneyards of personal and collective history.[17]

Austerlitz, we learn, had long been a "devotee" of this site, noting that before renovations began at the end of the 1980s, it "was one of the darkest and most sinister places in London, a kind of entrance to the underworld" (127–28/184). Austerlitz tells the narrator of his habit of sitting in the station for hours waiting for the feeling to begin to wrench inside him that he describes as "a kind of heartache which, as I was beginning to sense, was caused by the vortex of past time" (129/186). He relates to the narrator the history of the site, beginning with the so-called Little Ice Age when the site consisted of marshy meadows where Londoners would skate when the water froze over; he tells of the drainage and development of the meadows, the construction of parks and country houses; of the building, in the seventeenth century, of the priory of the order of St. Mary of Bethlehem and of the hospital for the insane that became famous under the name Bedlam. Austerlitz's reflections on this bit of London history give us a version of what Benjamin meant when he claimed that for the baroque poets history merged into the setting. Whenever he passed through the station, Austerlitz tells the narrator,

I kept almost obsessively trying to imagine . . . the location of that huge space of the rooms where the asylum inmates were confined, and I often wondered

---

window into the well I saw, with a shudder that went to the roots of my hair, a beetle rowing across the surface of the water, from one dark shore to the other" (190/228). In Hofmannsthal's "Letter," Lord Chandos insists that the sort of intense solidarity he had begun to feel with creaturely life after his crisis cannot be characterized as sympathy or compassion—as *Mitleid*: "For what did this have to do with compassion, with a comprehensible concatenation of human thoughts, when, on another evening, I found under a nut tree a half-filled water-pitcher left by a gardener boy, and this pitcher and the water in it, darkened by the shade of the tree, and a beetle, swimming on the surface of the water from one dark shore to the other—when this grouping of nullities sends through me . . . a shudder at the presence of the Infinite." Hugo von Hofmannsthal, "Ein Brief," in *Gesammelte Werke: Erzählungen, Erfundene Gespräche und Briefe, Reisen,* ed. Bernd Schoeller (Frankfurt a.M.: Fischer, 1979), 469.

17. Austerlitz's description of his suicidal fantasy of throwing himself over a banister in a certain house "into the dark depths of the stairwell" (125/181) is no doubt an allusion to Primo Levi's suicide.

whether the pain and the suffering accumulated on this site over the centuries had ever ebbed away, or whether they might not still, as I sometimes thought when I felt a cold breath of air on my forehead, be sensed as we passed through them. (129–130/186–87)

He imagines, further, the bleachfields and burial grounds "where the dead were buried once the churchyards of London could hold no more" (130/187–88). As Austerlitz explains,

When space becomes too cramped, the dead, like the living, move out into less densely populated districts where they can rest at a decent distance from each other. But more and more keep coming, a never-ending succession of them, and in the end, when the space is entirely occupied, graves are dug through existing graves to accommodate them, until all the bones in the cemetery lie jumbled up together. (130/188)

In the seventeenth and eighteenth centuries, we learn, "the city had grown above these strata of soil mingled with the dust and bones of decayed bodies into a warren of putrid streets and houses for the poorest Londoners" (130/188–90). Finally, Austerlitz relates that when in 1984 demolition work uncovered over four hundred skeletons, he would regularly return to the site to photograph the remains of the dead, "partly," as he puts it, "because of my interest in architectural history and partly for other reasons which I could not explain even to myself" (130/188; Sebald inserts here a photograph of skeletons and skulls embedded in earth, one of which seems to be laughing demonically).

In the course of this foray into urban archaeology, we learn that many of the slums—along with the bones buried beneath them—had already been cleared in the second half of the nineteenth century for the laying of rail lines that, as Austerlitz notes, "on the engineers' plans looked like muscles and sinews in an anatomical atlas" (132/190). The depiction of flayed flesh, along with that of skull and skeleton, is perhaps the single most potent image of exposure one could imagine. We have already encountered it in the narrator's commentary on Rembrandt's painting of the anatomy lesson. Here the image suggests a more generalized dimension of exposure, as if modernization—the introduction of railway lines into the city—had opened the skin of the city, exposing it to never-ending streams of traffic and commerce. The image of flayed flesh returns at the end of the novel when Austerlitz recalls a visit, during his first stay in Paris, to a museum of veterinary medicine. There, among the cabinets displaying deformed animals and body parts that call to mind Grünewald's *Temptation of St. Anthony*, Austerlitz comes upon a glass case exhibiting "the life-sized figure of a horseman, very skillfully flayed in the post-Revolutionary period by the anatomist and dissector Honoré Fragonard" such that "every strand in the tensed muscles of the rider and his mount . . . was clearly visible in the colors of congealed blood, together with the blue of the veins and the ocher yellow of the sinews and ligaments" (266–68/376). Finally, Austerlitz speculates that Fragonard, who "had apparently dissected over three thousand bodies and parts of bodies in the course of his career" and so was constantly surrounded by death and decay, sought in the process of vitrification the possibility of saving "some semblance of eternal life" from the corruptible body (268/376). It was shortly after his exposure to this horrific emblem of absolute, bodily exposure that Austerlitz suffered a series of fainting fits and losses of memory that landed him in Salpêtrière with a diagnosis of hysterical epilepsy.[18]

Thomas Browne, like Fragonard, sought out signs of eternity in the materiality of creaturely life. At the end of the long section on Browne in *The Rings of Saturn,* the narrator suggests that for Browne the capacity for transformation and transmigration manifest in the natural world invites us to believe that something survives the destruction that otherwise befalls all things earthly. This capacity is visible, above all, in such creatures as caterpillars and moths, and even more, perhaps, in our capacity to produce human artifacts of beauty—in this case, *silk*—from the by-products of such metamorphoses (we later learn that Browne's father was a silk merchant). The chapter ends on a note of uncertainty as to the value of such a capacity: "The purple

---

18. In good Foucauldian fashion, Austerlitz characterizes the famous clinic as "that gigantic complex of buildings where the borders between hospital and penitentiary have always been blurred" (269/378).

piece of silk he refers to, then, in the urn of Patroclus—what does it mean?" (26/39).

Such vague, existential qualms get taken up into the remarkable history of the silk trade that dominates the last chapter of *The Rings of Saturn*. The rise and fall of silk production in various countries from Asia to Europe, the complex entanglement of silk production, court intrigue, and geopolitics, and finally the ways silk production gets caught up in the racial ideology of the Nazi state—all this becomes, for Sebald, yet another allegory of natural history on a global scale: of *globalization* as the ultimate form of *Naturgeschichte*. Against this background it makes good sense that one of the final images in *Austerlitz* is of a scrap of silk.

At the end of the novel, the narrator leafs through a book Austerlitz had given him in Paris, *Heshel's Kingdom*. The book tells of Dan Jacobson's search for his grandfather, Heshel, a Russian Jew whose only material legacy to his descendants consists of, among a few other items, "a faded and already disintegrating piece of silk" (297/415). The narrator reads Jacobson's memoir while visiting, for the second time, the fortifications at Breendonk near Antwerp. The first visit was occasioned by Austerlitz's long disquisition on fortifications during one of his early colloquies with the narrator. There Austerlitz held forth about the fantastic nature and inflated excesses of the entire art of military architecture, "the whole insanity of fortification and siegecraft," their "tendency towards paranoid elaboration" (17, 16/25, 24).[19] Once again Sebald reminds us that the very means of avoiding exposure, of living in the mode of *defense,* becomes the operator of our further exposure to the rhythms of natural history. This becomes palpable in the short history of Breendonk—it twice changed hands between

---

19. During his small lecture to the narrator, Austerlitz notes that at the end of the seventeenth century the "star-shaped dodecagon" emerged as the privileged design for military fortifications, a design that "strikes the layman as an emblem both of absolute power and of the ingenuity of the engineers put to the service of that power" (15–16/23). Austerlitz will later encounter this design when he visits Terezin/Theresienstadt, where his mother was interned. A cruel irony of his mother's story is that the star-shaped residence built by Archduke Ferdinand of Tyrol had been a favorite destination during excursions out of Prague before the war.

Belgium and Germany—as well as in the photograph provided of the surface of the buildings "encrusted by guano-like droppings and calcareous streaks" (21/30); it is, in a word, as if the structure is being reclaimed by the elements. During the second visit to Breendonk, the narrator cites Jacobson's memoir apropos of a series of fortifications the Russians built in Lithuania late in the nineteenth century, which, "despite the elevated positions on which they had been constructed, and for all the great number of their cannon, the thickness of their walls, and their labyrinthine corridors, proved entirely useless" (298/416–17). To cite, once again, Austerlitz's remark concerning such structures in general, they "are designed from the first with an eye to their later existence as ruins" (19/28).

IV

What has, I hope, become clear in this sketch of Sebald's "baroque" sense of the object world is that for him materiality does not merely signify the "natural" corruptibility of all things earthly; rather, this corruptibility is an index of their participation in the violent rhythms of human history.[20] As I have emphasized throughout, for both Benjamin and Sebald creatureliness signifies a materiality dense with "deposits" of unredeemed suffering, deposits bearing witness to contact with what Benjamin characterized as the "mythic violence" that attends the foundation, preservation, and augmentation of institutions in the human world. Benjamin, as we have seen, tried to transfer his understanding of such "historical depositions" to an analysis of capitalist modernity, suggesting that the commodity itself becomes a

---

20. To Sebald's privileged materials and objects—dust, ash, moths, bones, flayed skin, and silk—we might add salt and herring. In *The Rings of Saturn,* for example, the narrator ends a brief history of herring fishing by recalling a series of cruel experiments undertaken by an inspector of the Rouen fish market. "This process," the narrator writes, "inspired by our thirst for knowledge, might be described as the most extreme of the sufferings undergone by a species always threatened by disaster" (57/74). The German original contains the word *Leidensgeschichte* ("history of suffering"), which is, of course, the word used for the passion of Christ.

key bearer of this spectral materiality in the guise of its seeming opposite, the fetish (promise of happiness, completion, the "real thing"). Michel Foucault, for his part, theorized the threshold of modernity as the moment when "mythic violence" begins to proliferate beyond the recognizable historical framework of sovereign power and authority and into the multiple contact points between expert knowledge and bodies, the domain of what he called disciplinary power and "biopolitics." But what I have argued with regard to both of these thinkers pertains, I think, even more emphatically to Sebald. The history of suffering that becomes visible under Sebald's saturnine gaze is not simply one of dissolution, of loss of energy, not merely one of going dead; it is equally one of perpetual intensification and agitation—of *ex-citation* in the sense I have been elaborating. For Sebald too, natural history has a *manic* dimension, a dimension testifying to that peculiar sort of animation I have referred to as "undeadness."

There is perhaps no better place to begin thinking about this dimension than in Sebald's use of Kafka's famous story about the undead, "The Hunter Gracchus."[21] Kafka's short prose piece is one of a series of famous invocations of undead wanderers one finds in nineteenth- and early twentieth-century literature and culture. One thinks, for example, of the figure of the flying Dutchman or the rise to cultural prominence of that of the wandering Jew (*der ewige Jude*), not to mention that most popular figure of the undead, the vampire.[22] Kafka's text tells of a hunter who falls to his death while hunting in the

---

21. In this context it is worth citing Adorno's remarks about undeadness in Kafka: "The zone in which it is impossible to die is also the no-man's land between man and thing: within it meet Odradek, which Benjamin viewed as an angel in Klee's style, and Gracchus, the humble descendant of Nimrod. The understanding of these most advanced, incommensurable productions, and of several others that similarly evade current conceptions of Kafka, may one day provide the key to the whole." Theodor Adorno, "Notes on Kafka," in *Prisms,* trans. Samuel Weber and Shierry Weber (Cambridge: MIT Press, 1997), 263.
22. Sebald alludes to Bram Stoker's *Dracula* in the Max Ferber story. When he settles into his new home in Manchester, the narrator is disturbed to find that the backyard is full of rats. They disappear just before Christmas when "a little ratcatcher by the name of Renfield turned up several times with a battered bucket full of rat poison" (153/225–26).

Black Forest. Because the mythic boat that was to take him to the realm of the dead went off course, he is condemned to a "life" of constant mobility, to sail the earthly waters for eternity according to the winds blowing in "the undermost regions of death." The story opens with the hunter's bark entering the harbor city of Riva, where two men in dark coats and silver buttons carry his bier to town. There, during an audience with the mayor, he tells the sad story that has left him stranded in that "extraterritorial" domain between real and symbolic death: "My death ship lost its way; a wrong turn of the wheel, a moment's absence of mind on the pilot's part, the distraction of my lovely native country, I cannot tell what it was; I only know this, that I remained on earth and that ever since my ship has sailed earthly waters."[23]

Kafka's Gracchus, this figure of spectral wandering, haunts Sebald's first major work of prose, *Vertigo,* from start to finish. In the first part of the book, which deals with the "coming of age" of Henri Beyle (Stendhal) during and after his years with Napoleon's army in northern Italy, we find the first clear allusion to Kafka's undead hunter. The context is a journey across Lake Garda that Beyle, in his autobiographical writings, claims to have undertaken with a certain Mme Gherardi. Sebald's narrator expresses some skepticism as to her actual existence, suggesting that she functions as a cipher for a series of love interests, that she "was merely a phantom, albeit one to whom Beyle remained true for decades" (22/27). Arriving in the port of Riva,

Beyle drew Mme Gherardi's attention to an old boat, its mainmast fractured two-thirds of the way up, its buff-coloured sails hanging in folds. It appeared to have made fast only a short time ago, and two men in dark silver-buttoned tunics were at that moment carrying a bier ashore on which, under a large, frayed, flower-patterned silk cloth, lay what was evidently a human form. The scene affected Mme Gherardi so adversely that she insisted on quitting Riva without delay. (25/30–31)

23. Franz Kafka, "The Hunter Gracchus," trans. Willa Muir and Edwin Muir, in *The Complete Stories,* ed. Nahum Glatzer (New York: Schocken, 1971), 230, 228.

The scene is framed, in Sebald's narrative, by two brief discourses on love, one in which Mme Gherardi characterizes love as a fantasy testifying to our distance from nature and one in which Beyle compares the emergence of love to the process by which salt crystallizes around a dead twig.[24]

Gracchus briefly returns in the second part of *Vertigo,* "All' estero," when the narrator confesses to conversing with a group of jackdaws during his emotionally troubled wanderings through Vienna in October 1980 (*graculus* and *kavka* are both names for jackdaws). The Gracchus allusion throws into relief the "undead" quality of the narrator's perambulations through Vienna. Like other Sebald texts, this one begins with the narrator taking a trip to get away from England after a difficult period.[25] The narrator very soon comes to realize that his restless wanderings through the city were mysteriously constrained by an unknown pressure:

Early every morning I would set out and walk without aim or purpose through the streets of the inner city, through the Leopoldstadt and the Josefstadt. Later, when I looked at the map, I saw to my astonishment that none of my journeys had taken me beyond a precisely defined sickle- or crescent-shaped area. . . . If the paths I had followed had been inked in, it would have seemed as though a man had kept trying out new tracks and connections over and over, only to be thwarted each time by the limitations of his reason, imagination or will-power, and obliged to turn back again. (34/42)

24. Salt, another of Sebald's privileged substances, returns at the end of the story of Max Ferber when the narrator visits the old salt frames in Bad Kissingen after visiting the Jewish cemetery there. In both cases the crystallizing process is seen to occupy an uncertain domain between inanimate and animate nature. Salt crystals embody, that is, the central question pertaining to the undead: *Is it alive?*
25. The text begins: "In October 1980 I traveled from England . . . to Vienna, hoping that a change of place would help me get over a particularly difficult period in my life" (33/41). One might compare this opening with that of *Austerlitz*: "In the second half of the 1960s I traveled repeatedly from England to Belgium, partly for study purposes, partly for other reasons which were never entirely clear to me" (3/5). Or the beginning of *The Rings of Saturn*: "In August 1992, when the dog days were drawing to an end, I set off to walk the county of Suffolk, in the hope of dispelling the emptiness that takes hold of me whenever I have completed a long stint of work" (3/11).

This pattern of constrained though agitated mobility renders exactly what Benjamin referred to as *erstarrte Unruhe,* or petrified unrest and what I have called "undeadness."

This constrained, "undead" pattern of *flânerie* finds its psychic correlate in repeated instances of compulsive thinking registered throughout Sebald's work. In *Vertigo,* the constrained agitation of such mental activity—more a kind of quasi-articulated pressure than thinking in any conventional sense—transforms the narrator himself into a kind of Gracchus figure. On the first of November 1980, still in Venice and caught up in reflections and memories of All Saints' Day and All Souls'—"nothing in my childhood seemed to possess more meaning than those two days of remembrance devoted to the suffering of the sainted martyrs and poor unredeemed souls" (64/77)—the narrator reports lying immobilized in his hotel room, enclosed by "ever widening and contracting circles of . . . thoughts." "It seemed to me," he remarks, "that one could well end one's life simply through thinking and retreating into one's mind." When room service finally arrives with a bottle of wine, he notes that his limbs had grown so cold and stiff that "I felt as if I had already been interred or laid out for burial" (65/78; the German original resonates more closely with the language of "The Hunter Gracchus": "Wie ein Bestatteter oder doch zumindest *wie ein Aufgebahrter*").[26]

Gracchus returns several more times in *Vertigo*. In the course of his efforts, in 1987, to repeat his 1980 journey from Vienna to Italy for the

26. Another similar moment of constrained physical and mental agitation—of *erstarrte Unruhe*—is recorded in *The Rings of Saturn,* when the narrator finds himself covering the same ground over and over again on the heath outside Dunwich: "Lost in the thoughts that went round in my head incessantly, and numbed by this crazed flowering, I stuck to the sandy path until to my astonishment, not to say horror, I found myself back again at the same tangled thicket from which I had emerged about an hour before, or, as it now seemed to me, in some distant past" (171/204). When he finally manages to emerge from what we might characterize as a spatialized repetition compulsion, the narrator notes that "the horizon was spinning all around as if I had jumped off a merry-go-round" (172/205). He furthermore notes that months later he has a dream about this episode in which his panic and exhaustion mutate into a visual image of a labyrinth—a recurring motif in Sebald—which in the dream he knows to be a cross section of his own brain (173/206).

purpose of working through his recollections of "those fraught and hazardous days" (81/97), the narrator simultaneously follows the tracks of Kafka, who in 1913 passed through northern Italy on a business trip.[27] Washing his hands in the bathroom of the train station in Desenzano, the narrator wonders whether Kafka too had glanced into the mirror above the sink. He feels confirmed in his fantasy when he notices a graffito, *il cacciatore,* to which he adds the words, *nella selva nera,* "in the black forest." After a series of strange experiences, including his encounter, on the bus to Riva, with two young twins who exhibit an uncanny likeness to Kafka, the narrator returns to Verona, where he has a vision taken directly from Kafka's story (and already cited in the first part of *Vertigo*); it is one he has had numerous times: "Two men in black silver-buttoned tunics, who were carrying out from a rear courtyard a bier on which lay, under a floral-patterned drape, what was plainly the body of a human being" (125/147).

At the end of the third story in *Vertigo,* "Dr. K. Takes the Waters at Riva," Sebald inserts a lengthy passage from "The Hunter Gracchus" and even reproduces a hazy image of a bark. The story concludes with reflections on the nature of the guilt that condemns Gracchus to his eternal wanderings. The narrator speculates that behind the false turn of the pilot's wheel that condemned the hunter to his miserable immortality lies Kafka's own "penitence for a longing for love" (*Abbuße einer Sehnsucht nach Liebe*) (165/188). After indicating the troubled nature of Kafka's sexuality—and suggesting its uncertain orientation—the narrator paraphrases one of the letters to Felice in which Kafka comments on a photograph of his fiancée's niece (the activity of "reading" photographs is, of course, quite familiar to readers of Sebald): "Yes, this little child deserves to be loved. That fearful gaze, as if all the terrors of the earth had been revealed to her in the studio. But what love could have been sufficient to spare the child the terrors of love, which for Dr. K. stood foremost among all the terrors of the

27. The year 1913, this crucial year before the outbreak of the Great War, is, of course, a central motif of *Vertigo.* Reading through the Verona newspapers from that year in the municipal library, the narrator writes, for example, "1913 was a peculiar year. The times were changing, and the spark was racing along the fuse like an adder through the grass" (121/142).

earth?" (167/190). What is at stake here, I suggest, is just the sort of love that could intervene into the petrified unrest, the undeadness embodied in the Gracchus figure.[28]

Gracchus returns in the final story of *Vertigo* in several different guises. In the fall of 1987, the narrator returns for the first time to the village of his birth and early childhood. In the course of his varied efforts to recapture aspects of his past, he visits the attic of a neighbor's house that had played a significant role in his childhood imagination. The excitement associated with this attic was in no small measure provoked by one of the neighbors, who had warned the narrator as a young child that the "grey hunter" lived there. When in the course of his small search for lost time, he finally enters the attic, it turns out that this gray hunter was a tailor's dummy dressed in the uniform of an Austrian *chasseur* who had fallen in the Battle of Marengo against Napoleon's army. In good Sebaldian fashion, when the narrator actually touches the sleeve of the uniform, "it crumble[s] into dust" (227/258). Finally, in the context of the narrator's most graphic memory of sex and death, we encounter the figure of Hans Schlag, a hunter who, it is noted, had managed extensive hunting grounds in the Black Forest before arriving in the narrator's native village. The narrator recalls witnessing Schlag having sex with Romana, the barmaid at the village pub.[29] What is crucial in this memory is, I think, the clear association the narrator makes (or made as a child) between sex and lifelessness understood, on the one hand, as a machinelike, senseless movement and, on the other, as inertness (these aspects are, in the passage, distributed by gender):

28. Kafka's letter to his childhood friend Oskar Pollak on the task of literature becomes especially resonant in this context: "A book must be the ax for the frozen sea within us." Cited in Ernst Pawel, *The Nightmare of Reason: A Life of Franz Kafka* (New York: Vintage, 1985), 158. One might also recall, in this context, Marie's remark to Austerlitz during their ill-fated trip to Marienbad: "Why, she said, have you been like a pool of frozen water ever since we came here?" (215/307).

29. The name Hans Schlag, as well as the inspiration for the episode in the neighbor's attic, comes from the draft of a story—"In the Attic"—that Kafka wrote shortly before "The Hunter Gracchus." As I noted earlier, the description of this scene is taken almost verbatim from Peter Weiss's *Schatten des Körpers des Kutschers.*

It was Schlag the hunter, who, holding onto the slatted frame of the shed with one hand, stood there in the darkness like a man leaning into the wind, his entire body moving to a strange, consistent and undulating rhythm. Between him and the slatting he gripped with his left hand, Romana lay on a heap of cut turf, and her eyes, as I could make out in the light reflected from the snow, were turned sideways and as wide open as those of Dr. Rambousek when his head had fallen lifeless on the top of his desk. (238/271)

Hans Schlag eventually suffers the fate of Kafka's hunter; he too falls to his death at the bottom of a ravine while hunting. The narrator's memory of encountering the hunter's fresh corpse clearly places Schlag in the company of the undead: "I . . . was not able to get the matter out of my mind all day long. When I was at my schoolwork, all I had to do was lower my eyelids a little and I beheld Schlag the hunter lying dead at the bottom of the ravine. And so it was no surprise to me when, at midday, I came upon him on my way home from school" (246/280). In the course of the autopsy, it is discovered that Schlag had, on his left arm, a tattoo of a small bark.

v

Kafka's Gracchus is a close relative of the wandering Jew, that mythic figure cursed to eternal wandering for having scoffed at Jesus on the way to the crucifixion. The legend, whose origins are in the New Testament, was consolidated in early modernity and returned with some regularity in the popular culture of a number of European countries well into the nineteenth century. In this context one might also recall the "scientific" reception of the legend, which creates a link to Austerlitz and his brief institutionalization at Salpêtrière for hysterical epilepsy (the very name "Austerlitz" already seems to echo the traditional name of the wandering Jew, "Ahasverus").[30] In 1893 one of Jean-Martin Charcot's pupils, Henri Meige, wrote a brief monograph on the Jewish predisposition to nervous illness with the telling title *Le*

30. As critics have noted, "Austerlitz" also sounds like "Auschwitz."

*Juif-errant à la Salpêtrière: Études sur certains nevropathes.*[31] Meige begins his remarkable essay by citing one of Charcot's case presentations from 1889, that of a Hungarian Jew named Klein who was apparently subject to compulsive wanderings and migrations: "I introduce him to you," Charcot reported, "as *a true descendant of Ahasverus or Cartophilus,* as you would say. The fact is that, like the compulsive (neurotic) travelers of whom I have already spoken, he is constantly driven by an irresistible need to move on, to travel, without being able to settle down anywhere. That is why he has been crisscrossing Europe for three years in search of the fortune which he has not yet encountered."[32] Meige's typical Wandering Jew is not so much a man in search of fortune as one driven to wander in search of a cure for the compulsion to wander:

They are constantly obsessed by the need to travel, to go from city to city, from hospital to hospital, in search of a new treatment, an unfindable remedy. They try all the recommended medications, avid for novelty, but they soon reject them, inventing a frivolous pretext for not continuing, and, with the reappearing impulse, they flee one fine day, drawn by a new mirage of a distant cure.

Meige adds to this description the following *racial* diagnosis:

Let us not forget that they are Jews, and that it is a characteristic of their race to move with extreme ease. At home nowhere, and at home everywhere, the Israelites never hesitate to leave their homes for an important business affair and, particularly if they are ill, to go in search of an effective remedy.

In Meige's view, what is ultimately pathological about these modern Wandering Jews, whose trajectory is not surprisingly from an

31. This short monograph has been published in English as Henri Meige, "The Wandering Jew in the Clinic: A Study of Neurotic Pathology," in a collection of essays on the figure of the Wandering Jew in history: *The Wandering Jew: Essays in the Interpretation of a Christian Legend,* ed. Galit Hasan-Rokem and Alan Dundes (Bloomington: Indiana University Press, 1986), 190–94.
32. Cited in Meige, "Wandering Jew," 191.

impoverished Eastern to a more affluent Western Europe, is their *drivenness,* the intensity of their compulsion "to be always seeking *something else and somewhere else.* What is pathological is not to be able to resist this need to keep moving, which nothing justifies and which may even be detrimental."[33]

Also significant in this context is the image of the *caravan,* the very icon of wandering, Jewish and otherwise, indeed of every kind of nomadism and collective *deterritorialization.* I have been able to count no fewer than nine references (including images) to desert caravans in Sebald's writings.[34] In *Austerlitz* the image recurs over and over again. Recalling his childhood in Wales, Austerlitz remembers his profound identification with an image from a children's Bible showing Israel's encampment in the wilderness: "I knew that my proper place was among the tiny figures populating the camp" (55/81). Later, during one of his visits to the Andromeda Lodge, his friend Gerald's mother, Adela, asks him, as they gaze together at the play of light and shadows on the walls of the ballroom at dusk, "Do you see the fronds of the palm trees, do you see the caravan coming through the dunes over there?" (112/162). And after a long hiatus in their contact, Austerlitz invites the narrator to visit him at his home by sending him a postcard "showing a camp of white tents in the Egyptian desert" (117/169; the image is reproduced in the text) and bearing as message only the date and place of the future meeting. Finally, in a disturbing reversal of the usual sense of the image, Austerlitz's childhood nanny, Vera, recalls his father's remarks after seeing *Triumph of the Will* in a Munich cinema:

Maximilian told us that a bird's-eye view showed a city of white tents extending to the horizon, from which as day broke the Germans emerged singly, in couples, or in small groups, forming a silent procession and pressing ever

33. Meige, "Wandering Jew, 192, 194.
34. The motif of the caravan merges with that of dust and death in the remark, attributed to Maxime du Camp, author of the study of nineteenth-century Paris cited by both Benjamin and Austerlitz, that "the deserts of the Orient . . . are formed . . . from the dust of the dead" (287/402).

closer together as they all went in the same direction, following, so it seemed, a higher bidding, on their way to the Promised Land at last after long years in the wilderness. (169/243–44)[35]

It is perhaps in just such perverse appropriations of the image of Jewish wandering that the full meaning of the German title of Sebald's first book of prose fiction registers. The word translated as *Vertigo*—*Schwindel*—means, of course, not just a feeling of dizziness but also deception, swindle, simulation.[36]

35. Other significant invocations of nomadism occur in *The Emigrants* and *The Rings of Saturn*. In the earlier book, in the story about Max Ferber, the narrator describes the painter's favorite bar, the "Wadi Halfa," a hole-in-the-wall in the basement of an otherwise unoccupied building run by African immigrants from the Masai tribe. Whenever the narrator tries to recall his meetings with Ferber there he sees him "sitting in the same place in front of a fresco painted by an unknown hand that showed a caravan moving forward from the remotest depths of the picture, across a wavy ridge of dunes, straight towards the beholder" (164/243). In this case, of course, the image alludes not only to Ferber's exile but also to the proprietor's experience of dislocation and nomadism. And in *The Rings of Saturn*, the narrator-wanderer comes upon a series of tentlike shelters along the beach south of Lowestoft and remarks that "it is as if the last stragglers of some nomadic people had settled there, at the outermost limit of the earth, in expectation of the miracle longed for since time immemorial, the miracle which would justify all their erstwhile privations and wanderings" (51–52/68).

36. Alain Badiou has characterized such forms of simulation as one of the faces of evil. For Badiou the form of evil he refers to as "simulacrum and terror" involves an appropriation of the language of "truth-events"—events that take the "void" of creaturely life as their point of departure and in principle bear a universal address—for the consolidation of closed particularities: "When a radical break in a situation, under names borrowed from real truth-processes, convokes not the void but the 'full' particularity or presumed substance of that situation, we are dealing with a *simulacrum of truth*." Indeed, for Badiou it is just such simulacra that emphatically condemn those excluded from the closed particularity consolidated in the "pseudo-event" to the status of creaturely life. "'Simulacrum' [and here Badiou is thinking above all of the "event" of Nazism] must be understood in its strong sense: all the formal traits of a truth are at work in the simulacrum. Not only a universal nomination of the event, inducing the power of a radical break, but also the 'obligation' of a fidelity, and the promotion of a *simulacrum of the subject*, erected—without the advent of any Immortal—*above the human animality of the others*, of those who are arbitrarily declared not to belong to the communitarian substance whose promotion and domination the simulacrum-event is designed to assure." Alain Badiou, *Ethics: An Essay on the Understanding of Evil*, trans. Peter Hallward (London: Verso, 2001), 73–74.

VI

Aside from Kafka's hunter Gracchus, there is another literary figure that embodies, in Sebald's work, the sort of undying persistence proper to the place "between two deaths." If Gracchus's status as undead derives from the interruption of his symbolic death—he really dies, but something goes awry in the symbolic passage to the realm of the dead—then Balzac's Colonel Chabert, referred to several times in *Austerlitz,* owes this status to the fact that his real dying was interrupted while his symbolic death was fully consummated. Chabert is left for dead during the battle at Eylau. His death is announced to Napoleon, and a death certificate is issued; his wife remarries, and his estate is redistributed. The bulk of the story is taken up with Chabert's efforts at revoking his symbolic death, that is to say, at reinstating his name and his marriage and reclaiming his property. These efforts ultimately come to nothing, and he ends his days in an almshouse. The futility of Chabert's efforts are summed up in his lawyer's remark, at the very end of the story, that of priests, doctors, and lawyers, the lawyers are the unhappiest; when a man comes to a lawyer, he laments, "we see the same ill feelings repeated again and again, never corrected. Our offices are gutters that cannot be cleansed."[37]

During his visit to Prague, Austerlitz's old nanny, Vera, happens upon two old photographs of special importance to him. One shows the stage of a provincial theater where his mother had performed in the years before her Prague debut; the other is a photograph of himself as a child in the costume of a page. Vera discovered the two photographs when she happened to pick up a volume of the edition of the *Comédie humaine* she inherited in 1933 along with her apartment. The volume she picks out and in which the photographs had been slipped between pages—most likely by Austerlitz's mother—is the one containing *Colonel Chabert.* Later, in the course of his efforts to research the fate of his father, Austerlitz takes a break from his work and undertakes to read Balzac, beginning with *Colonel Chabert.* During one

---

37. Honoré de Balzac, *Colonel Chabert,* trans. Carol Cosman (New York: New Directions, 1997), 100.

of his meetings with the narrator in the boulevard Auguste Blanqui, he quotes a long passage of the novella from memory. It describes Chabert's returning to consciousness in the mass grave where he had been left for dead (the passage is quoted in French): "I heard, or thought I heard . . . groans coming from the pile of corpses I was lying in. Even though the memory of these moments is murky, and despite the fact I must have endured even greater suffering, there are nights when I still think I hear those muffled moans!"[38] These *gémissements poussés par le monde des cadavres*—this murmuring of undeadness—which Austerlitz too is apparently unable to get out of his head, had already been evoked by Vera when she handed over the two photographs to Austerlitz. Speaking of "the mysterious quality peculiar to such photographs when they surface from oblivion," Vera registers the impression "of something stirring in them, as if one caught small sighs of despair, *gémissements de désespoir* . . . as if the pictures had a memory of their own and remembered us" (182/262). These *gémissements* return us to the realm of the creaturely in the sense I have been elaborating throughout this book. Indeed, they recall the Pauline vision of creation groaning in travail to which Heidegger alludes when he argues that the forms of exposure proper to both animal and human life generate an "essential disruption" (*wesenhafte Erschütterung*) in their respective being.

The relevant passage comes from Paul's letter to the Romans 8:21–22: "Because creation itself will be set free from its bondage to decay and obtain the glorious liberty of the children of God. We know that the whole creation has been groaning in travail until now."[39] The "miracle" to which Paul bears witness here is the emancipation not from mortality but from the *bondage* to decay that Paul correlates throughout his writings with a certain relation to the law, one he famously ascribes to the Jews. This is a relation in which law not only regulates and pacifies but also agitates and excites (to

---

38. Ibid., 22.
39. *The Writings of Saint Paul,* ed. Wayne A. Meeks (New York: W. W. Norton, 1972), 81. The passage in Latin contains the root of the French *gémissements*: "Scimus enim, quod omnis creatura ingemiscit et parturit usque adhuc."

transgressive enjoyment). In a word, Paul's conception of such an emancipation pertains to the mode of subjectivization proper to what I have been calling *Naturgeschichte*. We might think of it as a mode of subject formation in which the ambivalence proper to the superego finds no adequate supplement in an equally powerful commandment of neighbor-love (again, Paul seems to attribute this lack to the Jews).

In Paul's writings, then, the key name of death and decay is *law,* or rather the dimension of law that *undeadens,* renders subjects creaturely (in Paul's terms, binds them to decay, makes them carnal in an emphatic sense). The most famous and difficult passage in Paul's letters linking death and law is no doubt in Romans 7:

Likewise, my brethren, you have died to the law through the body of Christ, so that you may belong to another, to him who has been raised from the dead in order that we may bear fruit for God. While we were living in the flesh, our sinful passions, aroused by the law, were at work in our members to bear fruit for death. But now we are discharged from the law, dead to that which held us captive, so that we serve not under the old written code but in the new life of the Spirit.

Paul continues along this path of paradoxical formulations by claiming, in effect, that *death first comes alive* through the law:

What then shall we say? That the law is sin? By no means! Yet, if it had not been for the law, I should not have known sin. I should not have known what it is to covet if the law had not said "You shall not covet." But sin, finding opportunity in the commandment, wrought in me all kinds of covetousness. Apart from the law sin lies dead. I was once alive apart from the law, but when the commandment came, sin revived and I died; the very commandment which promised life proved to be death to me. For sin, finding opportunity in the commandment, deceived me and by it killed me. . . . Did that which is good, then, bring death to me? By no means! It was sin, working death in me through what is good, in order that sin might be shown to be sin, and through the commandment might become sinful beyond measure.

Finally, Paul seems to offer a solution to this set of paradoxes by suggesting that one differentiate between different registers, levels, or dimensions of law: the law articulated in commandment and what he calls the "law in my members":

I do not understand my own actions. For I do not do what I want, but I do the very thing I hate. Now if I do what I do not want, I agree that the law is good. So then it is no longer I that do it, but sin which dwells within me. For I know that nothing good dwells within me, that is, in my flesh. I can will what is right, but I cannot do it. For I do not do the good I want but the evil I do not want is what I do. Now if I do what I do not want, it is no longer I that do it, but the sin which dwells within me. So I find it to be a law that when I want to do right, evil lies close at hand. For I delight in the law of God, in my inmost self, but I see in my members another law at war with the law of my mind and making me captive to the law of sin which dwells in my members.

What we are offered here is nothing short of a theory of unconscious mental activity as generated by the *seductions of law* or, as I would prefer to put it, a theory of the unconscious understood as *creaturely expressivity* (the laws of which dwell "in my members"). As Alain Badiou has put it, "Paul's fundamental thesis is that the law, and only the law, endows desire with an autonomy sufficient for the subject of this desire, from the perspective of that autonomy, to come to occupy the place of the dead."[40] Badiou underlines here the exact admixture of animation and constriction that I have been attending to under a variety of headings throughout this book: "The law is what *gives life* to desire. But in so doing, it *constrains* the subject so that he wants to follow only the path of death" (79; my emphasis). We are back, in other words, at the notion of a form of exposure that both intensifies and constrains life:

What is sin exactly? It is not desire as such, for if it were one would not understand its link to the law and death. *Sin is the life of desire as autonomy, as automatism.* The law is required in order to unleash the automatic life of desire, the automatism of repetition. For only the law *fixes* the object of desire,

40. Alain Badiou, *Saint Paul: The Foundation of Universalism,* trans. Ray Brassier (Stanford: Stanford University Press, 2003), 79. Subsequent references will be made in the text.

binding desire to it regardless of the subject's "will." It is this objectal automatism of desire, inconceivable without the law, that assigns the subject to the carnal path of death. (79)

It is, in this view, the fixity of drive destiny manifest in the compulsion to repeat that is at issue in Paul's understanding of creaturely "flesh," "sin," and "death." For Paul, the glad tidings of the Christ-event are just this: It is possible, thanks to grace, to unplug from this destiny, to intervene into creaturely life and the processes of its production. What is at stake in the Pauline notion of resurrection, of the overcoming of death, is in other words not some phantasmal reanimation of the dead but the possibility of a deanimation of the undeadness that makes creatures of us all.[41]

## VII

In his own recent commentary on Paul's letters, Agamben has persuasively argued that Benjamin's theses "On the Concept of History" are deeply Pauline in their terminology and conceptualization of messianic time.[42] Agamben argues, in effect, that in his theses Benjamin engaged in the practice of unmarked citation he had proposed as the methodological principle of his *Arcades Project* (for Benjamin, it is Luther's translation of Paul that is at issue). Thus Benjamin's invocation of a "weak Messianic force" (*eine schwache messianische Kraft*) is read as an allusion to 2 Corinthians 12 : 9–10, where Paul speaks of the messianic power finding its fulfillment in weakness (Luther's translation reads, *denn meine Kraft ist in den Schwachen mächtig*). The phrase

41. In this context we might recall Benjamin's claim in "The Storyteller" that Leskov understood the Resurrection "less as a transfiguration than as a disenchantment" (158) as well as Adorno's remark, in his "Notes on Kafka," suggesting that an understanding of figures like the hunter Gracchus—figures who are unable to die—may one day provide a key to Kafka's work (263).
42. See Giorgio Agamben, *Le temps qui reste*, trans. Judith Revel (Paris: Bibliothèque Rivages, 2000). In this Agamben is following the lead of Jacob Taubes, who had already suggested a strong link between Benjamin and Paul. See Taubes, *The Political Theology of Paul*, trans. Dana Hollander (Stanford: Stanford University Press, 2004).

appears in a passage that addresses the possibility not so much of discovering in the past resources for working through crises in the present as discovering in the present a new legibility of the past that in some sense redeems it:

There is happiness—such as could arouse envy in us—only in the air we have breathed, among people we could have talked to, women who could have given themselves to us. In other words, the idea of happiness is indissolubly bound up with the idea of redemption. The same applies to the idea of the past, which is the concern of history. The past carries with it a secret index by which it is referred to redemption. Doesn't a breath of the air that pervaded earlier days caress us as well? In the voices we hear, isn't there an echo of now silent ones? Don't the women we court have sisters they no longer recognize? If so, then there is a secret agreement between past generations and the present one. Then our coming was expected on earth. Then, like every generation that preceded us, we have been endowed with a *weak* messianic power, a power on which the past has a claim.[43]

In Benjamin's Kafka essay, this weak messianic power is, so to speak, brought to bear on the figure whose emblematic cringe—the signature of his creaturely life—we have been tracking throughout this book: *das bucklicht Männlein,* the hunchback. Let me cite this remarkable passage once more: "This little man is at home in distorted life [*des entstellten Lebens*]; he will disappear with the coming of the Messiah, who (a great rabbi once said) will not wish to change the world by force but will merely make a slight adjustment in it [*nur um ein Geringes sie zurechtstellen werde*]."[44] Before we address head on the presence or absence of a messianic force, weak or otherwise, in Sebald's writings, I would like to note some further echoes of Benjamin's language in the novelist's work.

---

43. Walter Benjamin, "On the Concept of History," trans. Harry Zohn, in *Walter Benjamin: Selected Writings,* vol. 4, *1938–40,* ed. Howard Eiland and Michael W. Jennings (Cambridge: Harvard University Press, 2003), 389–90.
44. Walter Benjamin, "Franz Kafka: On the Tenth Anniversary of His Death," trans. Harry Zohn, in *Selected Writings,* 2:811. In *After Nature,* Sebald speaks of the deformation/distortion of life in Grünewald's late work: "The deformation of life slowly proceeds" (*Die Entstellung des Lebens geht langsam vonstatten*) (36/32).

Kafka suggests that the fate of the hunter Gracchus was the consequence of a brief lapse of attention: "My death ship lost its way; a
wrong turn of the wheel, a moment's absence of mind [*ein Augenblick
der Unaufmerksamkeit*] on the pilot's part, the distraction of my lovely
native country."[45] The "slight adjustment" introduced by the
Messiah might thus be thought as a correction to the absence of mind
that culminates in Gracchus's undeadness, as a shift of optics, the assumption of a new perspective or mode of attention. And indeed, almost immediately after the remark about the Messiah, Benjamin addresses the quasi-religious status of attentiveness in Kafka's work. The
passage in question is already familiar to us: "Even if Kafka did not
pray—and this we do not know—he still possessed in the highest degree what Malebranche called 'the natural prayer of the soul': attentiveness [*Aufmerksamkeit*]. And in this attentiveness he included all
creatures, as saints include them in their prayers."[46]

In *Vertigo*, the work that is, as we have seen, most deeply haunted
by Gracchus, a series of passages point to the slight displacements
in human life that somehow change everything. After arriving in
Venice, the narrator of "All' estero" wanders through this most
haunted of European cities—one of the first things he sees is the
ghost of King Ludwig II of Bavaria—and finally settles down in a bar
where he leafs through a copy of Grillparzer's *Italian Diary* that he
purchased in Vienna. Aside from Grillparzer's general dissatisfaction
with the city, what strikes the narrator most is a series of remarks the
Austrian writer makes apropos of the doge's palace, which he refers to
as "an enigma in stone": "The nature of that enigma was apparently
dread, and for as long as he was in Venice Grillparzer could not shake
off a sense of the uncanny. Trained in the law himself, he dwelt on that
palace where the legal authorities resided and in the inmost cavern of
which, as he put it, the Invisible Principle brooded" (54/65).

The Kafkan flavor of these reflections finds an echo in Austerlitz's
description of the inner architecture of the Palace of Justice in
Brussels: "This huge pile of over seven hundred thousand cubic meters

45. Kafka, *Complete Stories*, 228.
46. Benjamin, "Kafka," 812.

contains corridors and stairways leading nowhere, and doorless rooms and halls where no one would ever set foot, empty spaces surrounded by walls and *representing the innermost secret of all sanctioned authority*" (29/43; my emphasis).[47]

Among the victims of such power and authority—among those who, as it were, had most intimate contact with this "invisible principle"—Grillparzer mentions Giacomo Casanova, whose account of imprisonment by and escape from the Venetian authorities was, as the narrator notes, first published in Prague. Reflecting on the point at which depression and physical pain merge into a single sensation of pure, creaturely life, Casanova writes that "while it might be rare for a man to be driven insane, little was required to tip the balance. All that was needed was a slight shift, and nothing would be as it formerly was" (*Es bedarf nur einer geringfügigen Verschiebung, und nichts mehr ist, was es war*) (56/68).[48] In this context we might also recall Jacques Austerlitz's remark on the crucial shifts in the directions of one's life: "We take almost all of the decisive steps in our lives as a result of slight inner adjustments of which we are barely conscious" (*Austerlitz*, 134/193). Austerlitz makes this remark in regard to his decision to follow the porter into the Ladies' Waiting Room at Liverpool Street Station, a decision that inaugurated the long and arduous process of "self-analysis" that would indeed change the direction of his life.

VIII

If I am right that Sebald's work is, at its core, an ingenious literary project aimed at grasping the creaturely dimension that persists in the

47. The word Sebald favors to characterize such spaces is "extraterritorial." He uses it, for example, to capture the peculiar ethicopolitical topology of Terezín, the place where, to use Agamben's formulation, the state of exception had become the norm (see *Austerlitz*, 236/335). In *The Rings of Saturn*, the word is used to characterize the peculiar status of an immigrant neighborhood in The Hague as well as an abandoned military installation from the Cold War period (82/101, 233/278).

48. Casanova is recalling here the point during his imprisonment when "melancholy had him in its grip and would not let go. The dog days came. The sweat ran down him. For two weeks he did not move his bowels. When at last the stone-hard excrement was passed, he thought the pain would kill him" (56/68). In this instance, we might say that the sensation of creaturely life arises at the point of intersection between the "enigma in stone" and the "stone-hard excrement."

midst of our lives now (though for the most part in the mode of forgetting), the question remains whether his approach leaves open *a way out,* a way of intervening into this dimension that otherwise seems to foreclose the possibility of new possibilities for collective life.[49] One thing is certain. Sebald is utterly uninterested in what we might call the "new age" solutions to the dilemma, that is, the various therapies and techniques that proliferate throughout contemporary culture for reducing stress, enhancing well-being, and optimizing the pleasure/reality principle—in a word, for *soothing* the agitations of creaturely life. The relevant question with respect to Sebald is whether his way of constructing our historical situation leaves open the possibility of an event, a radical shift of perspective whereby something genuinely new could emerge. Is there really a place for the "weak messianic power" in Sebald's universe, or does the very way he constructs our situation—a construction that delivers, of course, a substantial degree of readerly pleasure—foreclose such an opening? Or to return to Judith Ryan's question about Sebald, does the fact of the Holocaust definitively undo, for Sebald, the possibility of breakthrough because it is branded in advance as either hopeless or, even worse, *dangerous*?[50]

In his essay on Paul, Badiou formulates this question in somewhat different though related terms. There Badiou expresses profound skepticism about the postmodern obsession with memory, an obsession that at least at first glance Sebald seems to embody as no other.

---

49. As Benjamin put it apropos of the remembrance and forgetting of this dimension in Kafka: "Kafka did not consider the age in which he lived as an advance over the beginnings of time. His novels are set in a swamp world. In his works, the creature [*die Kreatur*] appears at the stage which Bachofen has termed the hetaeric stage. The fact that this stage is now forgotten does not mean that is does not extend into the present. On the contrary: it is present by virtue of this very oblivion. An experience deeper than that of the average person can make contact with it" (Benjamin, *Selected Writings,* 2:808–9).
50. Already Thomas Mann, in *Doktor Faustus,* aroused our suspicion that any longing for breakthrough—aesthetic, moral, political—is always already caught up in the totalitarian temptation. More recently, Slavoj Žižek has repeatedly warned about the ideological uses of such suspicions and anxieties: "Today, reference to the 'totalitarian' threat sustains a kind of unwritten *Denkverbot.* . . . [T]he moment one shows the slightest inclination to engage in political projects that aim seriously to challenge the existing order, the answer is immediately: 'Benevolent as it is, this will necessarily end in a new Gulag!'" Žižek, *Did Somebody Say Totalitarianism? Five Interventions in the (Mis)Use of a Notion* (London: Verso, 2001), 3–4.

Indeed, he presents his study of Paul as a countermeasure to this very obsession. "At a time," he writes, "when the importance of 'memory' as the guardian of meaning and of historical consciousness as a substitute for politics is being urged on us from all sides, the strength of Paul's position cannot fail to escape us."[51] What Badiou means is that memory, as he puts it, "cannot settle any issue. There eventually comes a moment when what matters is to declare in one's own name that what took place took place, and to do so because what one envisages with regard to the *actual* possibilities of a situation requires it."[52] With regard to Paul, Badiou writes that "the interest of Christ's resurrection does not lie in itself, as it would in the case of a particular, or miraculous, fact. Its genuine meaning is that it testifies to the possible victory over death, a death that Paul envisages . . . not in terms of facticity, but in terms of a subjective disposition."[53] Our question is, then, whether Sebald's world leaves any opening for such a shift in subjective dispositions. Is there a conception, in his work, of what it might mean to suspend our bondage to *Naturgeschichte*? Or is Sebaldian jouissance so thoroughly tied up with the sex appeal of decay, so addicted to dust, ash, and bones, that there is no longer even a desire for a way out?[54]

The first thing to say in response to such questions is that Sebald's project is above all a literary one, not a political or even an ethical one in any straightforward sense. Whatever he achieves unfolds within the framework of an aesthetic experience that, though it may have political, ethical, and even religious meanings and consequences, is an

---

51. Badiou, *Saint Paul,* 44.

52. Ibid., 44.

53. Ibid., 45. We might think of such a disposition as a failure to separate, to even grasp the possibility of a separation, from the cringe of creaturely life.

54. My question is the very one that Terry Eagleton raises concerning Benjamin. According to Eagleton, Benjamin's work leaves three options available to modernity: to regress to an imaginary past; "to remain disconsolately marooned in the symbolic order, like all those melacholiasts from the *Trauerspiel* to the *Fleurs du Mal,* therapeutically demystified but to the same degree impotent"; and finally, what Eagleton characterizes as Benjamin's own option, "for which the second is a *sine qua non* yet with which it forms no obvious continuum. This is to re-channel desire from both past and present to the future: to detect in the decline of the aura the form of new social and libidinal relations, realizable by revolutionary practice." Terry Eagleton, *Walter Benjamin, or Towards a Revolutionary Criticism* (London: Verso, 1985), 42.

"intervention" in the world in only a very limited and particular sense. But even given the framework of expectations and possibilities proper to a literary artifact and its modes of reception in contemporary Western societies, the question remains of the ways the work opens or closes, energizes or depletes, our capacity *to imagine* new ways of being in the midst of life. Here I would say that Sebald indeed makes a number of rather significant contributions that help us to think more deeply about the relation between the saturnine immersion in the creaturely and the domain of ethical and political acts.

The first thing to emphasize in this context is the ubiquitous role of chance and coincidence in Sebald's writings. They contain numerous passages noting odd coincidences concerning dates of birth or parallel experiences across space and time. When, for example, the narrator in *The Rings of Saturn* visits the writer and translator Michael Hamburger, he becomes so preoccupied with the strange parallels in their lives that he loses a sense of the boundaries between them. The narrator notes, among other things, that both had known a certain Stanley Kerry at different, though somehow parallel, points in their lives:

When I now think back to Stanley Kerry, it seems incomprehensible that the paths of Michael's life and mine should have intersected in the person of that extraordinarily shy man, and that at the time we met him, in 1944 and in 1966 respectively, we were both twenty-two. No matter how often I tell myself that chance happenings of this kind occur far more often than we suspect, since we all move, one after the other, along the same roads mapped out for us by our origins and our hopes, my rational mind is nonetheless unable to lay the ghosts of repetition that haunt me with ever greater frequency. (187/223)[55]

---

55. I might add to this an autobiographical detail. The narrator visits Hamburger in the village of Middleton, which happens to be the name of another distinguished British Hölderlin translator and poet—Christopher Middleton. Middleton supervised my dissertation on Hölderlin at the University of Texas at Austin in the early 1980s, a project that led to my role as editor of a new edition of Hölderlin's poetry in English. In the course of that project I corresponded with Michael Hamburger regarding some translations I reprinted in my edition. At the University of Chicago, an endowment left by Hildegard Romberg allowed the Department of Germanic Studies to bring Sebald to Chicago in 1999 to read from *The Emigrants;* in 2004 I was named the Romberg Professor in Modern Germanic Studies at Chicago.

The role of chance and coincidence becomes absolutely central in Sebald's final novel, *Austerlitz,* where the chance meetings between the narrator and Austerlitz accumulate to such a degree that the documentary pretense of the novel actually becomes attenuated. More significantly, one of the most important events in Austerlitz's life—his entering the Ladies' Waiting Room at Liverpool Street Station—is presented as a chance occurrence (it is there that he begins the process of "recovered memory" that will determine the trajectory of the rest of his life). At the end of his account of the experience, reflecting on the vague memory of losing his native tongue after arriving in England, he remarks to the narrator, "And certainly the words I had forgotten in a short space of time, and all that went with them, would have remained buried in the depths of my mind had I not, through a series of coincidences, entered the old waiting room in Liverpool Street Station that Sunday morning, a few weeks at the most before it vanished for ever in the rebuilding" (138/199).

In his speculations on human happiness and, more specifically, on what it means, in psychoanalytic terms, to catch a lucky break in life, Jonathan Lear comes close, I think, to capturing the dynamic of at least certain experiences of chance in Sebald's work. Such breaks, are, as Lear puts it, a sort of "existential sabbath," "an occasion for opening up new possibilities, possibilities not included in any established structures." Happiness, Lear suggests, arrives when it becomes possible to appropriate the "possibilities for new possibilities" that are, as he puts it, "breaking out all the time":

But if psychoanalysis lies outside the ethical [that is: addresses the *meta*ethical self; ELS], how does it promote happiness? Here we need to go back to an older English usage of happiness in terms of happenstance: the experience of chance things working out well rather than badly. Happiness, on this interpretation, is not the ultimate goal of our teleologically organized strivings—but the ultimate ateleological moment: a chance event going well for us. Quite literally: a lucky break. *Analysis puts us in a position* to take advantage of certain kinds of chance occurrences: those breaks in psychological structure which are caused by too much of too much. This isn't a teleological occurrence, but a taking-advantage of the disruption of previous attempts to construct a teleology. If one thinks about it . . . one will see that it is in such fleeting moments that we find real happiness.[56]

In this context, it is significant that the path that opens up for Austerlitz by way of his coming upon the Ladies' Waiting Room at Liverpool Street Station is one that seems to include, perhaps for the first time since early childhood, the opening to the possibility, tenuous though it may be, of *love*.[57] When Austerlitz parts from the narrator for the last time, he says to him, "I am going to continue looking for my father, and for Marie de Verneuil as well" (292/410). The connection between the two events—the chance opening to his own past and the possibility of love—is made explicit by Austerlitz himself during his reflections on his experience in the Ladies' Waiting Room. In the course of his experience there, he says, "scraps of memory [began to] drift through the outlying regions of my mind: images, for instance, like the recollection of a late November afternoon in 1968 when I stood with Marie de Verneuil . . . when we stood in the nave of the wonderful church of Salle in Norfolk . . . and I could not bring out the words I should have spoken then" (136/196). What is at stake here is, I think, precisely what Benjamin had in mind when he spoke about the difference between historical knowledge and the form of remembrance he calls *Eingedenken*. "History is not simply a science but also and not least a form of remembrance [*Eingedenken*]. What science has 'determined,' remembrance can modify. Such mindfulness can make the incomplete (happiness) into something complete, and the complete (suffering) into something

56. Jonathan Lear, *Happiness, Death, and the Remainder of Life* (Cambridge: Harvard University Press, 2000), 129; my emphasis.
57. Concerning the notion of adding new possibilities to one's life, Lear writes, "The possibility for new possibilities is not an addition of a special possibility to the world; it is an alteration in the world of possibilities." Jonathan Lear, *Therapeutic Action: An Earnest Plea for Irony* (New York: Other Press, 2003), 204.

incomplete."[58] The missed opportunity of 1968—this fly in the amber of Austerlitz's past—persists as a symptom that begins to mutate after the experience at the Liverpool Street Station. What is clear, however, is that the actualization of the missed opportunity—the decision to look for Marie—becomes possible only by way of the special sort of relationship Austerlitz has developed with the narrator. This becomes explicit immediately after Austerlitz announces his decision, for that is the moment when he gives the narrator the key to his apartment, inviting him to study his collection of photographs—the very ones that (we are to assume) fill the pages of *Austerlitz*. The crucial dimension of the relationship, the one that places Austerlitz in a position to "own" the chance disruption of his drive destiny—to become uncringed, as it were—is, then, that of *testimony* and *transmission*.

When Lear claims that analysis can put us in a position to make use of breaks in psychic structure, to transform such breaks into the "slight adjustment" with which Benjamin associates the messianic unburdening of our hunched backs, it is crucial to remember that the analyst is *not* simply another human being we talk to, get advice from, bounce ideas off, a person whose empathy we enjoy. The analyst is a kind of nonhuman partner with whom a new sort of relationship takes shape—a new kind of social link. What is at stake in analysis is, I have been arguing, not so much human as *creaturely* expressivity. The Sebaldian narrator-witness-listener establishes bonds with his "informants" in ways that stand in a family resemblance to the social link elaborated in analysis.[59]

58. Walter Benjamin, *The Arcades Project,* trans. Howard Eiland and Kevin McLaughlin (Cambridge: Harvard University Press, 1999), 471. Regarding this understanding of remembrance that, according to Agamben, goes back to some early reflections Scholem shared with his friend on the verb forms of Hebrew (where one finds the aspects of accomplished vs. unaccomplished rather than the tenses of past and future), Agamben writes that it perfectly captures the essence of the typological relation in Paul: "It is a field of tension in which the two times enter into a constellation which the apostle calls *ho nun kairos,* where the past (the complete) again finds its actuality and becomes incomplete, while the present (the incomplete) acquires a sort of completeness or fulfillment" (*Temps,* 124).

59. At the conclusion of an essay on Kafka, Mladen Dolar suggests that the most promising "line of flight" out of one's subjection to creaturely life is presented in one of

Another way to approach the status of chance in Sebald's work is to recall Benjamin's reflections on what is no doubt the crucial literary model for the aleatory dimension of Sebaldian anamnesis: Proust's poetics of involuntary memory. Benjamin argues that the very massiveness of Proust's project demonstrates the enormous efforts required, under conditions of modernity, to mobilize the mnemonic resources of storytelling. "From the outset," Benjamin writes, the effort to do so "involved him [Proust] in a fundamental problem: reporting on his own childhood. In saying *that it was a matter of chance* whether the problem could be solved at all, he took the measure of its difficulties" (my emphasis). It was, Benjamin adds, in the context of these difficulties that Proust came up with the notion of *mémoire involontaire*. "This concept bears the traces of the situation that engendered it; it is part of the inventory of the individual who is isolated in various

---

Kafka's most difficult prose texts, "Investigations of a Dog," written two years before the author's death. In a final twist of this enigmatic story, the research of the narrator-canine turns toward the possibility of a new science, indeed an ultimate science, *eine allerletzte Wissenschaft,* that concerns itself with the sources of nourishment as well as with the sources of the voice, with pure immanence as well as with pure transcendence. "A border region between these two sciences . . . had already attracted my attention. I mean the theory of incantation, by which food is called down." Cited in Mladen Dolar, "Kafka's Immanence, Kafka's Transcendence," in *Transcendence: Philosophy, Literature, and Theology Approach the Beyond,* ed. Regina Schwarz (New York: Routledge, 2004), 191. Dolar suggests that this intersection of food and voice, nourishment and song, points to the dimension of the *drive* in Freud: "By speech [the] mouth is de-naturalized, diverted from its natural function, seized by the signifier (and for our purposes, by the voice which is but the alterity of the signifier). The Freudian name for this deterritorialization is the drive" (192). That is to say, the mouth itself becomes the rim or threshold of a zone of exception, is made into an organ of creaturely life. What Kafka's story suggests, however, is that it is precisely the "science" of such thresholds that holds the promise of a kind of freedom: "Freedom! Certainly such freedom as is possible today is a wretched business. But nevertheless freedom, nevertheless a possession" (cited in Dolar, 192). As Dolar concludes his essay: "The freedom that might not look like much, that might actually look wretched, but is there at all points, and once we spot it there is no way of going away from it, it is a possession to hold on to, it is a permanent line of flight, or rather the line of pursuit. And there is the slogan, the program of a new science which would be able to treat it, to take it as its object, to pursue it, the ultimate science, the science of freedom. Kafka lacks the proper word for it, he cannot name it, this is 1922, but he would only have to look around, to examine the ranks of his fellow Jewish Austrian compatriots. Of course, psychoanalysis" (193).

ways." What has been lost in Proust's—and Sebald's—universe is the regular *synchronizing* of individual and collective occasions of remembrance that define the liturgical time of the religious calendar:

> Where there is experience (*Erfahrung*) in the strict sense of the word, certain contents of the individual past combine in the memory (*Gedächtnis*) with material from the collective past. Rituals, with their ceremonies and festivals (probably nowhere recalled in Proust's work), kept producing the amalgamation of these two elements of memory over and over again. They triggered recollection (*Eingedenken*) at certain times and remained available to memory throughout people's lives. In this way, voluntary and involuntary recollection cease to be mutually exclusive.[60]

The question raised by all of Benjamin's work pertains to the possibility of actively mobilizing the resources of remembrance in a post-Proustian world without direct or immediate recourse to the language and structures of religious life. And once again, what is at stake in such a mobilization is above all the possibility of suspending that dimension of our lives where we are delivered over to our creatureliness.

It would, I think, be fair to say that Sebald has radicalized the Proustian model according to which any such mobilization retains its dependence on chance. There seems little prospect, hope, or even desire in Sebald's world for any sort of synchronizing of individual and collective remembrance. What remains, however, is the literary project itself and its own precarious capacity to establish communities of readers reflecting on the very dispersion that keeps them isolated from one another. More than that, Sebald's multiple portrayals of acts of testimony and transmission—in their very dependence on chance—leave us, I think, rather more open to the possibility of an encounter and engagement with the creaturely dimension of our

---

60. Benjamin, "On Some Motifs in Baudelaire," trans. Harry Zohn, in *Selected Writings*, 4:316. In the final part of *The Star of Redemption*, Rosenzweig addresses the different ways Judaism and Christianity undertake to synchronize occasions of *Eingedenken*.

neighbor. This is, then, not so much a substitution of memory-work for politics as it is the imaginative construction of the kind of sites where such encounters might take place; it is furthermore an ambitious and exemplary performance of the specific sorts of *labor*—of *study*—involved in sustaining fidelity to such encounters. If I might put it that way, love of neighbor is, for Sebald, among other things, a kind of ongoing research project.

# On the Sexual Lives of
# Creatures and Other Matters

I would like to address a series of further important themes and aspects of Sebald's writings, only some of which seem at first glance to belong in any manifest way to the topic of creatureliness. Perhaps the most obvious materials that I have until now touched upon only in passing are Sebald's numerous descriptions of animals. In the previous chapter I noted Gerald's great-uncle Alphonso's claim "that all mankind's misfortunes were connected with its departure at some point in time from that norm [of animal temperature] and with the slightly feverish, overheated condition in which we constantly found ourselves" (*Austerlitz*, 92/134–35). Sebald's writings contain numerous descriptions of animals that have been forcibly drawn into this overheated condition and that themselves come to display the imbalance, the surplus animation, here associated with humankind. The paradox at work here is that only animals that have been "deterritorialized," removed from their natural habitat, become creatures in the sense I have been elaborating. In a word, we get a glimpse of creaturely life not by seeing or imagining animals in "the open" but by observing them in various states of *disorientation* (these are, we might say, animals whose *instincts* have mutated into *drives*). What I have been calling creaturely life, then, does indeed mark our resemblance to animals, but precisely to animals who have themselves been thrown off the rails of their nature.

One thinks, for example, of the narrator's description of the Nocturama in *Austerlitz*. Recalling his first visit to this exhibition of nocturnal animals in Antwerp in the late 1960s, he remembers above all a remarkable display of repetition compulsion by a raccoon:

The only animal which has remained lingering in my memory is the raccoon. I watched it for a long time as it sat beside a little stream with a serious expression on its face, washing the same piece of apple over and over again, as if it hoped that all this washing, which went far beyond any reasonable thoroughness, would help it to escape the unreal world in which it had arrived, so to speak, through no fault of its own. (4/6–7)[1]

He further recalls that several of the animals in the exhibition "had strikingly large eyes, and the fixed, inquiring gaze found in certain painters and philosophers who seek to penetrate the darkness which surrounds us purely by means of looking and thinking" (5/7). The text includes photographs of two pairs of animal eyes—apparently of different kinds of owls—and of two pairs of human eyes, one of which is immediately recognizable as belonging to Ludwig Wittgenstein.[2]

1. One is perhaps reminded here of the first sentence of Kafka's *The Trial,* which states that Josef K. was arrested through no fault of his own (*ohne daß er etwas Böses getan hätte*).
2. Later in the novel, recalling his chance meeting with Austerlitz twenty years after their initial contact, the narrator writes, "Before approaching him I had been thinking at some length about his personal similarity to Ludwig Wittgenstein, and the horror-stricken expressions on both their faces" (40/58). In *The Emigrants,* Max Ferber tells the narrator that when he first arrived in Manchester he lived in "the selfsame house where Ludwig Wittgenstein, then a twenty-year-old engineering student, had lived in 1908." He goes to reflect that even though any connection with Wittgenstein was purely illusory, "it meant no less to him on that account. Indeed, he sometimes felt as if he were

It is as if each pair of eyes were staring out into that opacity the exposure to which produces what Heidegger had referred to as the essential disruption (*wesenhafte Erschütterung*) that brings animals and humans into an uncanny proximity.

Later in the novel, recalling his visit to Marienbad with Marie de Verneuil in 1972, Austerlitz relates how Marie had tried to alert him to his precarious mental equilibrium by telling the story of Schumann's descent into madness. Austerlitz's reflections are immediately drawn to the zone of this "natural historical" proximity:

As I listened to Marie and tried to imagine poor Schumann in his Bad Godesberg cell I had another picture constantly before my eyes, that of the pigeon loft we had passed on an excursion to Königswart. Like the country estate to which it belonged, this dovecote, which may have dated from the Metternich period, was in an advanced state of decay. The floor inside the brick walls was covered with pigeon droppings compressed under their own weight, yet already over two feet high, a hard, desiccated mass on which lay the bodies of some of the birds who had fallen from their niches, mortally sick, while their companions, surviving in a kind of senile dementia, cooed at one another in tones of quiet complaint in the darkness under the roof. (214/306)

Austerlitz goes on to say that "the torment inherent in both of these images . . . the mad Schumann and the pigeons immured in that place of horror, made it impossible for me to attain even the lowest step on the way to self-knowledge" (214–15/306). Austerlitz's inability to grasp his own implication in the dimension of creaturely life here manifest at the intersection of human and animal dementia is, at some level, noted in the following sentence in which he recalls that on the

---

tightening his ties to those who had gone before" (166/247–48). The other pair of eyes placed just above those of Wittgenstein belongs to the painter Jan Peter Tripp. One of Sebald's final projects, published posthumously, was a collaboration with Tripp consisting of a series of photorealist drawings of eyes of various writers, artists, and friends accompanied by short lyrical texts by Sebald: *Unerzählt* (Munich: Hanser, 2003). The link between the eyes of the owls and those of Tripp and Wittgenstein is conveyed by the German word *Kauz,* which denotes various kinds of owls as well as a strange, eccentric human being.

final days of their visit to Marienbad he and Marie "walked through the park and down to the Auschowitz Springs" (215/306), a clear allusion to the site that was designed to reduce human life to its creaturely minimum.

In *The Rings of Saturn,* we find another reference to demented birds. In the course of his extended account of the history of the country manor, Somerleyton Hall, the narrator first expresses the peculiar satisfaction he feels at the estate's decay ("How fine a place the house seemed to me now that it was imperceptibly nearing the brink of dissolution and silent oblivion") before noting the presence of a lone creaturely survivor portrayed in the accompanying photograph: "However, on emerging into the open air again, I was saddened to see, in one of the otherwise deserted aviaries, a solitary Chinese quail, evidently in a state of dementia, running to and fro along the edge of the cage and shaking its head every time it was about to turn, as if it could not comprehend how it had got into this hopeless fix" (36/50). In these and numerous other instances, Sebald draws us into the dimension of creaturely life by emphasizing a zone of "uncanny proximity" between animal and human life, one that takes shape at the point where both are in some fashion abandoned to a state of exception.

II

Against this background, it makes sense that the question of humor in Sebald's work has been little discussed in the critical literature. One rightly wonders whether there is room for humor in the bleak world of historical suffering his work seems to live and breathe. It is almost as if one were to ask whether Benjamin's angel of history was capable of a good laugh amid all that wreckage piling up before his eyes. But given the deep affinities we have observed between Sebald's work and that of Kafka, a writer with a considerable, if unusual, sense of humor, one might be prepared for encountering humor in Sebald as well. My sense is that it is at just those points of creatureliness I have been trying to isolate that Sebaldian humor arises; these are the points where the *nonsensical* aspect of what I have referred to as "signifying stress" becomes manifest to us, the point where we catch a glimpse of the mechanical stupidity of our jouissance, the very "Thing" that matters most to us. Here is one brief example to illustrate this strange feature where the point of greatest melancholy can become an occasion of laughter.

In the seventh chapter of *The Rings of Saturn,* the narrator recalls an earlier visit to Ireland during which he had occasion to live, very briefly, in the home of a Mrs. Ashbury and her four grown children. The Ashburys were among the last remnants of a British landowning class in Ireland whose impoverishment in the wake of the civil war left them in a state "like refugees who have come through dreadful ordeals and do not now dare to settle in the place where they have ended up" (210/250). We find the familiar Sebaldian motifs of *Naturgeschichte,* of a historical form of life succumbing to "natural" decay and decomposition: crumbling houses, rotting wood, walls stripped of paper "which had traces of whitewash with bluish streaks like the skin of a dying body" (210/251). In a certain sense, that is just what natural history means for Sebald: a form of life becoming manifest as a decomposing corpse. But in the midst of all this decay, the behavior of the "survivors," in this case Mrs. Ashbury and her children, assumes an aspect of utter and nonsensical purposelessness—of repetition compulsion as a weird sort of *comedy.* Edmund, the youngest of the Ashbury children, has spent years working on a boat that will never sail: "As he casually informed me, he knew nothing about boat-building and had no intention of ever going to sea in his unshapely barge. It's not going be launched. It's just something I do. I have to have something to do" (211/251). The three daughters, Catherine, Clarissa, and Christina, sew together vast quantities of fabric remnants and then take them apart, "like children under an evil spell" (212/252). At one point the daughters considered starting an interior decorating business, "but the plan came to nothing . . . both because of their inexperience and because there was no call in their neighborhood for such a service" (212/252). Mrs. Ashbury's main occupation was to collect flower seeds in paper bags that she would label, attach to the dead heads of the blooms, and hang from strings crisscrossing the library. Given the recurrence of the motif in the novel, it comes as no surprise that the family had also, at one time, considered raising silkworms. And of course the narrator turns out to have been the only guest at this "bed and breakfast" in the ten years of its existence. Sebald not surprisingly characterizes the meaningless and aimless aspect of the "work" the Ashburys perform as "an expression of a deeply engrained distress" (211/251). Nonetheless, it is in the absurd expressivity of this distress that Sebaldian humor emerges. To put it somewhat differently, it is precisely through the meaninglessness of their activity that the creaturely stuckness of the Ashburys becomes palpable, that their teleological strivings become manifest as nonsensical, as a parody and thus as a potential disruption of teleological activity—as the *stuff* of a lucky break, even if the Ashburys themselves are in no position to take advantage of it.

### III

Another feature of Sebald's work that I have thus far pushed to the margins, indeed the aspect of the work that has been recognized as a kind of Sebaldian signature, is the author's use of images and, above all, photography in his books. In his first literary work, the narrative prose poem *After Nature,* Sebald includes no photographs or reproductions of paintings. The poem does, however, contain numerous ekphrastic passages that underline the centrality of images for Sebald's project. The mode of attentiveness that I have placed at the heart of his enterprise clearly includes, quite literally, the practice of *looking*. In the first "canto" of the last, largely autobiographical section of the poem, Sebald describes two photographs that figure in his attempt to reconstruct his own origins. The first image is a class photograph from 1917 that includes one of the narrator's parents, who "stares out fearfully" among "forty-eight / pitiable coevals"; on the back of the photograph the narrator reads the words, "'In the future / death lies at our feet,'" calling this "one of those obscure oracular sayings / one never again forgets" (84/72).[3]

---

3. The German word translated as "coevals" is *Artgenossen,* signifying membership in the same species; the word choice thus emphasizes the dimension of biological life and, therewith, subjection to death. Here one might recall that other oracular pronouncement

The second photograph shows a peaceful scene from a botanical garden taken on August 26, 1943, and includes

Mother in her open coat,
with a lightness she was later to lose; Father,
a little aside, hands in his pockets,
he too, it seems, with no cares. (85/73)

The narrator goes on to link the apparent equipoise of the scene to a blindness—at least with respect to what is retained in memory—to extremes of both beauty and horror:

On the 27th Father's departure for Dresden,
of whose beauty his memory, as he
remarks when I question him,
retains no trace.
During the night of the 28th
528 aircraft flew in
to attack Nürnberg. Mother,
who on the next day planned
to return to her parents'
home in the Alps,
got no further than
Fürth. From there she
saw Nürnberg in flames,
but cannot recall now
what the burning town looked like

---

from the story about Paul Bereyter in *The Emigrants,* a story that itself includes two class photographs, one of Paul's class at his teacher training college and one said to be from the narrator's own childhood. After Paul's suicide on the railroad tracks, his friend Mme Landau recalls Paul's having told her that as a child his uncle had remarked concerning his nephew's obsession with trains that "he would end up on the railways" [*bei der Eisenbahn enden*] (62/92). It was precisely Mme Landau's failure to grasp the innocent meaning of the phrase—she commits a kind of auditory *Fehlleistung*—that led her to sense a dark foreboding in the words.

or what her feelings were
at this sight. (86/73–74)[4]

From these two brief descriptions, it is clear that the family photo album plays an important part in Sebald's project. Though only a relatively small number of the photographs reproduced in the books are taken from such albums—or rather, are presented as such—they play a greater role than many of the other photographs in the sense of providing rich occasions for narrative elaboration. This is clearly the case in the third story in *The Emigrants,* where the practice of going through old albums with one's relatives—typically of a different generation—not only is the occasion of storytelling but becomes itself an important site for one of the most important activities in Sebald's work: the transmission and negotiation of (family) history across various sorts of divides.[5]

---

4. This passage announces the topic that would preoccupy Sebald in the last work he published before his death, *On the Natural History of Destruction,* a series of lectures he first delivered in Zurich in 1997 on the failures of German authors to engage in any extended fashion with the trauma of Allied bombardments of German cities. In *The Rings of Saturn* Sebald returned to this topic, where he has a gardener at the once grand country estate Somerleyton Hall express his great disappointment at the paucity of literary representations of the aerial bombardment in Germany (the gardener's own obsession with the air war stems from having lived in the vicinity of one of the airfields from which the bomber squadrons departed): "At all events, ever since then I have tried to find out everything I could that was in any way connected with the war in the air. In the early Fifties, when I was in Lüneburg with the army of occupation, I even learnt German, after a fashion, so that I could read what the Germans themselves had said about the bombings and their lives in the ruined cities. To my astonishment, however, I soon found the search for such accounts invariably proved fruitless. No one at the time seemed to have written about their experiences or afterwards recorded their memories. Even if you asked people directly, it was as if everything had been erased from their minds" (39/53–54).

5. A "family album" that has clearly played a significant—perhaps even traumatic—part in Sebald's relationship to photographs is the one his father brought back from the Polish campaign of 1939. In the last section of *Vertigo,* "Il ritorno in patria," the narrator reproduces one of these photographs from a series showing "gypsies who had been rounded up and put in detention. They are looking out, smiling from behind the barbed wire, somewhere in a far corner of the Slovakia where my father . . . had been stationed for several weeks before the outbreak of war" (184–85/210). Next to the photograph one reads simply the word "gypsy" [*Zigeuner*] written, as the narrator says, in white ink.

And indeed, this practice of going through old albums, which Sebald places in the foreground of a number of sequences, can help us think about the status of photographs in his books more generally. My sense is that in one's engagement with the photographs in Sebald's work it is not especially productive to become overly preoccupied with the aesthetic quality of the photographs—typically quite poor—or the meaning of this or that photograph *for us,* the readers. First, one's "access" to the photographs is always mediated by the meanings of the images for particular figures in the texts (more often than not, the narrator); what is "for us" is not the photograph per se but the photograph qua photograph-for-someone. What we "see" is a photograph that forms a part of someone's life. This is most clearly and consistently the case in *Austerlitz,* where the photographs are by and large presented as taken—and obsessed over—by (the fictional character) Jacques Austerlitz. To put it more generally, what is at issue in Sebald's photographs is what we might call *our life with photographs,* the multiple ways they enter our lives—ways that have been and continue to be subject to radical historical shifts.

In interviews with critics, Sebald has offered a variety of hints about the nature of his own life with photographs. Apropos of his use of images in *Vertigo,* his first foray into this hybrid text-image genre, Sebald has said:

The process of writing, as I drifted into it, was in many instances occasioned by pictures that happened to come my way, that I stared at for long periods of time and that seemed to contain some enigmatic elements that I wanted to tease out. So they did form the instigation for trying to write this sort of thing. Because of that, they have kept their place. It eventually became some sort of habit, of including these pictures.

He goes on to note that photographs play a crucial role in his ambition "to produce the kind of prose which has a degree of muteness about it."[6] Such muteness is reinforced by the simple fact that the

6. Cited in James Wood, "An Interview with W. G. Sebald," in *Brick* 69 (Spring 2002): 87.

photographs interrupt the "noise" of the reading process, create breaks and pauses in the movement of narrative and descriptive language; we enter a zone of silence in which we continue to be engaged with the work though we are no longer reading, no longer inhabiting a strictly verbal universe.[7] In the same interview, Sebald emphasizes the element of chance in his relation to photographs, a dimension that intensifies what he characterizes as their ghostly dimension. Speaking about photographs taken when people had their pictures taken only a few times over the course of a lifetime, Sebald remarks that "they have something spectral about them":

It seems as if the people who appear in these pictures are kind of fuzzy on the edges, very much like ghosts. . . . It is this enigmatic quality which attracts me to these pictures. It's less a sense of nostalgia but [rather] that there is something utterly mysterious in old photographs, that they are almost destined to be lost, they're in an album which vanishes in an attic or in a box, and if they come to light they do accidentally, you stumble upon them. The way in which

---

7. In his study of Walter Benjamin's relationship with photography, Eduardo Cadava has argued that photography functions as a kind of allegory of Benjamin's mode of engagement with history more generally—of his Medusa's gaze on history, as Adorno once put it—one that assumes a variety of names over the course of Benjamin's career. Though I think Cadava blurs the boundaries between certain concepts—above all, between concepts pertaining to melancholy and those pertaining to the dimension of action—his insistence on the centrality of photography for Benjamin's mode of thinking and writing remains compelling. In each instance, the crucial dimension is that of *interruption*: "Like the stage setting that in Benjamin's *Trauerspiel* book names the spatial enclosing and freezing of history, photography names a process that, seizing and tearing an image from its context, works to immobilize the flow of history. . . . This moment of arrest is linked in Benjamin's thinking with what he sees in his essay on Goethe as the sudden emergence of the expressionless, in his 'Critique of Violence' as the interruptive character of the general strike, in his writings on Baudelaire as the petrified restlessness of the image, in his writings on the mimetic faculty as the flashlike perception of similarity, and in his 'Theses' as the messianic intervention into history. In each instance, Benjamin traces the effects of what he calls 'the caesura in the movement of thought.' This caesura—whose force of immobilization not only gives way to the appearance of an image but also intervenes in the linearity of history and politics—can be understood in relation to what we might call the photograph's Medusa effect." Eduardo Cadava, *Words of Light: Theses on the Photography of History* (Princeton: Princeton University Press, 1997), xx.

these stray pictures cross your paths, it has something at once totally coincidental and fateful about it.[8]

With the notion of spectrality we have returned once more to the double meaning of "medium" noted earlier. The photographic medium is privileged in this work at least in part because it seems to function as a unique locus of commerce with the dead (or rather, with the *undead*). As Roland Barthes has famously put it, "Photographs state the innocence, the vulnerability of lives heading toward their own destruction, and this link between photography and death haunts all photographs of people."[9] And in a set of reflections on the relations between photography and narration, John Berger, an author and critic whose work has much in common with Sebald's, inscribes this spectral dimension of the medium within a larger conception of the temporal rupture produced by every photograph:

Every photograph presents us with two messages: a message concerning the event photographed and another concerning a shock of discontinuity. . . .

8. Wood, "Interview," 90. Right after a series of reflections on the ghostly images in his adoptive father's photo album, Austerlitz recalls the figure of the cobbler, Evan, from his Welsh village, who was known for his traffic with ghosts. "At first glance," he recalls Evan's saying, "they seemed to be normal people, but when you looked more closely their faces would blur or flicker slightly at the edges" (54/78). In another interview, Sebald offers a variation on the theme of the chance encounter with the photograph: "I've always been interested in photographs, collected them, not systematically but randomly, whenever I came across one. As you know, photographs have something nomadic about them, they wander about and get lost for a while, somewhere in an attic, and then turn up again. And as they turn up, they have something of an appeal about them." Interview with Maya Jaggi in *In Other Words: The Journal for Literary Translators* 21 (Summer 2003): 13. Sebald has characterized the "call" emanating from certain photographs as an *ungeheuren Appel,* which can be translated as a "tremendous" or even "monstrous" call/appeal/demand. The phrase is cited in Heiner Boehncke, "Clair Obscur: W. G. Sebalds Bilder," in *Text + Kritik: Zeitschrift für Literatur,* vol. 158, *W. G. Sebald,* ed. Heinz Ludwig Arnold (Munich: Edition Text + Kritik, 2003), 51.
9. Roland Barthes, *Camera Lucida: Reflections on Photography,* trans. Richard Howard (New York: Hill and Wang, 1981), 70. At one point in his essay Barthes coins the term *spectrum* to denote the object or target of the photograph: "This word retains, through its root, a relation to 'spectacle' and adds to it that rather terrible thing which is there in every photograph: the return of the dead" (9).

Between the moment recorded and the present moment of looking at the photograph, there is an abyss. We are so used to photography that we no longer consciously register the second of these twin messages—except in special circumstances: when for example, the person photographed was familiar to us and is now far away or dead. In such circumstances the photograph is more traumatic than most memories or mementos because it seems to confirm, prophetically, the later discontinuity created by the absence or death.[10]

The twofold message of photographs is linked to the fact that they function both iconically and indexically; they not only "resemble" their referent but also bear a trace of its being, a bit of the real conveyed by light and preserved by photochemical process (Barthes speaks of the "ectoplasm of 'what-had-been'").[11] It is the indexical dimension that sustains photography's essential link to contingency, one of the crucial themes of all Sebald's work:

What the Photograph reproduces to infinity has occurred only once: the Photograph mechanically repeats what could never be repeated existentially. In the Photograph, the event is never transcended for the sake of something else: the Photograph always leads the corpus I need back to the body I see; it is the absolute Particular, the sovereign Contingency, matte and somehow stupid, the *This*. (Barthes, 4)

Again, it is not that Sebald is necessarily after all of these aspects of the photograph with every image he inserts in his books; it is that a certain spectrality belongs to the medium as such and so always enters into our life with photographs, whether consciously registered or not.

One might say the same thing about the now famous distinction Barthes makes in his idiosyncratic inquiry into our life with photographs, between the *studium* and the *punctum* of the photograph. For Barthes, the *studium* pertains to the kinds of knowledge and

10. John Berger, *Another Way of Telling* (New York: Pantheon, 1982), 86–87.
11. Barthes, *Camera Lucida*, 87. Subsequent references will be made in the text.

information that can be read off photographs—knowledge about culture, history, politics, forms of life (the *studium* is, we might say, the locus for the "cultural studies" of photographs). The *punctum*, a much more difficult concept, functions as a kind of small disturbance in the photographic image, a detail that in some way, at least for the viewer, sticks out from the cultural legibility of the photograph. Barthes associates such a detail with the psychoanalytic concept of the "partial object," a kind of organ without body in which the subject's enjoyment coalesces (in a locution that recalls Benjamin's notion of *erstarrte Unruhe*, Barthes speaks of an *"intense immobility"* at the site of the *punctum* [49]). And it is as such that the *punctum* functions as a placeholder for the singularity of the figure portrayed in the photograph, a dimension that, Barthes argues, can be *authenticated* but not *represented* (the *punctum* functions here, we might say, as a tiny condensation of what Celan called the "angle of inclination" of creaturely life).[12]

It is, moreover, what he refers to as the power of expansion proper to the *punctum,* its capacity, while remaining a detail, to fill a whole picture, that allows Barthes to fold his thoughts on this dimension into a series of reflections on a single photograph, the "Winter Garden" photograph" of his mother, the discussion of which takes up most of the latter part of Barthes's little book. Like the *punctum* in a single photograph, this photograph stands out from all the other photographs of his mother that "were merely analogical, provoking only her identity, not her truth; but the Winter Garden Photograph was indeed essential, it achieved for me, utopically, *the impossible science of the unique being*" (70–71). One might note here that it was just such a science that Freud thought he had invented with psychoanalysis, that peculiar mode of attending to the singular ways a human life gets (dis)organized around enigmatic signifiers and "partial objects." But it is also, I suggest, what Sebald was after in his practice of "spectral materialism." He includes photographs in his books not because they each function in the manner of Barthes's Winter Garden photograph— clearly this is not even the case for the narrators of Sebald's texts—but

---

12. In the photograph, "the power of authentication exceeds the power of representation" (89).

because our life with photographs always includes some registration of this spectral dimension in excess of any identity and manifest in the image as its "optical unconscious."[13]

In his various efforts at circumscribing this potential of photography, Barthes's language comes very close to the terms I have been using to develop the concept of creaturely life. We have already noted his comparison of the *punctum* with a partial object and his characterization of the reified agitation at work there as a kind of *intense immobility*. But the link between Barthes's understanding of the photographic medium and what we have been exploring under the heading of creaturely life comes most clearly to the fore where Barthes addresses the materiality of the photochemical process itself. What Barthes calls the *noeme* of photography—the aspect of the "That-has-been" manifest in every photographic image—"was only possible," he writes, "on the day when a scientific circumstance . . . made it possible to recover and print directly the luminous rays emitted by variously lighted objects. The photograph is literally an emanation of the referent. . . . A sort of umbilical cord links the body of the photographed thing to my gaze: light, though impalpable, is here a carnal medium, a skin I share with anyone who has been photographed" (80–81).

Barthes goes on to emphasize what he himself refers to as the quasi-mythic dimension of this materiality: "The loved body is immortalized by the mediation of a precious metal (monument and luxury);

13. The term is, of course, Benjamin's. Benjamin's reflections on this dimension clearly anticipate Barthes's notion of the *punctum*. Concerning an image of Karl Dauthendey with his fiancée, a woman who would, after bearing six children, slash her wrists, Benjamin writes: "No matter how artful the photographer, no matter how carefully posed his subject, the beholder feels an irresistible urge to search such a picture for the tiny spark of contingency, of the here and now, with which reality has (so to speak) seared the subject, to find the inconspicuous spot where in the immediacy of that long-forgotten moment the future nests so eloquently that we, looking back, may rediscover it. For it is another nature which speaks to the camera rather than to the eye: 'other' above all in the sense that a space informed by human consciousness gives way to a space informed by the unconscious." Benjamin, "Little History of Photography," trans. Edmund Jephcott and Kingsley Shorter, in *Walter Benjamin: Selected Writings,* vol. 2, *1927–1934,* ed. Michael Jennings, Howard Eiland, and Gary Smith (Cambridge: Harvard University Press, 1999), 510.

to which we might add the notion that this metal, like all the metals of Alchemy, *is alive*" (81; my emphasis). The spectrality of photography is, on this view, linked to an *undeadness* proper to the medium itself.

Finally, Barthes ties photography to the affective disposition in whose orbit this entire discussion of Sebald has unfolded, that melancholic immersion in creaturely life that resists any simple conversion—any dialectical sublation—into purposeful engagement in the world, into the work of culture. Gazing at the Winter Garden photograph, Barthes notes that he is unable to transform his grief:

No culture will help me utter this suffering which I experience entirely on the level of the image's finitude (that is why, despite its codes, I cannot *read* a photograph): the Photograph—my Photograph—is without culture: when it is painful, nothing in it can transform grief into mourning. And if dialectic is that thought which masters the corruptible and converts the negation of death into the power of work, then the photograph is undialectical. (90)

It is against this background that one can appreciate the conclusion of *Camera Lucida,* where Barthes, in his own way, points to that mode of attentiveness to creaturely life that Benjamin, thinking of Kafka, linked to a kind of natural prayer of the soul:

In the love stirred by Photography (by certain photographs), another music is heard, its name oddly old-fashioned: Pity. I collected in a last thought the images which had "pricked" me (since that is the action of the *punctum*). . . . In each of them, inescapably, I passed beyond the unreality of the thing represented, I entered crazily into the spectacle, into the image, taking into my arms what is dead, what is going to die, as Nietzsche did when . . . he threw himself in tears on the neck of a beaten horse: gone mad for Pity's sake. (116–17)

It is this madness in the face of the photograph—this unique site of exposure to the creaturely life of the other—that Barthes refers to as "the photographic *ecstasy*" (119).

IV

In an essay on *The Emigrants,* J. J. Long has suggested that Sebald's use of photographs must be understood as a performance of "postmemory," a term coined by Marianne Hirsch to capture the peculiarities of the memory of events that hover between personal memory and impersonal history, events one has not lived through oneself but that, in large measure through exposure to the stories of those who did experience them, have nonetheless entered into the fabric of the self.[14] When these events are traumatic, their memory is transmitted to the generations that follow not only through narrative but also through the complex symbolic communication of symptoms — modes of behavior that encrypt, as Freud suggested, a failure to experience anxiety in the face of past danger and duress. Recalling Celan's remarks on the impact of "dates" — each one's "January 20th" — we might say that postmemory takes up not only the explicit, conscious communications of the other but also the historical experience deposited/deposed in the "angle of inclination" of the other's creaturely existence.[15] If the constructions of postmemory are not to become so many flights of unregulated projection and fantasy, they must, Long argues, "exist in some kind of dialogue with the empirical, must be open to confirmation or contestation by the real. One way in which this can take place is through photography, whose perceived privileged relationship to reality, as icon or index, can check, correct, relativize, but also prompt both primary memory (based on recall) and postmemory (based on retrospective reconstruction)."[16]

---

14. J. J. Long, "History, Narrative, and Photography in W. G. Sebald's *Die Ausgewanderten,*" *Modern Language Review* 98, no. 1 (January 2003): 117–37. See also Marianne Hirsch, *Family Frames: Photography, Narrative and Postmemory* (Cambridge: Harvard University Press, 1997).

15. As Art Spiegelman's *Maus,* one of the most interesting and successful performances of postmemory, makes clear, the "post" in the term not only signifies a temporal position with respect to a primary event and its memory but also suggests something like "aftermath," that is, living in the aftermath of the effects an event has on another, in this case a parent. The very way that memory takes shape, the way it is lived by Vladek Spiegelman, the author's father, is in some ways the "event" in whose aftermath his son lives.

16. Long, "History," 124. Long's essay culminates in the claim that Sebald's photographs strive to overcome the entropy — the natural historical processes of decay — that

I have been arguing that one also needs to turn this claim on its head; because Sebald's methodology is a *spectral* materialism, the relation to reality constructed on the basis of photographs—on what Barthes calls their *studium*—must in turn be corrected, checked, and relativized by one's attention to what sticks out from or stains the surface of reality, to the *punctum* that functions as a kind of umbilical cord to the other's creatureliness.

I might note, finally, that Sebald appears at one point to equate the act of attention to the creaturely with photography. Toward the end of *The Rings of Saturn,* the narrator wanders out to Orfordness, the location of secret weapons research by the British during the Cold War and one of the sites Sebald characterizes as "extraterritorial" (the narrator recalls that it "resembled a penal colony in the Far East"; 233/278). Wandering alone through this abandoned military site and feeling as if "passing through an undiscovered country," the narrator accidentally flushes a hare out of the brush. The description of this fraction of a second combines Hofmannsthal's poetics of attunement with the creaturely and the rhetoric of photography:

It must have been cowering there as I approached, heart pounding as it waited, until it was almost too late to get away with its life. In that very fraction of a

---

otherwise dominates Sebald's gaze. "His reading of family albums allows him to suture himself into the stories of others and construct a sense of narrative and biological continuity as a compensation for exile and loss." Furthermore, the construction of patterns of repetition and reflexive reference across photographs and text "hint at a hidden, almost magical order behind the ostensible chaos of history and entropy of matter. The combination of narrative and photography . . . can thus be seen as an attempt, at the level of form, to counteract the dispersal, dissipation, and rupture inherent in the historical process. For Sebald . . . it is only through such aesthetic strategies that history can be redeemed" (137). Amir Eshel has made a similar argument, suggesting that Sebald achieves at a formal level a poetics of suspension or deceleration, an "actual reversal of time's gallop, and the production of a different temporality, one that suspends, at the metasemantic level, the ontology of past, present, and future." See Amir Eshel, "Against the Power of Time: The Poetics of Suspension in W. G. Sebald's *Austerlitz,*" *New German Critique,* no. 88 (Winter 2003): 94. I have been arguing that Sebald's work aims not at providing a vision of (aesthetic) redemption but rather at the construction of creaturely life—and the exemplification of the mode of attentiveness required for this labor—with the understanding that such sites might become the ground of new kinds of solidarity with others.

second when its paralyzed state turned into panic and flight, its fear cut right through me. I still see what occurred in that one tremulous instant with an undiminished clarity. I see the edge of the grey tarmac and every individual blade of grass, I see the hare leaping out of its hiding-place, with its ears laid back and a curiously human expression on its face that was rigid with terror and strangely divided; and in its eyes, turning to look back as it fled and almost popping out of its head with fright, I see myself, become one with it. (234/279–80) [17]

v

The productivity of the concept of "postmemory" does not stop with these reflections on photography. They help us to appreciate other dimensions of Sebald's work, most importantly, I think, his numerous reflections on the difficulties of historical reconstruction and, central to that, the question of the perspective of those engaged in such work. Sebald's most extended reflections on this matter concern the representation of war.

In an extended recollection of André Hilary, Austerlitz describes his beloved teacher's passion for history and his encyclopedic knowledge of the Napoleonic era (like everyone else in *Austerlitz,* of course, Hilary is a fictional character). Because the sequence in question concerns Hilary's presentation of the Battle of Austerlitz, one has to read it as a meditation not only on problems of historiography but also on the complexities the novel's protagonist faces in the reconstruction of his own history as well as on those the narrator faces in his mediation

---

17. Earlier in the book, recalling a night in Amsterdam, the narrator describes a similar conjunction of "photographic" seeing and creaturely life, though here the element of anxiety—of a profound disruption, or *Erschütterung*—that in the former instance "humanizes" the animal is missing: "Once, when lightning again flashed across the sky, I looked down into the hotel garden far below me, and there, in the broad ditch that runs between the garden and the park, in the shelter of an overhanging willow, I saw a solitary mallard, motionless on the garish green surface of the water. This image emerged from the darkness, for a fraction of a second, with such perfect clarity that I can still see every individual willow leaf, the myriad green scales of duckweed, the subtlest nuances in the fowl's plumage, and even the pores in the lid closed over its eye" (88–89/110; in the German edition, the narrator sees not a solitary mallard but rather a pair of ducks).

of that project (only the latter would represent the work of "post-memory" proper). During his lecture, Hilary bemoans the pitfalls of all attempts to capture the realities of just one day on the battlefield—December 2, 1805—of what it means to be in the midst of such an event, to have been, as it were, delivered over to *that date*: "It would take an endless length of time to describe the events of such a day properly, in some inconceivably complex form recording who had perished, who survived, and exactly where and how, or simply saying what the battlefield was like at nightfall, with the screams and groans of the wounded and dying" (71/104).[18] Hilary laments the recourse to cliché and set pieces already staged by others: "We try to reproduce the reality, but the harder we try, the more we find the pictures that make up the stock-in-trade of the spectacle of history forcing themselves upon us" (71/104–5). "Our concern with history," he concludes, "is a concern with preformed images already imprinted on our brains, images at which we keep staring while the truth lies elsewhere, away from it all, somewhere as yet undiscovered" (72/105).

These reflections recall the "vertiginous sense of confusion" experienced by Henri Beyle (in *Vertigo*) apropos of the discrepancy he registers between everything he had learned about the Battle of Marengo "from many and various tellings" and the site of the battlefield itself some fifteen months after the event where he could see, "scattered over a vast area, the bones of perhaps 16,000 men and 4,000 horses that had lost their lives there, already bleached and shining with dew" (17/22). The vertigo occasioned by this discrepancy is further heightened by the memorial column that had been erected at the battlefield: "In its shabbiness, it fitted neither with his conception of the turbulence of the Battle of Marengo nor with the vast field of the dead on which he was now standing, alone with himself, like one meeting his doom" (18/22).

One might note here one of Sebald's strategies for counteracting the illusion so often conveyed by historiographic representation and narration—that of being "in the midst" of historical events—namely

---

18. This sentence anticipates Austerlitz's later recitation from *Colonel Chabert* in which he cites the protagonist's recollection of the *gémissements poussés par le monde des cadavres*.

the recourse to the mathematical sublime, the evocation of a magnitude the mind cannot fully take in or metabolize. (What is it to see a field of 16,000 bleached skeletons?) It is there, in the encounter with an overwhelming magnitude, that one touches "the real" of the event rather than in the narrative or visual representation. In his reflections on the pictorial representations of famous sea battles in *The Rings of Saturn*, to take another example, Sebald writes that they "are without exception figments of the imagination. Even celebrated painters . . . some of whose versions of the Battle of Sole Bay I studied closely . . . fail to convey any true impression of how it must have been to be on board one of these ships" (76–77/95). Here too, using one of his most favored literary devices, the *list*, Sebald evokes excessive magnitudes as a placeholder for the reality of the event:

At that date there can have been only a few cities on earth that numbered as many souls as were annihilated in sea-battles of this kind. The agony that was endured and the enormity of the havoc wrought defeat our powers of comprehension, just as we cannot conceive the vastness of the efforts that must have been required—from felling and preparing the timber, mining and smelting the ore, and forging the iron, to weaving and sewing the sailcloth—to build and equip vessels that were almost all predestined for destruction. (78/96)[19]

Finally, in the course of his reminiscences about a visit to Belgium, the narrator recalls his impressions of the memorial site of the Battle of Waterloo.[20] As is so often the case in Sebald, the narrator is the sole visitor at the site. After watching a group of actors in period costume hired to simulate the look of life around 1815, the narrator enters the

19. The reference to a scene or magnitude that exceeds one's powers of comprehension—*unser Vorstellungsvermögen*—occurs no fewer than five times in *The Rings of Saturn*.
20. For the narrator, Belgium is a country whose population has been deformed as a consequence of its colonial past. He imagines that the pedestrians he sees all carried "that dark Congolese secret within them" and that this encrypted violence is the reason he encountered there so many "more hunchbacks and lunatics than normally in a whole year" (122–23/149). In a word, the *Neigungswinkel* of creaturely life—and this is already quite clear in Kafka's work—cannot be seen as a mark of belonging to the line of the *victims* in history.

so-called Waterloo Panorama. Like all such precinematic constructions, it is meant to create the impression of "being at the center of events" (124/151). Reflecting on the entirety of "the circus-like structure," the narrator muses, "This then, I thought, as I looked round about me, is the representation of history. It requires a falsification of perspective" (125/151). At this point the narrator evokes a scene of overwhelming suffering—again signaled by the *gémissements* of the dead and dying—and magnitude: "We, the survivors, see everything from above, see everything at once, and still we do not know how it was. The desolate field extends all around where once fifty thousand soldiers and ten thousand horses met their end within a few hours. The night after the battle, the air must have been filled with death rattles and groans" (125/152).

At this point the narrator asks the Benjaminian question concerning the link between the historian's gaze and the perspective of the victors—the link that both Benjamin and Sebald work to challenge with their distinctive mode of historical writing: "Whatever became of the corpses and mortal remains? Are they buried under the memorial? Are we standing on a mountain of death? Is that our ultimate vantage point? Does one really have the much-vaunted historical overview from such a position?" (125/152).

As these lines clearly indicate, it would be a mistake to assume that the problem with such a historical overview—the panoramic gaze on historical events—was merely epistemological, that the problem it presents was simply one of pretending to a view of events that, because of human limitations, can never truly be attained. In *Vertigo* Sebald reproduces one of the sketches Henri Beyle made in his autobiography depicting the moment when, during the transalpine march of Napoleon's army in 1800, his column came under fire near the village of Bard. Noting that Beyle marked the spot where he himself stood in all of this, Sebald's narrator writes, "Of course, when Beyle was in actual fact standing at that spot, he will not have been viewing the scene in this precise way, for in reality, as we know, everything is always quite different" (6–7/10). Sebald suggests, however, that the real problem with this discrepancy was that the sketch ultimately served as a kind of screen memory standing in the place of a traumatic gap in experience. Beyle writes that "he was so affected by the large number of dead horses lying by the wayside, and the other detritus of war the army left in its wake as it moved in a long-drawn-out file up the mountains, that he has no clear idea whatsoever of the things he found so horrifying then. It seemed to him that his impressions had been erased by the very violence of their impact" (5–6/9).

What are the consequences of these reflections for the way we conceptualize the "subject position" of postmemory? The first thing to note is that for writers who take the situation of postmemory seriously—and Sebald is in many ways exemplary here—being "in the midst" of history means, in large measure, being in the midst of the labor of reconstructing history, a history that is in turn transmitted in fragmentary fashion and along multiple "channels." The narrator of Sebald's works is crucial for this reason: he is forever exposing himself to the fragments and traces of other lives—traces often available only in objects, in bits of "material culture"—and to the enigmatic address that issues from them. These "irritants" of the other's alterity become the stuff of his own "dreamwork," the strange point of access to the other's "January 20th."

Sebald underlines the creaturely expressivity of these fragmentary transmissions in the scene of the narrator's final meeting with Max Ferber in *The Emigrants*. While trying to put Ferber's story into a narrative—the narrative we have just finished reading—the narrator learns that Ferber is in the hospital with pulmonary emphysema. Just before receiving this news, he expresses his frustration with regard to his writing in terms that exactly mirror the narrator's earlier description of Ferber's tortuous creative process as a portrait artist. First, the narrator's struggle:

Often I could not get on for hours or days at a time, and not infrequently I unraveled what I had done, continuously tormented by scruples that were taking tighter hold and steadily paralyzing me. These scruples concerned not only the subject of my narrative, which I felt I could not do justice to . . . but also the entire questionable business of writing. I had covered hundreds of pages with my scribble, in pencil and ballpoint. By far the greater part had been crossed out, discarded, or obliterated by additions. Even what I ultimately salvaged as a "final" version seemed to me a thing of shreds and patches, utterly botched. (230–31/344–45)

Earlier, describing Ferber's efforts to capture the singularity of his sitter's face—something Ferber claims to be ultimately unknowable—the narrator notes that each morning the artist "would erase the portrait yet again, and once more set about excavating the features of his model . . . from a surface already badly damaged by the continual destruction" (162/239). We now recognize the model for the narrator's own writing process:

He might reject as many as forty variants, or smudge them back into the paper and overdraw new attempts upon them; and if he then decided that the portrait was done, not so much because he was convinced that it was finished as through sheer exhaustion, an onlooker might well feel that it had evolved from a long lineage of grey, ancestral faces, rendered unto ash but still there, as ghostly presences, on the harried paper. (162/239)[21]

When the narrator finally visits Ferber in the hospital, the latter's voice assumes a nearly inhuman quality, offering, as it were, the vocal equivalent of the ghostly presences emerging from the worked-over paper of his own portraits: "Ferber was in the men's ward with well over twenty beds, where much muttering and groaning went on, and doubtless a good deal of dying. He clearly found it next to impossible to use his voice, and so responded to what I said only at lengthy intervals, in an attempt at speech that sounded like the rustle of dry leaves in the wind" (231/345–46). The uncanny quality of this vocalization is heightened once one realizes that the final simile is taken from Kafka's story "The Cares of a Family Man," in which the creature that Kafka called Odradek is described as having a laugh as if made without lungs:

21. Again, Sebald modeled Ferber's style—and life—on that of the German-born English painter Frank Auerbach. The German edition of *The Emigrants* contains an image of an Auerbach sketch that was withdrawn from the English edition. It gives a good visual sense of what Ferber describes here.

"It sounds rather like the rustling of fallen leaves."[22] Sebald's work aims at unpacking the dense natural historical materiality of such rustlings.[23]

We see, then, that Sebald takes considerable pains to dramatize the complex process of "inheriting," of taking responsibility for, the various symbolic and "proto-symbolic" transmissions from his various "neighbors." Sebald inscribes himself in this complexity as a crucial locus of ethical action with respect to those whose very way of being—whose "angle of inclination"—bears witness to traumatic histories. This ethical complexity is heightened, however, not only for the very obvious reason—one that he himself always places in the foreground—that Sebald is himself a German often dealing with people whose lives have been directly or indirectly scarred by the Shoah. Perhaps even more important, what Sebald seems to be after in his practice of self-implication—and the repeated allusions to the

22. Franz Kafka, "The Cares of a Family Man," trans. Willa Muir and Edwin Muir, in Kafka, *The Complete Stories* (New York: Schocken, 1971), 428. Recall also the narrator's recollection of his teacher's quasi-inhuman voice in the second story from *The Emigrants*: "In well-structured sentences, he spoke without any touch of dialect but with a slight impediment of speech or timbre, as if the sound were coming not from the larynx but from somewhere near the heart. This sometimes gave one the feeling that it was all being powered by clock-work inside him and Paul in his entirety was a mechanical human made of tin and other metal parts, and might be put out of operation for ever by the smallest functional hitch" (35/52).

23. There is another allusion to Odradek's laugh in Sebald's work, one that underlines the link between Kafka's text and Benjamin's thought about the allegorical quality of the commodity form. In the second part of *After Nature,* Sebald has the German explorer Georg Steller register an experience that recalls Benjamin's language about Dürer's engraving *Melancholia I;* the passage relates the mutation of objects of use (among native peoples of the Arctic) into objects of exchange: "Later, in a shelter made / out of joined fir-logs, he experienced / the effect of forsaken things / in a foreign space. A circular / drinking vessel of peeled-off bark, / a whetstone dotted with copper ore, / a fish-head paddle and / a child's rattle of fired clay / he carefully selects, and in their place / leaves behind an iron kettle, a string / of many-colored beads, / a little strip of Bokhara silk, / half a pound of tobacco and / a Chinese clay pipe." The allusion, at the end of the passage, to the sound of Odradek's laughter suggests that this mutation has been fateful for the inhabitants of the region: "After half a century this mute / exchange is still remembered, / as can be seen in a report by Commander Billings, / by an inhabitant of this remote region / with a laugh that's a rustling / turned inwards" (64/55).

narrator's own precarious mental equilibrium belongs in this context—is to indicate that the larger history he is reconstructing *has not ceased*. As I have suggested, Sebald's practice of "postmemory" is at the same time a writing of the natural history of the present. To put it somewhat differently, not only is Sebald's spectral materialism a mode of attention directed toward the past, it is also a way of registering structural turmoil at the heart of the present "empire" of social, political, and economic relations. In Benjaminian terms, Sebald—or at least Sebald's narrators—quite clearly writes out of a sense of inhabiting a moment of danger.

VI

Surely one of the most difficult aspects of Sebald's work is the way the narrator's precarious equilibrium, his own modalities of registering exposure to the diffuse workings of natural historical forces in the past and the present, comes to be linked to issues of gender and sexuality. In a body of work that has been understood as a work of memory and mourning, indeed as an exemplary (German) form of second-generation "Holocaust literature"—of "postmemory"—the proliferation of references to sexuality might come as a surprise. More noteworthy still is that so many of these references pertain to homosexuality (as far as I know, the topic of sexuality has for the most part been ignored in reviews and scholarly treatments of Sebald's work).

In his first work of fiction, for example, Sebald suggests that the sixteenth-century painter Matthias Grünewald, whose vision of a creation in torment provides something of an overture to Sebald's literary career, though married to a converted Jewish woman from the Frankfurt ghetto, was secretly homosexual. Sebald indicates that homosexuality functioned for the painter as a kind of fetish, that is to say, as a defense against the encounter with woman's "castration." Grünewald, he writes,

had more of an eye for men
whose faces and entire physique

he executed with endless devotion
whereas his women for the most part
are veiled, so relieving him of the fear
of looking at them more closely. (15–16/15)

He further suggests that Grünewald sustained a long-term homosexual relationship with a fellow painter named Mathis Nithart, a figure whose historical existence has never been definitively established.

In Sebald's second work, *Vertigo*, the topic of homosexuality enters much more into the foreground and often in combination with the narrator's paranoia about being watched or followed by men. In the second story of that work, "All' estero," the narrator travels from Vienna to Venice, a city already overdetermined as a site of errancy, of going astray, in all possible senses (the most obvious association is with Thomas Mann's *Death in Venice*). Upon arriving in the city the narrator notes that one's encounters in such a place have "an almost theatrical obscenity," even "an air of conspiracy" (52/63). On the evening of the first day he returns to the bar where he had leafed through Grillparzer's *Italian Diary* upon arriving in the city that morning. The return to the same bar is no doubt significant; the narrator himself notes later in the story that he is never quite sure what compels him to choose one bar, restaurant, or hotel over another (76/91). At any rate, it is there that he is befriended by an Italian astrophysicist, Malachio, who later takes him on a nocturnal boat tour of the city. During a rather Kafkaesque scene at a buffet at the train station where he takes a coffee before leaving for Verona, the narrator feels that he is being watched by two young men—they are first described as two pairs of eyes—who, he now feels, were also at the bar where he met Malachio (one begins to surmise that this was a gay bar). Indeed, he now fears that they have crossed his path a number of times over the course of his stay in Venice. The two men belong, it seems, to the theatrical obscenity of the city. Upon entering the amphitheater in Verona later that day, the narrator feels as if he is "being entangled in some dark web of intrigue" and feels sure that two men in the shadows at the far side of the arena are the same men who pursued him in Venice: "Like two watchmen they remained motionless at their posts until the sunlight had all but faded. Then they stood up, and I had the impression that they bowed to each other before descending from the tiers and vanishing in the darkness of the exit" (72/87). The narrator's response is one of paralyzing panic and compulsive thinking:

At first I could not move from the spot, so ominous did these probably quite coincidental encounters appear to me. I could already see myself sitting in the arena all night, paralyzed by fear and the cold. I had to muster all my rational powers before at length I was able to get up and make my way to the exit. When I was almost there I had a compulsive vision of an arrow whistling through the grey air, about to pierce my left shoulderblade and, with a distinctive, sickening sound, penetrate my heart. (72/87)

The jouissance associated with this fantasy of phallic penetration is clearer in the German, where the word translated as "sickening" — *satt* — also suggests "satisfied," "satiated," "full." Two threatening men appear in Milan some seven years later when the narrator attempts to retrace the still troubling steps of his original Italian journey (he is in Milan to replace a lost passport; he thus finds himself in a kind of caesura of his symbolic identity). Emerging from the train station, he is manhandled by two young men for no apparent reason; the corporeal proximity of his assailants manifests the same theatrical obscenity the narrator associated with Venice: "It was quite impossible to get out of their way: their breath was already upon my face, already I was seeing the knotty scar on the one's cheek and the veins in the other's eye and feeling their hands beneath my jacket, grabbing, tugging and pulling" (109/129).

These various pairs of men are no doubt meant to recall the two pallbearers in dark coats and silver buttons from Kafka's "The Hunter Gracchus." But this association only heightens the reader's sense that these figures hold the place of a kind of homosexual panic on the part of the narrator. For as we have already noted, the narrator suggests that Kafka's hunter represents a state of perpetual penitence for a longing for an illicit love. One of the "sources" for this reading is a letter Kafka wrote to Felice Bauer (February 23, 1913) in which he describes his curious fascination with the son of a Jewish bookshop owner in Prague. In the letter, Kafka notes that the man's first engagement was broken off owing to financial difficulties and that the woman he later married apparently had a psychotic breakdown just weeks after the wedding and had to be institutionalized. The man, now some forty years old, often sits in his father's store staring out at the street "through gaps between books which, Dr. K. expressly notes, are mostly of an obscene nature" (166/189). Kafka—or rather Sebald's Dr. K.—goes on to tell Felice how he had recently followed "this wretched creature, who feels himself (as Dr. K. knows) to be German and for that reason goes to the Deutsches Haus every evening after supper to nurture his delusion of grandeur as a member of the German Casino Club" (166/189). On this particular evening, the man became "an object of fascinated interest in a way he cannot entirely explain even to himself" (166/189). The narrator then cites verbatim Kafka's direct address to Felice: "Do you understand, my dearest . . . can you understand (*please tell me!*) why it was that I followed this man down Zeltnergasse, veritably lusting, turned into the Graben behind him, and watched him enter the gates of the Deutsches Haus with a feeling of unbounded pleasure?" (166–67/ 190). The narrator adds: "At this point Dr. K. surely came within an inch of admitting to a desire which we must assume remained unstilled" (167/190).[24] The conclusion of "Dr. K. Takes the Waters at Riva" returns us to the "Hunter Gracchus" story at the end of which—according to the narrator's interpretation—the hunter, apparently forgetting that the mayor might be in a position to redeem him (his name is Salvatore), places his hand on the latter's knee.[25]

Yet another episode belonging to this "complex" is the curious encounter on the bus ride to Riva between the narrator and the Italian twins who resemble Kafka as a young boy. The narrator's response is extreme, as if this experience of doubling is simply too much to bear: "My heart pounded, and a vertiginous feeling came over me. . . . I leaned my head against the window frame . . . and for a long time did

24. As Sebald clearly suggests, this story has to do not only with homosexual desire but also with the so-called German/Jewish symbiosis, which is itself a kind of story of unrequited love.

25. Earlier in the story, the ghost of Grillparzer places his hand on Dr. K.'s knee (142/164).

not dare look around. Not until we had left Salò far behind and were approaching Gargnano was I able to master the fright which had frozen my limbs and glance back over my shoulder" (89/106). When he approaches the boys' parents and asks them to send him a photograph of their sons it is clear that they consider him a pederast. When the narrator later asks a young man to take a photograph of a building's facade for him, the man's wife pulls him away, seemingly suspicious of the narrator's intentions (127/149). In both cases, homosexual desire is registered as a suspicion directed at the narrator, as something being projected on him from the outside.

In *The Emigrants,* when Henry Selwyn tells the narrator of his origins as a Lithuanian Jew, noting that he had concealed his background from his wife for a long time, there is a vague suggestion that there might be other secrets in this man's life. Indeed, Selwyn's retreat to the world of plants and animals, his remark to the narrator that he had sold his soul, and finally his act of suicide all seem to have as much to do with unlived homosexual desire as with the inability to integrate the experience of emigration into an English upper-class identity. This, at least, is what is suggested by the story of Selwyn's relationship with the alpine guide, Johannes Naegeli. Though separated by some forty years—they met in 1913 when Naegeli was sixty-five and Selwyn twenty-one—Selwyn tells the narrator that "never in his life, neither before nor later, did he feel as good as he did then, in the company of that man. . . . Even the separation from Elli, whom I had met at Christmas in Berne and married before the war, did not cause me remotely as much pain as the separation from Naegeli" (14/24). When he learned, during his military service, that Naegeli had fallen into a crevasse in the Alps, it plunged him, he recalls, "into a deep depression that nearly led to my being discharged. It was as if I was buried under snow and ice" (15/25).

The second "case" of same-sex love in *The Emigrants* is that of the narrator's great-uncle Ambros Adelwarth, whose longtime relationship with his employer, Cosmo Solomon, is presented as involving a strong homoerotic component. Indeed, it is suggested that the psychic turmoil and demise of both figures was a result of the impossibility of either renouncing or fully embracing this desire, of having to sustain it as a kind of public secret. (One should add, of course, that the love between Ambros and Cosmo was further complicated not only by issues of class but also by those of the German/Jewish divide.) The narrator strongly suggests that certain features of Ambros's personality are to be linked to the impasse of homosexual desire in a world in which such desire has no place, is condemned to perpetual internal and external emigration.

Indeed, the story of Ambros Adelwarth seems in many ways to be a kind of textbook case of what Judith Butler has analyzed as the *melancholy of gender*. Butler's theory is that abandoned—but unmourned—same-sex libidinal attachments become incorporated in the bodily ego as the very matter—we might say *erstarrte Unruhe*—of one's gender identity and sexual "orientation." Gender identity itself becomes, in this view, a primary locus of one's hauntedness, of the persistence of specters and phantasms of unnamed loss. The analysis of gender thereby becomes a crucial site of what I have referred to as *spectral materialism*. As Butler has put it,

When we consider gender identity as a melancholic structure, it makes sense to choose "incorporation" as the manner by which that identification is accomplished. Indeed . . . gender identity would be established through a refusal of loss that encrypts itself in the body and that determines, in effect, the living versus the dead body [I would say *undead* body—ELS]. . . . The localization and/or prohibition of pleasures and desires in given "erotogenic" zones is precisely the kind of gender-differentiating melancholy that suffuses the body's surface.[26]

Against this background, the extreme degree of *composure* that family members recall about Ambros becomes an index of such a melancholy at the very core of his being.[27] As the narrator's uncle

---

26. Judith Butler, *Gender Trouble: Feminism and the Subversion of Identity* (New York: Routledge, 1990), 68.

27. Dr. Abramsky, the psychiatrist who administered shock therapy to him in Ithaca, remarks that he had never experienced anyone as melancholic as Ambros: "Even when he was simply standing at the window looking out he always gave the impression of being filled with some appalling grief. I do not think, said Dr. Abramsky, that I ever met a more melancholy person than your great-uncle" (111/162).

Kasimir puts it, "I always felt sorry for him, because he could never, his whole life, permit anything to ruffle his composure," to which he immediately adds that "of course . . . he was of the other persuasion, as anyone could see, even if the family ignored or glossed over the fact" (88/129). Over the course of his life, this composure becomes a kind of reified decorum: "The older Uncle Adelwarth grew, the more hollowed-out he seemed to me, and the last time I saw him . . . it was as if his clothes were holding him together" (88/129).[28]

Even Ambros's facility with languages seems to be a sign of his capacity for such self-abnegating composure. Indeed, the irritant that in some sense forms the kernel of the narrator's interest in his great-uncle is the memory of hearing him speak at a family gathering in the early 1950s. "Although I do not remember what Uncle Adelwarth said in his rather formal address, I do recall being deeply impressed by the fact that his apparently effortless German was entirely free of any trace of our home dialect" (68/98).[29] Later the narrator's aunt Fini recalls that Ambros spoke perfect French and that "he had the special gift of acquiring a foreign language . . . solely by making certain adjustments (as he once explained to me) to his inner self" (78/114). We might say that Ambros has the capacity to adapt or assimilate to various symbolic systems without becoming libidinally implicated in them. In this way the "melancholy of gender" approaches the structure of psychosis in which the subject experiences such systems—including language—as a purely external mechanism parasitic upon his being. Indeed, the electroshock therapy that eventually destroys Ambros might serve as an emblem of such a relation.

Finally, there is the tragic case of Roger Casement, presented in the fifth chapter of *The Rings of Saturn*. Casement, who worked tirelessly on behalf of the victims of various colonial regimes in the

28. At the end of his life, the act of sustaining this last bit of self-composure becomes for Ambros the very substance of life. As Dr. Abramsky recalls, "After a while he had the greatest difficulty with everyday tasks. He took almost the whole day to get dressed. Simply to fasten his cufflinks and his bow tie took him hours. And he was hardly finished dressing but it was time to undress again" (115/169).
29. In German, the phrase used is *nach der Schrift reden,* which means to speak a kind of hypercorrect, written German, unmarked by regional intonation.

Congo, South America, and Ireland, is finally destroyed when the publication of a diary revealing his homosexual liaisons leads to his utter abandonment to his enemies in the British government. The narrator suggests that Casement's obsession with the nature and origins of power was deeply connected to his life as a homosexual, "that it was precisely Casement's homosexuality that sensitized him to the continuing oppression, exploitation, enslavement and destruction, across the borders of social class and race, of those who were furthest from the centers of power" (134/162).

One might hear in these last remarks an echo of Freud's famous case study of Judge Daniel Paul Schreber. There Freud argued that Schreber's paranoia was triggered by an upsurge of homosexual libido at an especially vulnerable point in his life. In the course of his discussion of the mechanism of paranoia, Freud posits that in the typical case of libidinal development, homosexual tendencies become deflected from sexual aims and are applied to fresh uses: "They now combine with portions of the ego-instincts and, as 'attached' [*angelehnte*] components, help to constitute the social instincts, thus contributing an erotic factor to friendship and comradeship, to *esprit de corps* and to the love of mankind in general." Freud goes on to claim that "it is precisely manifest homosexuals, and among them . . . those that set themselves against an indulgence in sensual acts, who are distinguished by taking a particularly active share in the general interests of humanity—interests which have themselves sprung from a sublimation of erotic instincts."[30] Though Sebald's reflections on Casement suggest a somewhat different link between homosexuality and the general interests of mankind, one having to do with identification with the marginal figures of society, both Freud and Sebald posit a

30. Sigmund Freud, "Psychoanalytic Notes upon an Autobiographical Account of a Case of Paranoia (Dementia Paranoides)," in *The Standard Edition of the Complete Psychological Works of Sigmund Freud*, trans. James Strachey (London: Hogarth Press, 1953–74),12:61. Freud based this study on a reading of Schreber's *Memoirs of My Nervous Illness (Denkwürdigkeiten eines Nervenkranken)*. For a detailed study of both, see Eric L. Santner, *My Own Private Germany: Daniel Paul Schreber's Secret History of Modernity* (Princeton: Princeton University Press, 1996).

connection between homosexuality and various forms of social, ethical, and political engagement and altruism.

But there is much more in Freud's case study that resonates with Sebald's treatment of homoeroticism. For as we have seen, one of the ways homoerotic desire seems to manifest itself in Sebald's work is paranoia with respect to the male gaze. It is, I should note, fairly certain that Sebald was familiar with Freud's study of Schreber. In an essay on Elias Canetti, Sebald gives considerable attention to the last chapters of Canetti's magisterial study of the nature and origins of power, *Crowds and Power* (*Masse und Macht*), in which Canetti offers a vehement critique of Freud's interpretation of the Schreber material. And in a speech delivered in Stuttgart shortly before his death—the occasion was the opening of the House of Literature there in 2001— Sebald noted a further, more personal, connection to Schreber, who apparently functioned for him as a kind of totem. In the course of his remarks, Sebald recalls his first visit to Stuttgart in 1976 to meet the painter Jan Peter Tripp. "At the time," he says, "Tripp gave me a present of one of his engravings, showing the mentally ill judge Daniel Paul Schreber with a spider in his skull—what can there be more terrible than the ideas always scurrying around in our minds?—and much of what I have written since derives from this engraving, *even in my method of procedure.*"[31]

In his study of Schreber, Freud tries to capture the link between paranoia and homosexual desire—and panic—by way of a kind of transformational grammar of symptom formation. Freud claims that paranoia is one way of negating the proposition "I (a man) love him (a man)." The core delusion of persecution emerges, that is, when the mind attacks this thought by negating the verb: I *don't love*

---

31. W. G. Sebald, "An Attempt at Restitution: A Memory of a German City," trans. Anthea Bell, *New Yorker*, December 20/27, 2004, 112; my emphasis. Much of the rest of the speech is dedicated to Friedrich Hölderlin, whose own psychotic break occurred only a few years after he wrote the elegy, "Stuttgart," to which Sebald refers. One can assume that Sebald was familiar with the most significant study of Hölderlin's psychosis, Jean Laplanche's *Hölderlin et la question du père*. Laplanche's study is deeply informed by Lacan's study of the Schreber case.

him, the paranoiac protests, I *hate* him, and I hate him because he *hates/persecutes* me.[32] But even more interesting for our purposes is Freud's suggestion that the paranoiac's symptoms of being watched, spoken about, being the object of grand conspiracies, being physically manipulated by malevolent agents and machines—and in Schreber's case, becoming God's own private whore—are all attempts, on the part of the subject, to *reestablish* a libidinal cathexis to the world after its catastrophic suspension triggered, in turn, by an initial homosexual panic. (In a sense, the paranoiac would rather sacrifice the world than do *that*.) For Freud, the crucial lesson of Schreber's *Memoirs,* a text rich with florid descriptions of global catastrophe, is that the paranoiac lives in a kind of permanent state of emergency.[33] As Freud puts it, "The patient has withdrawn from the people in his environment and from the external world generally the libidinal cathexis which he has hitherto directed on to them. . . . The end of the world is the projection of this internal catastrophe; his subjective world has

32. See Freud, *Standard Edition,* 12 : 63– 65. By negating the direct object (rather than the verb), homosexual panic mutates into erotomania: I don't love *him,* I love *her* (and her, and her . . . ); by negating the subject, we end up with pathological jealousy: I don't love him, *she* loves him.

33. As Freud notes, Schreber's delusions of the end of the world largely turned on the agency of his psychiatrist, Paul Flechsig. Though his delusions also included those of his own death, Freud writes that "the form of his delusion in which his ego was retained and the world sacrificed proved itself by far the more powerful. He had various theories of the cause of the catastrophe. At one time he had in mind a process of glaciation owing to the withdrawal of the sun; at another it was to be destruction by an earthquake, in the occurrence of which he, in his capacity of 'seer of spirits,' was to act a leading part. . . . Or again, Flechsig was the culprit, since through his magic arts he had sown fear and terror among men, had wrecked the foundations of religion, and spread abroad general nervous disorders and immorality, so that devastating pestilences had descended upon mankind. In any case the end of the world was the consequence of the conflict which had broken out between him and Flechsig, or, according to the aetiology adopted in the second phase of his delusion, of the indissoluble bond which had been formed between him and God" (69). In this context, we might recall that the figure of Cosmo Solomon in the third story of *The Emigrants* suffered his second serious nervous breakdown after seeing what we can only assume was the 1922 Fritz Lang film *Dr. Mabuse, the Gambler,* a film in which Mabuse's malevolent telepathic influences function in much the same way that Schreber experiences the power of his psychiatrist, Flechsig.

come to an end since his withdrawal of his love from it."[34] What we witness as a series of paranoid delusions are, in fact, efforts at healing, at rebuilding the world from the ground up:

> And the paranoiac builds [the world] again, not more splendid, it is true, but at least so that he can once more live in it. He builds it up by the work of his delusions. *The delusion-formation, which we take to be the pathological product, is in reality an attempt at recovery, a process of reconstruction.* Such a reconstruction after the catastrophe is successful to a greater or lesser extent, but never wholly so. . . . But the human subject has recaptured a relation, and often a very intense one, to the people and things in the world, even though the relation is a hostile one now, where formerly it was hopefully affectionate. We may say, then, that the process of repression proper consists in a detachment of the libido from people—and things—that were previously loved. It happened silently; we received no intelligence of it, but can only infer it from subsequent events.[35]

And as Freud concludes this line of interpretation, "What forces itself so noisily upon our attention is the process of recovery, which undoes the work of repression and brings back the libido again on to the people it had abandoned. In paranoia this process is carried out by the method of projection." The ultimate truth of paranoia is, thus, as Freud famously put it, "that what was abolished internally returns from without."[36]

One should add to this series of reflections Freud's remarks concerning the megalomania that is part of every paranoid formation. In his summary of the various ways the proposition "I (a man) love him (a man)" can be negated, Freud adds a final mode that negates not the verb, subject, or direct object but the entire proposition: *I don't love at all,* not anything, not anyone. And as Freud adds, "Since . . . one's libido must go somewhere, this proposition seems to be the psycholog-

34. Freud, *Standard Edition,* 12:70.
35. Ibid., 12:70–71.
36. Ibid., 12:71.

ical equivalent of the proposition: 'I only love myself.' So that this kind of contradiction would give us megalomania, which we may regard as a *sexual overestimation of the ego*." [37] One might be reminded here of the narrator in Sebald's texts, who at times exhibits the unnerving habit of writing himself into someone else's life story so that it seems almost to become about him. One thinks, for example, of the curious encounter with Michael Hamburger in *The Rings of Saturn* where the narrator seems to want to appropriate the latter's story of exile as his own.[38] Perhaps even more disturbing is the narrator's sense of being inscribed in the histories of the dead when he sees his own birthdate on a head-stone (in the last story of *The Emigrants*) or scratched into the wall of a casement (in the final paragraph of *Austerlitz*). In each of these in-stances the narrator manifests a peculiar will—one in which a certain megalomania mixes with envy—to write himself into another person's history (in these cases, both Jews named Stern).

Against this background, it is tempting to bring Freud's claims to bear on the "case" of Sebald, or rather on that of his narrators. Doesn't the combination, in Sebald's work, of visions of world destruction and ruin (by war, by erosion, by entropy, by natural disaster, by combus-tion), a certain preoccupation with homoerotic desire, and episodes of paranoia fit, rather neatly, into the matrix of Freud's account? Isn't there a kind of oscillation in Sebald's universe between homoerotically charged male bonding and an obsession with the end of the world? Or rather, aren't Sebald's narrators constantly forming bonds with other men by way of a shared sense of ruination and desolation? Is Sebald's peculiar "narratophilia," his erotically charged pursuit of what are for the most part men with stories of trauma and bereavement—of worlds coming apart—a sort of compromise formation that integrates, in an

37. Ibid., 12:65.
38. "But why it was that on my first visit to Michael's house I instantly felt as if I lived there, in every respect precisely as he does, I cannot explain. All I know is that I stood spellbound in his high-ceilinged studio room . . . in front of the heavy mahogany bu-reau at which Michael said he no longer worked because the room was so cold. . . . [W]hile we talked of the difficulty of heating old houses, a strange feeling came upon me, as if it were not he who had abandoned that place of work but I, as if the spectacles cases, letters and writing materials . . . had once been my spectacles cases, my letters and my writing materials" (183/218–19).

idiosyncratic way, the libidinal tensions that Freud locates at the heart of paranoia?

These questions become all the more vexing once one takes into account Sebald's largely affirmative commentary on Canetti's critique of Freud's case study. In *Crowds and Power,* Canetti argued that Schreber's delusional world revolved not around issues of homoerotic libido but around issues of *power.* Canetti defines paranoia as a *disease of power,* one that he places not only at the center of Schreber's delusional system but also at the heart of all forms of totalitarian leadership. The paranoiac and the totalitarian leader both manifest a pathological will to sole survivorship and a concomitant willingness, even drivenness, to sacrifice the rest of the world in the name of that survivorship; both want to be, as it were, *the last man standing* (one recalls in this context all the places in Sebald's work where the narrator walks through eerily depopulated streets, museums, parks, and other public spaces). Concerning Schreber's apocalyptic delusions in which the end of the world is staged in numerous permutations, Canetti writes,

We do not get the impression that these disasters came upon mankind against Schreber's will. On the contrary, he appears to feel a certain satisfaction in the fact that the persecution he was exposed to . . . should have had such appalling consequences. The whole of mankind suffers and is exterminated because Schreber thinks there is someone who is against him. . . . Schreber is left as the sole survivor because this is what he himself wants. He wants to be the only man left alive, standing in an immense field of corpses; and he wants this field of corpses to contain all men but himself. It is not only as a paranoiac that he reveals himself here. To be the last man to remain alive is the deepest urge of every seeker after power. . . . Once he feels himself threatened his passionate desire to see *everyone* lying dead before him can scarcely be mastered by his reason.

Because of this shared psychic disposition, because the paranoiac and the totalitarian leader are both caught up in the same drive for power—and for Canetti, power is the ultimate object of the drives—he concludes that a "madman, helpless, outcast and despised, who drags out a twilight existence in some asylum, may, through the insights he procures us, prove more important than Hitler or Napoleon, illuminating for mankind [power's] curse and its masters."[39]

I have argued elsewhere that Canetti misreads Schreber's *Memoirs* by equating the latter's delusions of global catastrophe with the apocalyptic dimension of the totalitarian imagination.[40] It should be quite clear that to link Sebald's imagination to such a perspective would represent an equally egregious misreading. Canetti's fundamental error is to have collapsed the tension we have been exploring throughout this book, namely that between the *sovereign exception* and what I have been calling *creaturely life,* the life utterly exposed, utterly abandoned to the state of exception. (Schreber's term for this state is "circumstances contrary to the Order of the World," *weltordnungswidrige Umstände.*) What makes Schreber's *Memoirs* unique, what makes them an unavoidable point of reference for so many theorists of culture, cultural crisis, and modernity, is that they offer us the gaze on the world *from the perspective of the creature.* And no doubt one of the great charms of Schreber's *Memoirs* is that he himself rather straightforwardly announces his unique attractiveness to anyone interested in the complex dynamics of political theology under conditions of modernity. (This was also, as both Benjamin and Agamben have argued, the primary object of Kafka's explorations.) In Schreber's *Memoirs, creaturely life speaks,* addresses readers in the most direct way possible, and even develops theories about its own genesis (one might say that Schreber offers a radical version of Schmitt's *Political Theology* as seen from *below*). But even if we follow this politicotheological line of thought, we are still faced with the fact that in Schreber's world creaturely life is

---

39. Elias Canetti, *Crowds and Power,* trans. Carol Stewart (New York: Seabury Press, 1978), 443, 448. One should add that for Canetti one of the archetypical sites where the mentality of the "survivor" manifests itself most clearly is the *cemetery.* Canetti argues that the secret at the heart of the emotional gravity one feels when one wanders through a cemetery is that one ultimately feels superior to the dead: "The seriousness that one feels and that one even more puts on display hides a secret feeling of satisfaction [*eine geheime Genugtuung*]." One can't help recalling here the numerous scenes in Sebald's books in which the narrator (or a character akin to him, like Austerlitz) walks through cemeteries. Sebaldian *flânerie* takes place not so much on the bustling streets of the metropolis as on the abandoned paths of the *necropolis.*

40. See once more Santner, *My Own Private Germany.*

fundamentally linked to matters of sexuality and gender. That is, even if we bracket Freud's interpretation linking Schreber's delusions to homosexual panic and accept that the latter's "testimony" pertains first and foremost to the workings of sovereign power in a state of exception, we are still confronted with the question of the connection between creaturely life and sexuality, a connection that manifests itself above all in what Schreber refers to as his *Entmannung*, his gradual transformation into a woman compelled to cultivate *weibliche Wollust*, feminine jouissance. As Schreber puts it in his inimical style, "As soon as I am alone with God, if I may so express myself, I must . . . strive to give divine rays the impression of a woman in the height of sexual delight."[41]

A logical move at this point would be to turn to Foucault's work correlating the exercise of power in the modern period and the emergence of sexuality as a distinct domain of human experience and knowledge. In his essay on Canetti, Sebald himself refers to Foucault's notion of the panoptical nature of power in the modern period, one he tries to capture by referring to a Thomas Bernhard story in which a supposedly mad character declares that the world *is a singular, monstrous jurisprudence.*[42] According to this view, Sebald writes, "the system of power is . . . not only one of hierarchization but also of contiguity. It proliferates downward, conquers the foundations, spreads out laterally, so that finally there is no more escape."[43] At this point, natural and historical being become indistinguishable. That is, once power assumes the form that Foucault referred to first as *disciplinary* and then as *biopower,* "the system of nature is also no longer that of a beautiful paradigmatic order. . . . It is itself already contaminated by the madness of society, if this doesn't already have its origin in a nature in

41. Daniel Paul Schreber, *Memoirs of My Nervous Illness,* trans. Ida Macalpine and Richard Hunter (Cambridge: Harvard University Press, 1988), 208. For a discussion of Schreber's association of feminization with the figure of the *eternal Jew,* see once more Santner, *My Own Private Germany.*
42. See W. G. Sebald, "Summa Scientiae: System und Systemkritik bei Elias Canetti," in *Die Beschreibung des Unglücks: Zur österreichischen Literatur von Stifter bis Handke* (Frankfurt a.M.: Fischer, 1994), 97.
43. Ibid.

which everything lives coldly side by side and the real functional unity
consists in the fact that one part is always being devoured by another."⁴⁴ It is against this background that Sebald understands
Canetti's ultimate abandonment of literature. "His creative energy,"
Sebald writes, "is directed in speculative fashion toward another existence [*ein anderes Dasein*] in which the conditions of life would be totally different."⁴⁵

Now Foucault famously argued that it was precisely in the context
of such a "natural historical" formation—those are admittedly not his
terms—that the modern conception of sexuality emerged, or rather
that sexuality, as understood in modernity, was itself produced as a
certain intensification of the body in strict correlation with its exposure to regimes of knowledge intent on maximizing the potentials of
life for the nation-state.⁴⁶ It was, in Foucault's view, precisely a form
of excessive and overproximate concern with the living body that

44. Ibid.
45. Ibid., 99. At this point, Sebald cites a remark in which Canetti muses that "it would
be sweet [*es wäre hübsch*], from a certain age on, from year to year, to become smaller
and to pass, in reverse order, through the same stages through which one once so
proudly ascended" (cited in ibid., 99). It is in this context that one can fully appreciate
Sebald's deep affinity with the work of Robert Walser.
46. As Foucault put it in the first volume of *The History of Sexuality,* "For the first time
in history, no doubt, biological existence was reflected in political existence; the fact of
living was no longer an inaccessible substrate that only emerged from time to time . . . ;
part of it passed into knowledge's field of control and power's sphere of intervention.
Power would no longer be dealing simply with legal subjects over whom the ultimate
dominion was death, but with living beings, and the mastery it would be able to exercise over them would have to be applied at the level of life itself; it was the taking charge
of life, more than the threat of death, that gave power its access even to the body. If one
can apply the term *bio-history* to the pressures through which the movements of life and
the processes of history interfere with one another, one would have to speak of *bio-power*
to designate what brought life and its mechanisms into the realm of explicit calculations
and made knowledge-power an agent of transformation of human life." Michel
Foucault, *History of Sexuality,* vol. 1, *An Introduction,* trans. Robert Hurley (New York:
Vintage, 1990), 142–43. As I suggested earlier, Lacan's theory of the discourse of the
university articulates the social bond that Foucault equates with relations of biopower.
In Lacan's matheme, these relations are represented as $S_2 \Rightarrow a$, the chain of knowledge
directly addressing the real of the subject. But for Lacan this relation stands above, so to
speak, another one, that of an *attenuated* relation between $S_1$ and $, the master signifier
and the subject. We can understand that attenuation as signifying a generalized investi-

produced that sexuality that would become the defining and essential feature of modern man's existence, the very substance of his selfhood:

> More than the old taboos, this form of power demanded constant, attentive, and curious presences for its exercise; it presupposed proximities; it proceeded through examination and insistent observation. . . . It implied a physical proximity and an interplay of intense sensations. . . . The power which . . . took charge of sexuality set about contacting bodies, caressing them with its eyes, intensifying areas, electrifying surfaces, dramatizing troubled moments. It wrapped the sexual body in its embrace. There was undoubtedly an increase in effectiveness and an extension of the domain controlled; but also a sensualization of power and a gain of pleasure. . . . Power operated as a mechanism of attraction; it drew out those peculiarities over which it kept watch. Pleasure spread to the power that harried it; power anchored the pleasure it uncovered.[47]

As illuminating and productive as Foucault's insights are about new forms of power ("knowledge-power," "disciplinary power," "biopower"), they posit, in my view, far too rigid an opposition between premodern and modern forms of power rather than seeing modernity as a widespread mutation of social bonds whereby the traditional forms and loci of sovereignty—along with the sovereign exception and its effects—disperse and proliferate along new pathways and relays, by way of new kinds of *Bahnungen,* to use a Freudian formulation. Indeed, it has been one of the great contributions of Agamben's work to have newly conceptualized Foucault's theories of power along these lines. To put it somewhat differently, Foucault was far too quick to abandon *the politicotheological dimension* of the subject's

---

ture crisis, a condition in which the subject is unable to metabolize, claim as his own, any symbolic mandate/identity. As I have emphasized in my study of the case, Schreber's psychotic break occurs shortly after he is named to the position of president of the highest court of Saxony; unable to identify with the symbolic status with which he was *invested,* Schreber feels himself to be literally *invaded* by particles and rays emanating first from his psychiatrist and then from God. In a word, Schreber's fate materializes *both* the upper and lower portion of the discourse of the university.

47. Ibid., 44–45.

inscription into power relations as a premodern relic that merely occludes one's gaze on the conditions and possibilities of modernity. Indeed, I have been arguing that one of the great virtues of the "German-Jewish" tradition of modern literature, philosophy, and social theory—a tradition at the heart of Agamben's project as well— has been to have sustained a focus on the vicissitudes of this dimension under conditions of modernity. I have also been arguing that W. G. Sebald should be seen as one of the great heirs to this tradition in the field of literary production. What remains, then, is to articulate more precisely the ways the domain of gender and sexuality is articulated in this work with the vicissitudes of political theology in modernity. To put it simply, how are we to understand the sexual dimension of creaturely life?

VII

Until now I have focused largely on the at times explicit, at times implicit presence of homoerotic desire in much of Sebald's work. It is hard not to see Sebald's representation of heterosexuality and, above all, of female sexuality, as forming a complement to this persistence of homoeroticism. The first thing to note in this context are the few rather odd references to heterosexual coupling in Sebald's fiction. Typical, I think, for the gaze on heterosexual desire in this work is the narrator's description of a couple on the beach from *The Rings of Saturn*. As the narrator stands precariously at the edge of a cliff largely hollowed out by nesting holes built by swallows ("I was . . . standing on perforated ground . . . which might have given way at any moment") and stares out over the sand and water, his gaze is suddenly seized by movement on the beach that quickly assumes the status of a *primal scene*:

As I tried to suppress the mounting sense of dizziness, breathing out and taking a step backwards, I thought I saw something of an odd, pallid color move on the shoreline. I crouched down, and overcome by a sudden panic, looked over the edge. A couple lay down there, in the bottom of the pit, as

I thought: a man stretched full length over another body of which nothing was visible but the legs, spread and angled. In the startled moment when that image went through me, which lasted an eternity, it seemed as if the man's feet twitched like those of one just hanged. Now, though, he lay still, and the woman, too was still and motionless. Misshapen, like some great mollusk washed ashore, they lay there, to all appearances a single being, a many-limbed, two-headed monster that had drifted in from far out at sea, the last of a prodigious species, its life ebbing from it with each breath expired through its nostrils. (68/88) [48]

The text leading up to this primal scene prepares us, to a certain extent, for the encounter with a monstrous excess of creaturely corporeality. Walking along the shore, the narrator registers a feeling of immobility at the sight of a ship on the horizon that clearly alludes both to the Flying Dutchman and the bark bearing the hunter Gracchus, two figures of creaturely undeadness: "Out on the leaden-colored sea a sailing boat kept me company, or rather, it seemed to me as if it were motionless and I myself, step by step, were making as little progress as that invisible spirit aboard his unmoving barque" (65–66/84). The narrator then comes upon a herd of hogs sleeping behind a fence. The quasi-erotic tenderness of his encounter stands in stark contrast to his horror at the scene of human coupling:

I climbed over the wire and approached one of the ponderous, immobile, sleeping animals. As I bent towards it, it opened a small eye fringed with light lashes and gave me an enquiring look. I ran my hand across its dusty back, and it trembled at this unwonted touch; I stroked its snout and face, and chucked

48. The narrator's immediate association with this clearly disturbing scene (he refers to the site as an *unheimlich gewordene Stelle,* a place that had become uncanny [68/88; translation modified], and even wonders if he had imagined the whole thing) is a passage from the Borges story "Tlön, Uqbar, Orbis, Tertius," one of the constant points of reference in *The Rings of Saturn.* The story, as the narrator recalls, is "a tale which deals with our attempts to invent secondary or tertiary worlds." In the course of the story, one of Borges's figures recalls "the observation of one of the heresiarchs of Uqbar, that the disturbing thing about mirrors, and also the act of copulation, is that they multiply the number of human beings" (70/90).

it in the hollow behind one ear, till at length it sighed like one enduring endless suffering. When I stood up, it closed its eye once more with an expression of profound submissiveness. (66/85)

At this point the narrator recalls the story from Mark 5:1–13, according to which Jesus heals a man possessed by unclean spirits by transferring them to a herd of swine that then, "some two thousand according to the evangelist, plunged down a steep slope and drowned in the sea" (67/86). Troubled by the parable, the narrator asks himself whether it meant that "human reasoning, diseased as it is, needs to seize on some other kind that it can take to be inferior and thus deserving of annihilation" (67/86). Shortly after these reflections he comes upon the couple on the beach. The entire sequence, which passes from the undead spirit on the sea, to the possessed Gerasene, to the swine consumed by a death drive, to the couple on the beach, seems to trace the migration of an excess vitality that persists at the boundary of the animal, human, and spirit world.

We have already noted another "primal scene" of heterosexual desire, one also linked to the motif of the undead hunter Gracchus. I am thinking of the episode from the final story of *Vertigo* where the narrator recalls his encounter, as a child, with the enigmatic sexual dance of Hans Schlag and Romana:[49] "From deep in the hunter's chest came a heavy moaning and panting, his frosty breath rose from his beard, and time after time, when the wave surged through the small of his back, he thrust into Romana, while she, for her part, clung closer and closer to him, until the hunter and Romana were but one single indivisible form" (239/271). The series of memories that follow upon this scene help to frame the symbolic space that sexuality comes to occupy for the narrator. He recalls his route home from school after a difficult day on which his teacher—next to Romana, the crucial object of the narrator's early sexual desire—relates the history of calamities that have afflicted his native village (Sebald perhaps wants to suggest that this is one of the sites where sexuality and disaster

---

49. Recall that the language of this scene was in large measure lifted from a story by Peter Weiss, thus embodying itself a form of mirroring multiplication.

became linked for him; he was, so to speak, *seduced* by the discourse of catastrophe). Along the way, the narrator describes the statue of St. George on the cemetery wall: "St. George was forever driving a spear through the throat of the griffin-like winged creature lying at his feet" (242/275). The force of this never-ending act of phallic violence is heightened by a reproduction, in triplicate, of an image of St. George slaying the dragon.[50] His route home then takes him past the shop of the village barber with the telling name Köpf—*köpfen* means beheading in German—the memory of which, especially after it becomes associated with the story of Salome and John the Baptist, still prevents the narrator from entering barbershops without a sense of panic and dread. This shift from phallic violence to what seem to be anxieties about violence done to the phallus—in a word, castration anxiety—is underlined by the diphtheria-induced delirium that followed upon the death of the hunter Schlag. Placing his hand in an earthenware crock where preserved eggs were stored for the winter, the narrator recalls the sensation of touching "something soft, something that slipped through my fingers and which I instantly knew could only be eyeballs gouged from their sockets" (250–51/284–85).[51]

Other passages in Sebald's work suggest that the real source of anxiety with regard to heterosexual coupling is female sexuality. I have already noted the passage in *After Nature* where Matthias Grünewald's homosexuality is correlated with a fear of looking too closely at women. In the second part of that *Elementargedicht*, Sebald clearly borrows from Kafka's repertoire of female characters—above all the figure of Leni from *The Trial*—to characterize Georg Steller's wife,

---

50. In *Vertigo*, the narrator visits the Church of Santa Anastasia in Verona to view a fresco by Pisanello of St. George and the Princess of Trebizond. Because one has to deposit a thousand-lire coin in a metal box to illuminate the painting, the entire episode takes on the aspect of a peep show.

51. The link between sexuality, death, and castration figured as endangerment to the eyes is underlined by the narrator's recollection in both *After Nature* and *Vertigo* of a Chinese optometrist whose touch is experienced as "something disembodied and ghoulish, something that went quite through me" (*Vertigo*, 97/115). In *After Nature*, a series of associations with the test pattern in the optometrist's office leads to an image of being the object of a male gaze; the chain of recollections culminates in a scene where a group of black sailors wave from the railing of a ship in Hamburg harbor (96/82).

whose sexuality is posited as a counterforce to her husband's pursuit
of science (here, the study of a colleague's papers):

He spends the whole summer
bent over the jumble of cards,
while the naturalist's neglected
wife, gaudily dressed, sits
beside him and with her split
fin strokes the glans that throbs
like his heart. Steller feels science
shrinking to a single slightly
painful point. (52–53/44) [52]

It is in this context too that one has to place the "orphic" decisions
of three of the writers Sebald portrays in his work—Stendhal,
Chateaubriand, and Kafka—to sacrifice a life with women for the sake
of becoming writers. It is also here that one needs to place the theory
of disembodied love—a love in which "there is no difference between
intimacy and disengagement," *Annäherung und Entfernung*—that
Dr. K. relates to the young Genovese woman he befriends at a northern Italian spa: "If only we were to open our eyes, he says, we would
see that our happiness lies in our natural surroundings and not in
our poor bodies *which have long since become separated from the natural
order of things*" (*Vertigo*, 158/180; my emphasis). That was the reason,
Dr. K. continues,

why all false lovers (and all lovers, he adds, are false) closed their eyes while love-
making or else, which came to the same thing, kept them wide open with craving. Never were we more helpless or lacking in rational sense than in that condition. Our dreams could then be constrained no longer and we became subject
to the compulsion of constantly going through the whole gamut of variations
and repetitions which, as he himself had often enough found, extinguished
everything, even the image of the lover one so wished to preserve. (158/180)

52. Benjamin characterizes Kafka's women as swamp creatures belonging to what
Bachofen called the hetaeric stage of human development. See *Selected Writings*,
2:808–9.

VIII

Here, as in the earlier passages concerning castration anxiety, we find ourselves on the terrain that Freud mapped out under the heading of the uncanny, *das Unheimliche*.[53] For as Freud notes in his essay on that peculiar quality of human feeling and experience, we register as uncanny anything that recalls the quality of demonic agency encountered above all in the compulsion to repeat, whether this be forms of thought or infantile complexes such as those connected to castration anxiety.[54]

In his essay, which he composed about the time he was also developing the concept of the death drive, Freud specifically rejects the view, proposed by Ernst Jentsch, that the effect of uncanniness is produced whenever uncertainty is created as to a thing's life or lifelessness. As Jentsch puts it, "One of the most successful devices for easily creating uncanny effects is to leave the reader in uncertainty whether a particular figure . . . is a human being or an automaton."[55] Jentsch refers here to the impression made by various kinds of constructed dolls and automatons as well as by any human behavior bearing an aspect of the mechanical, as in epileptic fits. Jentsch specifically refers to E. T. A. Hoffmann's achievements in the creation of uncanny effects, and Freud takes the reference to Hoffmann as his point of departure for delineating his own theory of the uncanny.

The primary focus of Freud's analysis is Hoffmann's story "The Sandman." We are therewith in a zone of intertextual proximity to

53. On the importance of "the uncanny" for Sebald, see also John Zilcovsky, "Sebald's Uncanny Travels," in *W. G. Sebald: A Critical Companion*, ed. J. J. Long and Anne Whitehead (Edinburgh: Edinburgh University Press, 2004).

54. As Freud puts it, "For it is possible to recognize the dominance in the unconscious mind of a 'compulsion to repeat' proceeding from the instinctual impulses and probably inherent in the very nature of the instincts—a compulsion powerful enough to override the pleasure principle, lending to certain aspects of the mind their daemonic character, and still very clearly expressed in the impulses of small children; a compulsion, too, which is responsible for a part of the course taken by the analyses of neurotic patients. All these considerations prepare us for the discovery *that whatever reminds us of this inner 'compulsion to repeat' is perceived as uncanny*" (*Standard Edition* 17:238; my emphasis).

55. Cited in Freud, *Standard Edition*, 17:227.

*Austerlitz*. One of Austerlitz's discoveries during his conversations with his former neighbor and nanny in Prague is that his mother, Agáta, had her Prague debut as an actress in the autumn of 1938 in the role of Olympia in Jacques Offenbach's *Tales of Hoffmann* (Jacques Austerlitz had indeed been named after his mother's favorite composer). In Hoffmann's story, the doomed protagonist, Nathanael, falls in love with Olympia, a mechanical doll constructed with the aid of his demonic nemesis, Coppola/Coppelius. A fellow student of Nathanael's tells his friend that because of her stiff and mechanical comportment Olympia makes an impression of utter soullessness: "Her step is peculiarly measured; all of her movements seem to stem from some kind of clockwork. . . . We found Olympia to be rather uncanny [*unheimlich*], and we wanted to have nothing to do with her. She seems to us to be playing the part of a human being." [56] Nathanael suffers his major breakdown when he can no longer deny Olympia's true status as an automaton, that is, when he realizes that he has fallen in love with a machine, that his love had been, as it were, artificially produced.

Freud, as I have noted, was highly critical of the view that the effect of uncanniness was primarily linked to the blurring of boundaries between the animate and inanimate, to uncertainty as to the question, Is it/Am I alive? Instead he places the emphasis on the protagonist's castration anxiety in the face of ever-repeated instantiations of a demonic paternal agency. That is, Freud emphasizes the repetition of a specific "infantile complex" as the key to the uncanny quality produced by Hoffmann in "The Sandman." One need not deny the value of Freud's insight here; one should simply note the compatibility of the insight with the views Freud feels compelled to reject. What Freud failed to see, that is, was the connection between Jentsch's notion of intellectual uncertainty (concerning the distinction animate/inanimate) and his own conception of repetition compulsion, which

---

56. *Tales of E. T. A. Hoffmann,* trans. Leonard J. Kent and Elizabeth C. Knight (Chicago: University of Chicago Press, 1969), 117 (I have changed the translation of *unheimlich* from "weird" to "uncanny").

*at a formal level* is, for Freud, the distinguishing feature of the uncanny effect. There is nothing that throws more into question our status as living beings than the sheer, quasi-mechanical automaticity of the compulsion to repeat. It is, in other words, in this compulsion that we recognize the workings of the drive, precisely that excessive "inhuman" vitality that sets us apart from the animal and in some sense first makes us distinctly human. I would also argue that the symbolic castration Freud considered to be a kind of bedrock in the formation of the psyche itself generates considerable uncertainty as to the subject's status as a living being. For the notion of castration ultimately means that one is called upon to exchange one's natural being for a relation to a symbolic representation—the phallus—that operates according to social and cultural laws that have a certain impersonal automaticity. The phallus is in this sense the ultimate prosthetic device or "machine part," an organ that never quite fits the body (recall again Dr. K.'s lament that our poor bodies "have long since become separated from the natural order of things").

But perhaps Freud's most productive insights about *das Unheimliche* concern the figure and theme of *the double,* a topic that covers a wide array of phenomena that have been exploited to great effect in romantic literature and early cinema. Freud praises Otto Rank's work on the topic, underlining his pupil's insight that the double was "originally an insurance against the destruction of the ego," that it functioned as a protection against death. Indeed, Freud writes that "the 'immortal' soul was the first 'double' of the body." He goes on to link the process of doubling to castration, suggesting that what was first "an assurance of immortality . . . becomes the uncanny harbinger of death."[57] Once one's being has been delegated to a symbolic representation, this "double" always—at least potentially—presents us with the prospect of our own extinction, of being survived by our

57. Freud, *Standard Edition,* 17:235. There Freud writes, "This invention of doubling as a preservation against extinction has its counterpart in the language of dreams, which is fond of representing castration by a doubling or multiplication of a genital symbol."

proxy. To a certain extent, then, the double functions as a kind of demonic index of our inscription in natural history:

> When all is said and done, the quality of uncanniness can only come from the
> fact of the "double" being a creation dating back to a very early mental stage,
> long since surmounted—a stage, incidentally, at which it wore a more friendly
> aspect. The "double" has become a thing of terror, just as, after the collapse of
> their religion, the gods turned into demons.[58]

In a brilliant essay on the importance of the gaze in psychoanalytic
thought, Mladen Dolar has suggested that Lacan's famous "mirror
stage" can be understood as an elaboration of Freud's insights regarding the double:

> To put it simply: when I recognize myself in the mirror, it is already too late.
> There is a split: I cannot recognize myself and at the same time be one with
> myself. With the recognition, I have already lost what one could call the "self-
> being," the immediate coincidence with myself in my being and *jouissance*.
> The rejoicing in the mirror image, the pleasure and the self-indulgence, had
> already to be paid for. The mirror double immediately introduces the dimen-
> sion of castration.[59]

Dolar extends these remarks to include Lacan's later concept of
the *objet a,* the elusive bit of the real that seems to materialize for the

---

58. Ibid., 17:236. Recall Benjamin's remark in the *Trauerspiel* book: "The attire of the
Olympians is left behind, and in the course of time the emblems collect around it. And
this attire is as creaturely as a devil's body. . . . Alongside the emblems and the attire, the
words and the names remain behind, and, as the living contexts of their birth disappear,
so they become the origins of concepts in which these words acquire a new content,
which is predisposed to allegorical representation. . . . The deadness of the figures and
the abstraction of the concepts are therefore the precondition for the allegorical meta-
morphisis of the pantheon into a world of magical, conceptual creatures." Walter
Benjamin, *The Origin of German Tragic Drama,* trans John Osborne (London: NLB,
1977), 225–26.
59. Mladen Dolar, "At First Sight," In *Gaze and Voice as Love Objects,* ed. Renata Salecl
and Slavoj Žižek (Durham, NC: Duke University Press, 1996), 138.

subject the lost jouissance of self-being, the ultimate object of desire that one struggles in vain to glimpse in the mirror reflection:

The mirror in the most elementary way already implies the split between the Imaginary and the Real: one can have access to imaginary reality, the world one can recognize oneself in and familiarize oneself with, on the condition of the loss, the "falling out" of the object *a*. It is this loss of the object *a* that opens the reality henceforth seen as "objective" reality, the possibility of subject-object relations, but since its loss is the condition of any knowledge of "objective" reality, it cannot itself become an object of knowledge.[60]

Any encounter with one's double thus always has a lethal aspect, always threatens to precipitate the dissolution of one's world: "We can see now what the trouble is with the double: the double is that mirror image in which the object *a* is included. It gains its own being, the Imaginary starts to coincide with the real, provoking a shattering anxiety. The double is the same as me—*plus the object a. . . .*" What this means is that anxiety, for Lacan, is not to be understood as a response to lack or loss but rather to a kind of excess or *too-muchness,* to an over-proximity of the object: "What one loses with anxiety is precisely the loss—the loss that made it possible to deal with a coherent reality . . . the lack lacks, and this brings about the uncanny."[61]

In the third part of *Vertigo,* Sebald suggests that during his journey to northern Italy in the fall of 1913 Kafka very likely saw one of the great early filmic elaborations of the theme of the double, *The Student of Prague* (in his essay on the uncanny, Freud notes that Rank's study begins with a discussion of this film). The narrator suggests that Kafka would have recognized in Balduin, the student-hero of the film, "a kind of *doppelgänger,* just as Balduin recognizes his other self in the dark-coated brother whom he could never and nowhere escape." Very early in the film, after the pact is sealed with the malevolent Scapinelli, "Balduin, the finest swordsman in all Prague, confronts his own

60. Ibid.
61. Ibid., 139.

image in the mirror, and presently, to his horror, that unreal figure steps out of the frame, and henceforth follows him as the ghostly shadow of his own restlessness" (151–52/173–74).[62] By then linking this scene to Kafka's fragment "Description of a Struggle," the first part of which stages a sometimes surreal, sometimes comical—and homoerotically charged—pas de deux between two men during a nocturnal walk through Prague, Sebald suggests that in the context of his own work, the question of homosexuality—and perhaps of sexuality more generally—needs to be seen in relation to the topic of the double and the uncanny.[63]

My sense is that one will understand what is at stake in such scenes only by returning to that other "couple" I have been exploring throughout this book, that of *the sovereign and the creature*. Though I certainly do not think Sebald had a consistent position on these matters, in my view his work nonetheless suggests that human sexuality can really be grasped only within the matrix of this relation. We become sexual in the human sense when we have, so to speak, been made over as creature, when our bodies have been intensified, amplified, by exposure not simply to the space of signification, the symbolic order, but to the point of exception that sustains this space, that "totalizes" it, establishes it as a consistent—if always unstable—matrix in which one is called upon to assume one's proper "orientation." We become creatures of *drive* (rather than animals of *instinct*) because our sexual life is organized in relation to the "agency" of exception, one

62. In a review of Hanns Zischler's book, *Kafka Goes to the Movies,* Sebald linked the proliferation of doppelgänger figures in early cinema to the nature of the medium itself, to the fact that the cinema, like photography, is one vast machine for the proliferation of copies. "And because the copy endured after the thing copied has long disappeared, there lingered the unpleasant intimation that the thing copied, the human being and nature itself, enjoyed a lesser degree of authenticity than the copy, that the copy hollows out the original, just as it is said that someone who encounters his double feels himself destroyed." Sebald, "Kafka im Kino," in *Campo Santo,* ed. Sven Meyer (Munich: Hanser, 2003), 200–201.

63. "Would this sort of scenario not have struck Dr. K. as the description of a struggle in which, as in the contest he himself had set against the backdrop of the Laurenziberg, the principal character and his opponent are in the most intimate and self-destructive of relationships, such that, when the hero is driven into a corner by his companion he is forced to declare: I am betrothed, I admit it" (*Vertigo,* 152/174).

that is no doubt subject to considerable historical mutation. In this sense, sexuality functions as a crucial locus of the persistence of political theology in modernity. It is no wonder, then, that the figure of the double is always linked to that of an obscene paternal agency—a kind of primal father, in Freud's sense—who both prohibits and commands enjoyment, who promises the greatest possible satisfaction and at the same time makes it impossible, who offers, in a word, *impossible enjoyment* (think of Coppola/Coppelius in "The Sandman" or Scapinelli in *The Student of Prague*). For human beings, sexual life is always, at some level, a "double life."

Slavoj Žižek has argued that the obscene, primal father whose murder Freud posited at the foundation of civilization is in fact a *modern* phenomenon, one that emerges precisely at the point where patriarchy no longer functions; the default of the symbolic father precipitates a systemic "investiture crisis" in which subjects can no longer identify with the symbolic roles with which they been invested (husband, professor, judge . . . ).[64] In modernity, Žižek suggests, the obscene father and his creature no longer live in some "closet" on the far side of the law, functioning as its hidden support (the classical structure of sovereignty); rather, their "outlaw" relationship enters the foreground, becomes the open secret of the social bond.[65] Referring to the universe of noir film and literature, Žižek writes that "the allegedly archaic figure of the 'primordial father' is actually a thoroughly *modern* entity, a result of the *decline* of the paternal metaphor." Žižek's remarks on the noir universe provide a concise inventory of the various faces of sexuality we have noted in Sebald's work:

This is what is ultimately at stake in the *noir* universe: the failure of the paternal metaphor (i.e., the emergence of the obscene father who supplants

---

64. See Santner, *My Own Private Germany* for an extended treatment of "investiture crisis."

65. See once more Alenka Zupancic, *The Shortest Shadow: Nietzsche's Philosophy of the Two* (Cambridge: MIT Press, 2003): "This could also be expressed in terms of what . . . Giorgio Agamben develops at the political level: modern politics is characterized by the fact that the 'state of emergency' (the state that is, at one and the same time, the exception to as well as the support of the rule of law) is itself becoming a rule of law" (51).

the father living up to his symbolic function) renders impossible a viable, temperate relation with a woman; as a result, woman finds herself occupying the impossible place of the traumatic Thing. The *femme fatale* is nothing but a lure whose fascinating presence masks the true traumatic axis of the *noir* universe, the relationship to the obscene father, i.e., the default of the paternal metaphor—all the usual babble about "latent homosexuality" misses completely the primordial dimension of this relationship.[66]

What this ultimately means is that the multiple manifestations of sexuality we have discovered in Sebald's texts do not represent an intrusion of a supplementary topic beyond the concerns we have focused on in the main body of the book; sexuality does not, in a word, befall creaturely life as an additional set of "properties" or "experiences" but is a fundamental mode in which this life takes shape and comes to be registered. It is also in this sense that the entire problem of how to "apply" psychoanalysis to social, collective life falls away as a pseudo-problem. Psychoanalysis, above all where it addresses what seems to be our most intimate and individual secrets—those pertaining to our sexuality—is always already a "social science," always already deeply engaged with the texture of social bonds. The natural history of modern life—and this is, as I have tried to show, Sebald's singular topic—is always already a history of sexuality.

66. Slavoj Žižek, *Enjoy Your Symptom! Jacques Lacan in Hollywood and Out* (New York: Routledge, 1992), 159–60.

# Epilogue

If I am indeed right about these connections, where then does the possibility lie for what I earlier alluded to as a "miracle" in the domain of ethical and political life? Where are the resources of a "weak messianic power"? What could it mean to traverse what looks more and more like the hopeless closure of creaturely life? That is to say, if sexuality itself, this classical site of transgression, can function as a mode of consolidating the entwinement of the sovereign (exception) and the creature, how might one imagine a passage beyond that lethally exciting embrace that binds us to the rhythms of natural history?

My sense is that this was the question that pushed Lacan in his efforts to formulate his later thinking on love and, above all, the thought of an "Other jouissance," a mode of enjoyment that yields, within the order of (phallic) sexuality, a remainder that "decompletes" the world of the sovereign and the creature, renders the space articulated by it—now understood not as sexuality *tout court* but rather as *masculine sexuality*—"not all." The great paradox of Lacan's approach here is that it proceeds not by way of transcendence—positing a space beyond the closure of the sovereign and the creature, one that would not be touched by symbolic castration and the "double life" it produces—but through a more radical gesture of "immanentization." The problem with the space of sexuality—and political life—articulated within the matrix of the sovereign and the creature is that it is in some sense *not closed enough*. As Suzanne Bernard has glossed this crucial feature of Lacan's theory,

> Thus while man is "whole" within the symbolic, the exception [i.e., the primal father—ELS] that delimits him precludes him from fully identifying with castration. One could say that while man is wholly subject "to," and hence "in," the symbolic, he is "in it with exception," that is, he "takes exception" to it in some way. As a result, the fantasy of a subject not subjected to Law—the fantasy of no limit—determines masculine structure in an essential way. The point here is that the masculine subject is effectively "caught" in the phallic function, ironically because he does not fully identify with it but maintains a kind of distance toward it through believing in an exception to symbolic Law.[1]

For Lacan, we might say, the possibility of experiencing miracles lies in suspending the hold of this structure of fantasy or at least of entering into a new kind of relationship with it.

Let me try to make this line of thought a bit more concrete by way of a final return to the work of Rainer Maria Rilke, specifically to what is perhaps his most famous poem, "The Archaic Torso of Apollo." Published in 1908 as the opening poem of the second part of the volume *New Poems,* this poem—and the entire volume of "new poems"—has generally been understood as marking a new phase in Rilke's development as an artist, one linked to a turn away from the poet's own (idealized) subjectivity toward the recalcitrant concreteness of *things* (as is well known, the *New Poems* have, for better or worse, been characterized as "thing poems," *Dinggedichte*). I am

---

1. Suzanne Bernard, "Tongues of Angels: Feminine Structure and Other Jouissance," in *Reading Seminar XX,* ed. Suzanne Bernard and Bruce Fink (Albany: SUNY Press, 2002), 177.

depending, in a word, on Rilke's own turn to the concrete—to the world of *things*—to make a still somewhat abstract conceptual scheme more concrete. Here, then, is the sonnet in German and in Stephen Mitchell's translation:

Wir kannten nicht sein unerhörtes Haupt,
darin die Augenäpfel reiften. Aber
sein Torso glüht noch wie ein Kandelaber,
in dem sein Schauen, nur zurückgeschraubt,

sich hält und glänzt. Sonst könnte nicht der Bug
der Brust dich blenden, und im leisen Drehen
der Lenden könnte nicht ein Lächeln gehen
zu jener Mitte, die die Zeugung trug.

Sonst stünde dieser Stein entstellt und kurz
unter der Schultern durchsichtigem Sturz
und flimmerte nicht so wie Raubtierfelle;

und bräche nicht aus allen seinen Rändern
aus wie ein Stern: denn da ist keine Stelle,
die dich nicht sieht. Du mußt dein Leben ändern.

[We cannot know his legendary head
with eyes like ripening fruit. And yet his torso
is still suffused with brilliance from inside,
like a lamp, in which his gaze, now turned to low,

gleams in all its power. Otherwise
the curved breast could not dazzle you so, nor could
a smile run through the placid hips and thighs
to that dark center where procreation flared.

Otherwise this stone would seem defaced
beneath the translucent cascade of the shoulders

and would not glisten like a wild beast's fur:
would not, from all the borders of itself,

burst like a star: for here there is no place
that does not see you. You must change your life.][2]

In the present context, I will focus on the famous last lines of
the poem (following the colon after the word "star"). These lines
bring to a head the "argument" of the poem—a poem that, of
course, begins with headlessness—suggesting that the aesthetic
encounter evoked in the body of the poem could be characterized,
ultimately, as exposure to a peculiarly dispersed and serialized gaze
of the work of art. The poem then proposes that such exposure
exerts a moral pressure on the poem's speaker (and readers), that it
injects into their life a disquietude about the shape and direction of
the life lived before the aesthetic encounter. It as if the poem is
making a claim—indeed a moral judgment—about the nature of a
life lived in ignorance of the object (or kind of object) evoked in
the poem.

When I say that the penultimate line of "The Archaic Torso
of Apollo" brings the poem's argument to a head, I mean that it
concentrates in a kind of logical formula—expressed in the form of
a double negation—the poem's evocation of the statue's nearly
overwhelming presence. That presence is characterized, in turn, as
the dazzling, even blinding glow of a gaze. The poem as a whole is
organized around this fundamental ambiguity concerning the status
of the gaze—an ambiguity palpable in a number of the *New Poems*—
whereby an object is endowed with a gaze that is in turn reinvested
with a kind of sublime, dazzling "thingness" (it is, I suggest, only
this second-order "thingness" that really allows us to speak here
of "thing poems"). The poem presents us, in a word, with the *gaze
as object*. Perhaps even more important, the oscillation staged in
the poem between seeing and being seen is mobilized by a missed
encounter, the fact that we are dealing with a fragmentary object.
That is, Rilke suggests that the aesthetic intensity of the artifact in
question—what I have characterized as its sublime, second-order

2. Rilke, *The Selected Poetry of Rainer Maria Rilke,* ed. and trans. Stephen Mitchell
(New York: Vintage, 1984), 60–61.

thingness—is a function of the fact that it is a kind of remainder and, indeed, one in a double sense. Not only is it an artifact left over from a culture that has disappeared, it is itself only a fragment of its original form. To use Barthes's terms, Rilke suggests that the object's status as remainder allows him to experience its surface as a pure surplus over any possible *studium,* as the locus of a kind of wandering *punctum.*[3]

Rilke, of course, places special emphasis on the *parts*—we might say *partial objects*—that have gone missing in this particular fragment, namely the eyes and the genitals. The second line deploys the catachresis *Augenäpfel* for the missing eyes of the statue, drawing heightened attention to the metaphoric status of the word by endowing the eyes with the capacity to ripen.[4] That we are dealing here with a catachresis, a metaphor that fills in, that substitutes for, a missing original or proper name—*Augapfel* or "eye apple" just *is* the German word for eyeball (a catachresis in English as well)—intensifies and complicates the topic of loss announced in the first line. We are put on alert as to a potential confusion between kinds of lack: the loss of something that was once there and an absence of something that was never there, could never have been there, could never be at the place where it is missed.[5] It is equally significant that Rilke uses a metonymy to signify the missing genitals: *Zeugung,* or "procreation." Once again,

3. In a letter to Lou Andreas-Salomé of August 15, 1903, Rilke no doubt greatly exaggerates this radical diminution of the *studium* in favor of the *punctum* in his relationship to ancient art: "The incomparable value of these rediscovered Things lies in the fact that you can look at them as if they were completely unknown. No one knows what their intention is and (at least for the unscientific) no subject matter is attached to them, no irrelevant voice interrupts the silence of their concentrated reality, and their duration is without retrospect or fear. The masters from whom they originate are nothing; no misunderstood fame colors their pure forms; no history casts a shadow over their naked clarity—: they *are*. That is all. This is how I see ancient art" (cited in Rilke, *Selected Poetry,* 303).
4. This point has been emphasized by, among others, Wolfram Groddeck in an essay dedicated to the logic of figuration in the poem. See "Blendung: Betrachtung an Rilkes zweitem Apollo-Sonnett," in *Interpretationen: Gedichte von Rainer Maria Rilke,* ed. Wolfram Groddeck (Stuttgart: Reclam, 1999), 87–103.
5. We might say that for Freud, the so-called erogenous zones are produced when a part of the body begins to serve as *the localization of an absence experienced as a loss.*

we encounter a verbal displacement at the site of lack. And both figures—the metaphor *Augenäpfel,* qualified as "ripening," and the metonymy *Zeugung,* emphasizing potency—underline the aspect of intensification or "potentiation."[6]

A link between these two missing parts is furthermore suggested by the verb *blenden* in the second strophe, a word that can mean not only to dazzle, as Mitchell has translated it, but also *to blind.* And as Freud compelling argues in his essay "The Uncanny," the semantic field of blinding/blindness and that of castration are fundamentally linked. As Freud puts it there, "A study of dreams, phantasies and myths has taught us that anxiety about one's eyes, the fear of going blind, is often enough a substitute for the dread of being castrated," suggesting, for example, that "the self-blinding of the mythical criminal, Oedipus, was simply a mitigated form of the punishment of castration—the only punishment that was adequate for him by the *lex talionis.*"[7] But if the poem makes an argument for the potentiation of aesthetic presence and intensity by way of a passage through a lack correlated with castration, the penultimate line points to a rather specific way of understanding such a submission (to castration) and potentiation (of aesthetic presence and force). It points, I suggest, to what Lacan characterizes as the feminine mode of "sexuation," the feminine mode of structuring a relationship with the jouissance (of self-being) lost to the "phallic signifier."[8]

In Lacan's view, the masculine structure of enjoyment involves a fundamental irony. The determination of the set of men—those subject to the limitation of jouissance that Freud called castration—is achieved by way of reference to the exceptional figure of the primal father, the one who is not subject to castration, the one whose sexual life is, precisely, not a double life. Masculine "sexuation" is thus

6. Groddeck is very helpful on this point as well.
7. Sigmund Freud, *The Standard Edition of the Complete Psychological Works of Sigmund Freud,* trans. James Strachey (London: Hogarth Press, 1953–74), 17:231.
8. That the phallus is indeed a signifier—a central one, to be sure, as the diction of the poem suggests—that it marks the mutation of the body into a matrix of symbolic intensities, is underlined in the poem by the use of a metonymy at the place of (the name of) the missing genitals.

organized according to two seemingly contradictory propositions: All men are subject to the phallic function (or perhaps: Man is wholly determined by it); there is at least one man who is not subject to the phallic function. Man can, in other words, bear his castration because there is—in fantasy—at least one who "has it all," who has access to unlimited enjoyment. But as I have indicated, Lacan did not feel that these propositions and the structure of fantasy implied in them formed an unsurpassable horizon of human experience (or in Freud's terms, the bedrock of psychic structure). Lacan posited, namely, an alternative pattern of sexuation, one he characterized as "feminine." The reference to the phallic function remains, but the logic by which this function is assumed is new. Lacan tries to capture this new logic by way of an alternative pair of propositions that read more or less as follows: There is *no* woman who is *not* subject to the phallic function; *Not all* woman is subject to the phallic function (or perhaps: She is not wholly determined by it).[9] Lacan clearly felt he had discovered something quite significant, even revolutionary, with this logic of the "not all." He refers to it as "a never-before-seen function" that ultimately means "that when any speaking being whatsoever situates itself under the banner 'woman,' it is on the basis of the following—that it grounds itself as being not-all in situating itself in the phallic function."[10] This is the point of the infamous claim about woman's nonexistence: "There's no such thing as Woman, Woman with a capital *W* indicating the universal. There's no such thing as Woman because . . . she is not-all."[11] Lacan adds that "being not-all, she has a supplementary *jouissance* compared

---

9. There is an interesting parallel worth pursuing here with Heidegger's conception of authenticity. Heidegger characterizes authenticity as an "existenziell modification" of the way selfhood for Dasein is standardized, submitted to the "function" he refers to as *das Man* (the "they" or the "anyone"). Heidegger specifically says that such a modification ought not be thought of as "a state of exception of the subject detached from *das Man* [*vom Man abgelösten Ausnahmezustand des Subjekts*]." See Heidegger, *Sein und Zeit* (Tübingen: Max Niemeyer, 1993), 130.

10. Jacques Lacan, *The Seminar of Jacques Lacan,* Book XX, *Encore,* trans. Bruce Fink (New York: W. W. Norton, 1998), 72. I have changed Fink's translation of *pas tout* from "not whole" to "not all."

11. Ibid., 73.

204 | EPILOGUE

to what the phallic function designates by way of *jouissance*."[12] As Kenneth Reinhard has emphasized, Lacan's understanding of the difference between masculine and feminine "sexuation" is fundamentally "set theoretical":

There is no figure of the sovereign woman who might adjudicate the claims of individual women to participate in feminine sexuality, and determine the boundaries of the set. In the language of set theory, if a man *belongs* to the subset of humanity called "all men," a set that constitutes a unified group, guaranteed by the transcendental exceptionality of the primal Father, a woman is *included* in the subset of women without belonging to it, insofar as that subset has no border that would determine membership, and delimit inside from outside. Men are part of the group Man insofar as they are all equivalent in their failure to represent the primal Father: the set of "all men" functions according to the principles of group formation around a leader that Freud describes in *Group Psychology and the Analysis of the Ego*. And although women are no less irrecusably marked by the phallus, the terms of their reprieve are not given by a transcendental sovereign who represents the possibility of eventual satisfaction, but *immanently,* in the contingencies of their particular inhabitations of the not-all.[13]

What Lacan is after here is, in my view, a new conception of what it means to encounter the *singularity* of the "other" (rather than its *particularity* qua member of a set delimited by such and such attributes). At least this is how I understand what Lacan means when he characterizes the field of "women" as infinite, as an open domain or "neighborhood" in which individuals appear "one by one": "When I say that woman is not-all and that that is why I cannot say Woman, it

12. Ibid. Lacan takes pains here to underline the difference between such supplementarity over against any notion of complementarity that would ultimately return us to the fantasy of a unified cosmic whole, that is, to a picture of a cosmic harmonization of contrasting principles.
13. Kenneth Reinhard, "Toward a Political Theology of the Neighbor," in *The Neighbor: Three Inquiries in Political Theology,* by Slavoj Žižek, Eric Santner, and Kenneth Reinhard (Chicago: University of Chicago Press, 2005).

is precisely because I raise the question of a *jouissance* that, with respect to everything that can be [encompassed] in the [phallic] function, is in the realm of the infinite."[14] Or, "You know that the not-all has been essential to me in marking that there is no such thing as *the Woman* which is, namely, that there are only, if I may say, different ones, and in some way, [they enter] one by one."[15] The crucial point here is that this new space is opened by the suspension of the force of a spectral excess—a haunting—constraining the possibility of encounter in the field organized according to the logic of masculine sexuation. As Bernard has put it, "Lacan suggests that feminine structure (and hence, Other jouissance) is produced in relation to a 'set' that *does not* exist on the basis of an external, constitutive exception. In other words, it is produced in relation to a set *not haunted* by a figure operating as a limit."[16]

To return to Rilke, a poet who throughout his life was obsessed with the dilemmas of "object love," I suggest that what is at issue in the ethical injunction at the end of "The Archaic Torso of Apollo" is precisely an opening to a new field and logic of encounter, in this case with the work of art, one whose very status *as work,* as unified, consistent, self-identical artifact, thereby becomes transformed. The injunction of the final line invites the speaker/reader to open to a space of possibilities "framed" by the double negative of the penultimate line, "for here there is no place / that does not see you."[17] The commandment "You must change your life" ultimately calls for a suspension of the (superego) imperative haunting the conception of the self-identical work of art and a hermeneutics guided by such a conception. This is the imperative that would have been implied had the poem insisted that the speaker/reader of the poem was exposed to

14. Lacan, *Encore,* 103.
15. Jacques Lacan, *Le séminaire, Livre 21, Les non-dupes errent,* cited in Reinhard, "Toward a Political Theology," 58.
16. Bernard, "Tongues of Angels," 178.
17. The homology I have been proposing (between Lacan's formulas of sexuation and Rilke's poem) is complicated by the fact that in the poem both the object and the speaker undergo the shift to the logic of "not all." What is at stake, then, is a new *Werkästhetik* and a new mode of encounter—a new way of being submitted to the (now dispersed, "serialized") gaze of the object—correlative to it.

the *whole work*—even qua fragment—the vision, that is, of being in the meaningful presence of *it all*.[18] This is an imperative that both demands and constrains interpretation, that measures interpretation against the phantasm of full access to the work's final and ultimate meaning: the phantasm of the *reader-interpreter as sovereign*. What we get instead is an open and infinite field of encounter in which there is no "place," no detail, no aspect of the work to which you are not called upon to respond, though you are not thereby held responsible for a final and definitive meaning of the work as a whole.

It is important in all of this to keep in mind Lacan's insistence on the supplementarity of the relation of the logic of "not all" to that of the "all" and its exception. To move from the sphere of aesthetics to that of ethics and politics—a shift that is constantly rehearsed in Sebald's own literary work—what is at stake in this relation of supplementarity is ultimately that between the space of the *neighbor,* on the one hand, and that of the *sovereign and the creature,* on the other. That is, just as in the sphere of sexuality elaborated by Lacan woman remains subject to the phallic function, in the spheres of ethics and politics—spheres correlated, as we have seen, with that of sexuality— the domain of neighbor-love does not represent a space apart from that delimited by the sovereign and the creature but serves as a mode of intervening into that space, of opening up the possibility of new possibilities foreclosed within the agitated immobility of that fateful entwinement.

II

At this point I would like to return one last time to the German-Jewish tradition that has informed this entire investigation. Franz Rosenzweig has characterized such an intervention as the *Beseelung,* or "ensoulment," of the creature by acts of neighbor-love—small

---

18. There is another alternative to the two options I have mentioned ("there is no place that doesn't see you" and "it all sees you"), namely, *every place* sees you. My problem with this alternative is that it seems to presuppose the existence of "places" in advance of any encounter, something not implied, or at least not so strongly implied, in the use of the double negative. What is suggested in the double negative is that each "place" is in some sense co-constituted by the responsiveness of the viewer.

miracles, as it were, performed *one by one,* moving from one neighbor to the next (rather than by way of a love directed immediately to *all* humankind):

> If then a not-yet is inscribed over all redemptive unison, there can only ensue that the end is for the time being represented by the just present moment, the universal and highest by the approximately proximate [*das jeweils Nächste*]. The bond of the consummate and redeeming coming together [*Verbindung*] of man and world is to begin with the neighbor and ever more only the neighbor, the well-nigh nighest [*zunächst der Nächste und immer wieder nur der Nächste, das zu-nächst Nächste*]. . . . Where . . . someone or something has become neighbor to a soul, there a piece of the world has become something which it was not previously: soul.[19]

Rosenzweig imagines this work of ensoulment—this transformation, this "sublimation" of the creature to the status of the neighbor—as occurring within a field of tension between what he calls the "dual" and the "plural," the I-thou and the world of the third person. The "dual," he writes, is

> that formation which is not durable in language, which is absorbed by the plural in the course of development, for admittedly it nowhere maintains itself securely except, at most, with the few things which *per se* appear in pairs. Otherwise it glides from one bearer on to the other, the next one, from one neighbor to the next neighbor. It is not satisfied until it has paced off the whole orbit of creation. But it only appears to have thus surrendered its dominion to the plural; in fact it leaves its traces everywhere in its migrations by providing the plurals of things everywhere with the sign of singularity.[20]

I don't think there is a better characterization of the insistent and —why not?—quietly *miraculous* stride of Sebald's narratives through the domain of creaturely life.

19. Franz Rosenzweig, *The Star of Redemption,* trans. William W. Hallo (Notre Dame, IN: University of Notre Dame Press, 1985), 234–35; translation modified. The shift from *der Nächste* to *das Nächste* in the passage suggests that neighborliness is a factor not simply of spatial proximity but also of the urgency of a situation.
20. Rosenzweig, *Star of Redemption,* 235.

# Index

for, 77n41; in creaturely life, 16–18; in critical engagement with Sebald's work, 43–45; ethical status of, 89–91; ethicopolitical agency vs., 62–63, 91; of gender, 172–73; manic side of, 80–84; objects as allegories in, 87; as occasion for laughter, 147; photography linked to, 157; posture of, 20–21, 86; remembrance vs. futurity in, 88–89; as resistance, 44–45. *See also* spectral materialism

memory: Austerlitz's archaeology of, 109–12; chance and coincidence in recovering, 136–38; discrepancies as screening of, 163–64; poetics of involuntary, 139–40; postmodern obsession with, 133–34; of sex and death, 120–21. *See also* postmemory; remembrance *(Eingedenken)*

Mendes-Flohr, Paul, 38n59

messianism: awakening in, as deanimation of undead, 88; Benjamin's creaturely life and, 86; conception of Israelites' Exodus and, 77n40; journal concerned with, 38; thought and action in, xi–xii. *See also* redemption; Resurrection

Middleton, Christopher, 135n55

miracles: as dependent on witnessing, 75; dimension of, 16n28; expectation of (baroque), 86–87; possibility of, 197, 198; state of exception as, 15–16

Mitchell, Stephen, 4n4, 199–200, 202

modernity: aesthetic modernism vs. forces of, 77n41; Benjamin on, 12, 134n54; Benjamin's work on baroque linked to, 76–80; creaturely life as product of exposure to, 12–16; excess of animation in, 80–82; exposure to, in Rilke's *Malte*, 48–49; Freud's primal father foregrounded in, 195–96; of Kafka's position and law, 93; mobilizing storytelling under, 139–40; politicotheological dimension under, 183–84, 195; premodern mutations

continuing in, 183–84; sexuality as conceived in, 182–83

monumentalism, 55, 66, 108

mood *(Stimmung)*, 45–47

moths, 105, 112–13

mourning, 89–91, 157

Muselmann figure, xvi n7, 25n40

myth: critique of, 92–93; dimensions of, 75; of ethnogenesis, 73–74; fixations on, xix; totemism and, 69–72

mythic violence: deposits bearing witness to, 114–15; fortifications as emblem of, 108; in life cycle of capitalist production, 76–80; natural history and, 17n31, 65; pure violence that could interrupt, 94–95; repetition compulsion as defining, 67–68; as sustained and suspended in superego, 74–75

Nancy, Jean-Luc, 68n30

natural history *(Naturgeschichte)*: allegory as proper mode of representing, 18–19; ambiguity underlying, 80–82, 99; baroque vision of, 86–87; birth of unconscious and, 33–34; combustion and destruction in, 104–6; conception of, xiv–xv, 16–18, 97; of destruction, 63–65, 76; faith in progress countered in, 107; as form of life manifest as decay, 147–48; globalization as form of, 113; human history as species of, 58, 63–64, 76; manic dimension of, 115–21; museums of, 78, 104–5n11; mythic violence linked to, 17n31; nihilism and, 78; paradox of man's subordination to, 105–6; Paul's conception in relation to, 126–27; practice of postmemory as writing, 167; sexuality and, 31–32, 186–87; temporality and, 21

neighbor: creature elevated to, 36n56; responsibility for transmissions from, 166–67; singularity of, xxi; supplementarity and space of possibilities for, 206. *See also* love of neighbor